ANDREW J. POPPLETON

FIGHTER

for

Omaha City,
the Union Pacific Railroad,
and Chief Standing Bear

Lawrence A. Dwyer, JD

ANDREW J. POPPLETON:

Fighter
for
Omaha City,
the Union Pacific Railroad, and
Chief Standing Bear

KLD Books, Inc.
Omaha, Nebraska
www.KLDbooks.org

ISBN: 979-8-9927035-0-4 (paperback)
ISBN: 979-8-9927035-2-8 (ebook)
ISBN: 979-8-9927035-1-1 (hardcover)

Library of Congress Control Number:

Cover Photo
Andrew J. Poppleton (1869)
Courtesy of A.J. Poppleton III Personal Collection.

Editor
Karen L. Dwyer, PhD

Dedication

I dedicate this book to the memory of two mentors who inspired in me a love for the law and history and taught me the principles of legal and historical research

Judge Louis T. Carnazzo
(1905-1992)

Professor A. Stanley Trickett
(1911-1994)

Tribute to A.J. Poppleton III

In November 2023, I received a phone call at my law office from A.J. Poppleton III, identifying himself as the great-grandson of Andrew J. Poppleton. He wondered if I would like to see his personal collection of letters, journals, correspondence, scrapbooks, newspaper clippings, photographs, and various other materials belonging to his great-grandfather. We met on a Saturday in my office, and when he opened the boxes, and without touching anything, I knew immediately what was before my eyes – an unbelievable treasure trove of primary history.

I told A.J. that I had been considering writing a small biography on his great-grandfather ever since I studied his work when I was writing my book on Chief Standing Bear and the landmark federal court habeas corpus trial which took place in 1879 in Omaha, Nebraska. I was fascinated by the brilliance of his closing argument and by his compassionate desire to defend those Ponca prisoners, pro bono. I thought he deserved a biography for what he and his co-counsel John Webster had done for Native Americans. Little did I know of his importance as one the first 15 settlers in Omaha City, his leadership role in the first session of the territorial legislature, writing our first Code of Laws, serving for 24 years as head legal counsel for the Union Pacific Railroad, and the vital civic, legal and cultural organizations he helped to found and lead, which are still operating 150 years later.

This book is the result of the kindness of A.J. Poppleton III, allowing me the great privilege of seeing, touching, and reading the materials contained in his collection. By all accounts, Andrew J. Poppleton was the head lawyer of his day, a giant among many of the greatest lawyers in Nebraska history. His passion, eloquence, and command of the English language were evident from the journal he kept at age 22 while a student at Union College, to the memoirs he wrote just before his death.

Impressive as well was the correspondence he shared with his wife Caroline during their 40 years of marriage. He called her the foundation and sunshine of his life. But she was much more than just a support to him; she was an influential leader herself in the community, most notably in the arts, work for the poor in the community, and development of a first-class school for nurses. A.J. and Caroline Poppleton were at the forefront of a group of "couples" who piloted the course of growth and development for Omaha in its first fifty years.

Someday, the wish of his close friend Dr. George Miller will come to fruition, and "a monument shall be erected in our public parks to the memory of Andrew J. Poppleton." When it does, I know his family will be there to witness this long overdue recognition of one of the titans in Omaha history.

Thank you, A.J., for preserving this early history of Omaha and the legacy of your great-grandparents.

TABLE OF CONTENTS

1

Heritage

The ancestral homeland of Andrew J. Poppleton was located a few miles west of York in North Yorkshire, England, in two small medieval villages, Upper Poppleton and Nether Poppleton, meeting on the river Ouse. The Great Survey of England and Wales completed at the behest of King William the Conqueror in 1086 identified the two villages as "Popeltun," derived from the Old English names *popel*, meaning 'pebble' and *tun,* meaning 'a hamlet farm.' [1]

Andrew Poppleton's great-grandfather, Samuel Poppleton, came to America in his mid-twenties with his wife Rosanna Whalley and settled in Vermont. Their youngest son Samuel Poppleton II, Andrew's grandfather, was born on Christmas day in the year of their arrival, 1751.[2]

When the War for American Independence broke out in 1775, Samuel Poppleton II, served with Ethan Allen at Ticonderoga and fought in the crucial battle at Saratoga. After a distinguished military service, he settled in Bennington, Vermont and married Caroline Osborne in 1783.[3]

Parents: William and Zada Poppleton

In his memoirs, Andrew wrote fondly of his grandparents Samuel Poppleton II and Caroline Osborne, who had nine children "of whom my father, William Poppleton, was the youngest, he being born at Poultney, Vermont, June 1795."[4] His grandparents moved to Richmond, New York where William Poppleton, age 19, married Zada Crooks, age 18, on October 10, 1814.

In 1823, Andrew's father traveled to Michigan to determine whether the newly opened land for settlers was suitable for farming and raising his family. He liked what he saw, purchased a tract from the government and returned home. Two years later. William and Zada left New York for Oakland County, Michigan, an arduous journey of 32 days, described by Andrew's older brother Orrin:

> He [William Poppleton] took his departure from Richmond, Ontario County, New York with his wife [Zada] and two children [Orrin age 8 and Sally age 5], with a horse team and covered wagon, bidding relatives and friends a long farewell, resolutely pushed westward to the frontier for newer and vaster scenes, for larger and grander prospects. Being late in the season, steamboats on Lake Erie having laid up for the season, he took the road through Canada ... an unbroken wilderness. Early in December 1825 after a tiresome journey of thirty-two days, in a covered emigrant wagon, struggling along over rough and dangerous roads, much of the way half-frozen and covered with snow, he arrived safely at his future homestead, and at once, with ax in hand, began unflinchingly to fell the giant forest trees, and to carve out of it a home, a competence, an honorable position and name among the early pioneers, with an intensity of purpose which never for a moment was shaken or wavered.[5]

Fig 1. William Poppleton (1795-1869)

Fig 2. Zada Crooks Poppleton (1796-1861)
Both Photos Courtesy of A.J. Poppleton III Personal Collection

Over the years, William Poppleton purchased more farm land from the government and other settlers, so that within 20 years, he owned more than twelve-hundred acres. Zada Poppleton gave birth to seven children: an unnamed baby who died in infancy, Orrin, Sally, Hannah, Carrie, Zada, and Andrew. In his memoirs, Andrew wrote that his mother was a woman of vigor and support to her husband and children, and a leader of the other women in the community:

> My mother was a woman of vigorous health, who had both the disposition and ability to second her husband's efforts in every enterprise in which he was engaged. In doing this and in rearing a family of five children, of which I was the fourth, she lived an arduous and laborious life, bearing much the same relation to the women of that region as a leader and counsellor, as that which was borne by her husband to the men.[6]

Andrew described his father as "a strong man, mentally, morally, and physically, and a leader all his life in his community. He was a farmer by trade but always found time to fill many local offices. In 1842, he was a member of the Michigan legislature."[7] Later he served as Commissioner of Highways, County Assessor, and a member of the County Board of Supervisors for Oakland County, Michigan. Orrin Poppleton also wrote that his father was a man of resoluteness, intensity of purpose, and unwavering confidence in his ability to handle whatever came his way and pass on to his children a love of land and family.[8]

Zada Crooks Poppleton died on December 28, 1861, age 65; and William Poppleton died on May 7, 1869, age 74. They had been married 47 years, and were buried in the Crooks Road Cemetery, Oakland County, Michigan. They provided a lifetime of strength and encouragement to their children, emphasizing education, hard work, and public service.

Early Education

Andrew's early education began in a schoolhouse one mile from his home, for which he had fond memories:

> [M]y earliest recollections of school center in this building. I attended this school not to exceed two or three sessions, when a schoolhouse was built nearer my father's house, which for many years was known as the Poppleton schoolhouse. The balance of my district school education was acquired in this schoolhouse.[9]

William Poppleton, a self-educated man, insisted his children receive a good education, feeling he had not received such advantages in his own childhood. Andrew wrote of his father:

> [He] was rigid and exacting in requiring continuous attendance upon all sessions of the school, both summer and winter, and at a suitable age supplemented this elementary education with one or two sessions at some academy.[10]

In 1844, when Andrew was 14, his parents sent him to Romeo Academy in Macomb County, 30 miles from home. His father believed the school's affiliation with Michigan University would help Andrew gain admission to the university. Andrew wrote: "I had grown up strong and vigorous in health and developed an aptitude for acquisition which made my father anxious to give me a college education, a plan with which my mother was in full sympathy."[11] At Romeo Academy, Andrew developed a close friendship with A.J. Hanscom, a fellow student who, a decade later, would play a pivotal role in his life and the future of Omaha.

Michigan University

After three years at Romeo Academy, Andrew returned to teach at the district school, receiving a monthly stipend of $16.00. With his parents' encouragement, he began the process of applying to Michigan University:

> In September 1847, I took my examinations for entrance to Michigan University at Ann Arbor. When they were finished, I was told that while they were satisfactory in all other studies and especially in mathematics, that I was exceedingly deficient in Greek; in consideration of my good standing in other studies, upon a promise to devote special attention to Greek until I had overtaken the requirements of the university, I was allowed to enter. At the examination at the close of the first term, I took the first rank in Greek in my class and held it until I left the institution.[12]

At the end of the first term in his freshman year, Andrew had no difficulty mastering the required curriculum, including Greek, and felt unchallenged. So, in addition to attending the required classes, he was determined to learn subjects of greater interest:

> From the first, therefore, I devoted considerable attention to general and especially historical reading and also to investigations necessary for the discussion of pending questions in debating societies to which I belonged. This part of my education during the three years that I remained at Michigan University, I have always regarded as the most profitable portion of the time.[13]

An Unjust Situation and a Life-Changing Decision

In September 1850, Andrew returned to Ann Arbor for his senior year. Immediately, he faced a tough decision. For unknown reasons, the Michigan University faculty adopted a rule that required "all members of Greek letter societies to abandon them or leave the University."[14] Andrew found great fraternal support and camaraderie with Beta Theta Pi, the Greek Letter Debating Society of which he was a member and became distraught at this new rule. He thought it was unfair and without justification, so he disenrolled:

> I had then been two years a member of a Greek Letter Society, at that time social and literary in character, which I regarded with the greatest affection, and which had been a source of great benefit to me. I declined to abandon my society and left the University.[15]

Andrew left Michigan University and the friends he loved less than nine months before graduation because the university administrators were unwilling to rescind their new policy. He could have complied and finished the year with his degree, but Andrew was a fighter. He saw injustice in the new policy and the administration's unwillingness to discuss it with the students, so he went home.

He hoped his parents would understand his decision and not be too disappointed.

2

Union College: The Most Profitable Year

William and Zada were heartbroken when Andrew came home in September 1850. He had studied diligently and gained many friends in Ann Arbor. He was already sad, but facing his distraught parents in his senior year made the situation even more difficult because no one in the Poppleton family had ever graduated from college:

> When I reached home, I found a sorrowing family. This sudden termination of my university career seemed to them the greatest of calamities. It was difficult to reconcile my father and mother to the decision I had reached, but I finally prevailed upon them to allow me to finish my collegiate course at Union College, then presided over by Dr. Nott. About the first of October 1850, I left home for that institution.[16]

Union College

Located in Schenectady, New York, Union College was over 300 miles from home. Andrew had never been so far away from his family. He missed their closeness, but he was determined to make the best of it and complete his college degree.

Union College was founded in 1795 as the first non-denominational liberal arts college in the country. After Columbia, it was the second oldest institution of higher learning chartered by the New York State Board of Regents.[17] By the time Andrew arrived, President Eliphalet Nott had expanded the curriculum from its original emphasis in the classics, mathematics, and languages (Latin, Greek and Hebrew), to include courses in science and civil engineering. Dr. Nott taught classes in recitation and critical thinking, which Andrew loved.

Both Michigan University and Union College emphasized teaching students Greek and Latin languages, in order to equip students with the ability to read the works of the ancient philosophers and historians in their original languages. Andrew excelled in both languages, and was deeply moved by what he read, so much so that he made a list of the books he read that year in Latin by Cicero, Livy, Caesar, and Tacitus; and in Greek by Homer, Sophocles, and Euripides.[18]

Glancing at his list of extra reading materials, it is obvious that Poppleton also enjoyed great works of literature by Washington Irving, James Fenimore Cooper, and Oliver Goldsmith, among others. But his favorite fiction writer that year was Charles Dickens, as he read Oliver Twist, David Copperfield, and Notes on America. Poppleton collected and read all of Dickens' work his entire life.

From an early age, books of poetry were never far from his side. He loved Longfellow, Bryan, and especially Shakespeare. If he wasn't reading poetry, he was composing it for his own pleasure or including it in a major address. Poetry seemed to calm his soul and uplift his spirit.

Searching His Soul

Andrew recorded his daily activities, thoughts, and feelings in a journal of over 138 pages. He wrote every word and phrase in clear, precise sentences. He entitled his writing, "A Journal of the Thoughts, Feelings and Lucubration's of Andrew J. Poppleton While a Student in Union College, Class of 1850-1851." Note: *Webster's Dictionary* defines lucubration as "study, mediation, a piece of writing."[19]

Shortly after arriving on campus, he began to question his decision to come to Union College because it was quite different from Michigan University. Even his dorm room seemed dirty compared to his room at Ann Arbor. The first entry he wrote in his journal reflected his disappointment:

> Today, it being the 1st day of November 1850, I begin the record of my joys and sorrows, hopes and fears - affirmations and disappointments – loves and hates – during the coming year. Yet before I begin, I must take a brief review of the first two weeks, confirming the time which I have already put in "Old Union." It has been a lonesome two weeks, in this uncouth almost filthy room. I have sat and brooded over serious trust, until my heart has grown bitter, my feelings melancholy - and in fact I have wished myself anywhere else than here. But this is wrong – there is no reason for it. I have found busyness here as well as elsewhere and my treatment by all has been more than I could reasonably expect. During the first week I was the most lonely from the uncertainty I was in. It was still doubtful whether I should remain here or try some other college, and I waited anxiously for the return of Orrin [his older brother] from New York which was to put an end to any uncertainty. He came, saw Dr. Nott and was satisfied, and thus it was decided that I should graduate here. I have felt contented since and have addressed myself to my studies with my accustomed earnestness.[20]

From thoughts of melancholy, loneliness, and uncertainty about leaving Michigan University, Andrew was comforted by his brother's assurance that Union College was a good place to finish his college degree. On November 1, 1850, he wrote of his growing admiration for Dr. Nott:

> During this last week I have been regular in my attendance at Chapel and recitations ... I am bound to recite as well as the Best. Dr. Nott's recitation has been to me thus far, a perfect luxury ... He takes up a great deal of time talking, and his remarks are always worth four times what we get in the book. He is a perfect example of that union of the scholastic and the ideal, with the practical, which makes a perfect man. He is at the same time a thorough dramatist, and a thorough actor, a thorough scholar, and a thorough speaker.[21]

Fig 3. Dr. Eliphalet Nott, President of Union College

Profile: Dr. Eliphalet Nott (1773-1866)

Eliphalet Nott was born in East Haddam, Connecticut, on June 25, 1773. His parents named him after a son of King David (Bible, 2 Samuel 5:16). He began his teaching career at the age of 16 and a year later became principal of Plainfield Academy. He obtained a master's degree from Rhode Island College (now Brown University) at age 17. Like his brother Samuel, he became a licensed minister in the Congregational church and later a licensed minister in the Presbyterian church. In 1796, at the age of 23, he married Sarah Benedict and took a teaching position at Cherry Valley Academy in Connecticut, where he also pastored a Presbyterian church. Two years later, he and Sarah moved to Troy, New York to pastor a Presbyterian church. After six years of marriage, Sarah died in 1804. In that same year, he became president of Union College, a position he would hold for 62 years. The school was in debt, but with his fundraising abilities and administrative talents, he was able to expand and modernize the campus. In 1807, he married Gertrude Tibbits, who died in 1841. He then married Urania Sheldon who survived him. Nott was a prolific inventor, holding 30 patents in designs related to the heating and cooking stove industry, including the "Nott Stove". In 1829, while still serving as president of Union College, he was invited to become president of Rensselaer Institute in Troy, a school devoted to science and engineering. He resigned from Rensselaer in 1845 but added science and engineering courses to the curriculum at Union College, an innovative idea at the time for a liberal arts college. In 1850, he was elected president of the American Association for the Advancement of Education. Dr. Nott died in January 1866 and was buried in the cemetery behind the college. He was the longest-serving president at any American college during the 19th Century.[22]

Andrew attended chapel services on a regular basis. His journal entries revealed that his faith had an important influence on his life. On Sunday, November 3, 1850, he wrote:

> How have I spent this holy day of rest? I spent the time after breakfast in walking about the city with Tuts [a classmate] until half past ten, and thus retreated to the Sanctuary. There, we listened to a very just sermon from Dr. Nott – the first time I have heard him preach. It was a fine effort. He held the audience in breathless silence for an hour, doubtless as much by his serious expression as by the beauty of his style. The afternoon we spent in rambling about the country to the Mohawk [river]. In the evening, we went to the Episcopal church. And now I will lay me down to rest thankful for the just favors and sanguine in the hope of future good.[23]

Andrew focused his mental energy on the required courses. He became a serious student and could apply himself to learning even when he was deficient in a particular subject, such as he did with Greek at Michigan University. This ability to focus on a particular subject or task was refined at Union College and served him well later in life. He wrote of his admiration for lectures given by Dr. Taylor Lewis, a professor of languages. Dr. Lewis's ability to articulate ideas and convey information in an eloquent manner, with passion, was something Andrew never forgot. Dr. Nott and Dr. Lewis were important mentors in his life.

Onset of Illness

In a journal entry dated November 6, 1850, Andrew wrote for the first time of an eye affliction that would affect him periodically the rest of his life:

> I have today experienced a very strange feeling about my eyes - a bout of dizziness which almost makes me stagger. Sometimes, and tonight, I took a long walk in the hope that increased air and exercise might make me feel better, but I have found no relief, and I now go to bed at eight o'clock to try to sleep it off. I have perhaps written too much nights. I know not what else it can be.[24]

The next day's entry reflected no change in the way he felt yet revealed a growing sense of discontent. He concluded his thoughts with a touch of poetry:

> This has been a dull day to me. That dizziness sticks to me yet and for that reason, I have done little today. I have been left to the companionship of my own thoughts ... thoughts within my own heart, and thus, I felt that all was dark there. The fact is I am discontented and unhappy. Why should I be so I won't put it in black and white:
>
> O, could I be what I have been –
> O, could I see what I have seen.[25]

Andrew's dizziness and headaches continued for days thereafter, with journal entries expressing his continued uneasiness:

> November 10, 1850. This is again the Sabbath day of rest or rather should be for it has not been a day of rest to me. My eyes are so bad that I cannot do anything, and I am in a continual state of uneasiness. In fact, they are so bad that I am unable to write and, therefore, can make but a meager record of events during this "Season of my Calamity.[26]

> November 11, 1850. The sore weight of affliction, which was upon me yesterday, shortens my scrawlings today.[27]

Andrew walked the countryside and went to Sabbath services, even if for a short time, but nothing seemed to help his "calamity." His early journal entries never mention any comfort from fellow students. He was alone and wrote of a desire to quit school and return home. Gradually, he found an inner strength and determination to fight through his suffering and stay the course:

> I must endure it another year. I am tired of college life ... Patience and forbearance and some other Christian virtues must be experienced, I suppose. I will try, though the struggles be hard indeed.[28]

On November 16, 1850, two weeks after the onset of his eye affliction, Andrew wrote: "I begin to have some hope that I shall be in working order again soon."[29] Yet, his brief glimmer of hope was tempered by a ever-present concern that his dizziness and eye issues would return, which made him even more homesick:

> What is to be the effect on my eyes?
> I am afraid - not good.
> I have this day thought much of home.[30]

First semester examinations became a deep concern for Andrew. He wondered if he was sufficiently prepared and at least could achieve a passing grade. On November 19, 1850, he wrote:

> This has been a perplexing day. My thoughts have been turned toward the embarrassment of my situation, and it almost makes me sick to think of it. I cannot study – examination is coming, and I am altogether unprepared – what shall I do? There can be but one answer – press it through if I can. It is a heaviness of heart and must be played with some boldness. Things went altogether wrong with me in regard to the speaking today. I ought to have spoken but I think I can address that. At any rate I shall try hard. All these thoughts and perplexities have left me in bad spirits, and I go to rest, moody and melancholy. I shall be heartily glad when examination is past, and this suspense is ended.[31]

Finally, Andrew's journal entry on November 21, 1850, expressed his determination to press on and get his illness and bouts of melancholy behind him. He realized he had no other choice if he wanted to make something of his life – he must fight:

> The last six months have given me some foretaste of the crossings
> and perplexities of life. Experience is a sad school.
> But I must pass through it as well as others.
> Good night! my melancholy thoughts.[32]

"The Law is My Field"

As Andrew began to recover from his illness, he wrote of his thoughts about a future career. He knew he could teach Latin and Greek or work on the family farm. But another option soon outweighed the others. On December 17, 1850, he wrote:

> The law is my field (by my late decision), and I must try to turn all my thoughts to it and accustom them to swim in that channel. In short, make dry detail and perplexing intricacy my heaven. Every man who succeeds in any profession must give his whole soul to it – especially is this true of the law. It is jealous in its nature and will tolerate no rival in the heart of its devotee. Out there ye distracting passions![33]

In his memoirs, Andrew wrote how he began working toward a law career while at Union: "After examining the prescribed courses at Union, I came to the conclusion that I could do a large amount of outside work during the year. I accordingly provided myself with Kent and Blackstone's [legal commentaries], with the intention of reading them during the year."[34] These two commentaries provided a good introduction to the law for many aspiring lawyers of his day.

During winter break, 1850-51, Andrew spent several days watching and listening to some of the leading trial lawyers in New York courtrooms display their eloquence and the power of the legal profession. He wrote:

> A fortunate thing happened to me during my year at Union. The winter vacation at that time was six weeks. I remained at the college during this period. At the same time the Court of Record was in session in that city, and the judges themselves were not more punctual in their attendance upon their respective courts than myself during the whole period. The men I saw there engaged in trials, arguments, and other business, left a lasting impression on me. They were mostly men of national reputation: Nicholas Hill, at that time conceded to be the head of the profession; Charles O'Connor, afterwards conducting the prosecution in the celebrated Forest divorce case, whose last professional work was his appearance in the Supreme Court of the United States before the electoral commission on behalf of Samuel J. Tilden; John K. Porter, who led the prosecution of Guiteau for the murder of President Garfield; John Van Buren, the brilliancy of whose powers as a popular orator were fully matched by his solid acquirements and logical power as a lawyer.[35]

Reading Kent and Blackstone became "old" and "dull" and a "drudgery" to Andrew, but he fought thru the tedious work. He always had a love for reading and writing poetry, but on February 16, 1851, he wrote: "I must stop reading poetry. It does not do my mind any good ... Another week is before me. I must devour 250 pages of Kent. If I do this, I shall be satisfied with my weeks work."[36]

Skipping School to Hear Daniel Webster

Andrew shared an entertaining story in his journal about his determination to hear Daniel Webster, attorney and senator from Massachusetts, considered the greatest orator in the country. Webster was scheduled to speak in Albany, and Andrew and other students wanted to attend the event. Dr. Nott learned there could be a mass exodus of students to see Webster, so he issued a circular letter prohibiting students from going. But the ban did not stop Andrew who figured out a way to attend:

> Securing permission to visit Michigan friends at Ballston, from that point I made my way to Albany on the appointed day. I there found four other students who had left the college notwithstanding the prohibition, and at the suggestion of one of them, Needham, we organized a committee and waited upon Mr. Webster. Mr. Needham made a brief speech, presenting the compliments of the college, to which Mr. Webster replied in fitting terms. This resulted in our being assigned good seats when his speech was made, and also seats at the banquet which followed in the evening. Very much to our surprise the Albany papers contained full accounts of our proceedings and of course before noon the next day were in the hands of Dr. Nott. We anticipated a reckoning, but for some reason, doubtless thinking silence the wisest and best course, the whole matter was ignored and no reference whatever made to it by him.[37]

Final Semester Reflection: "I have Done Well"

Andrew often included in his journal, reflections on what might have been, or what could be. He liked to think about his past, as well as contemplate his future, writing on April 24, 1851:

> Sunday – the first in my last term of college. How many memories come hurrying back as the thought rises in my mind. I have entered on the last journey of my four-year pilgrimage. The academy where I first began to cover Latin and Greek – the old school room radiant with smiling faces - small and joyous – the hailing days of my freshman year which will undoubtedly long remain in memory – the hot breath of indignation and scorn - and the now various incidents of my brief sojourn here – come with a freshness and fullness. It is a pleasant thing to look back upon time well spent and moments well improved, but it is a sad thing to wander over the wreck of departed years and find it strewn with broken resolutions and promises unfulfilled. Of the latter I

have had my share. I have not done what I might have done, but I have done well.[38]

In August 1851, at age 21, Andrew Poppleton wrote five resolutions he determined to follow after leaving Union College:

1. I will think upon the current news, Shakespeare, and the Bible.
2. I will play no games but whist and chips and these not so much for amusement as profit.
3. All days except Sunday afternoon shall be working days with me.
4. I will resume and search upon my questions once or more.
5. I will try to live up to the maxim: "be accurate in all things. [39]

Despite his sadness in leaving his friends and the Greek Letter Society at Michigan University, Andrew believed the year he spent at Union College was the most profitable of his life:

> After forty years of struggle with the world I look back upon the period I spent at Union College as the most profitable year in my whole life. Here, as in Michigan, I became a member of the leading literary society and never missed an opportunity of writing or speaking during the entire year. At the close of the year, I received my diploma and returned home.[40]

A Transformational Year

The year Andrew spent at Union College had a transformational impact on his life. First, he found a way to overcome his loneliness living far away from family and friends for an entire year. He missed the love and comfort of home. However, his exposure to a broad course of study in multiple disciplines from dynamic teachers, helped expand the possibilities for him that life could provide beyond Troy, Michigan.

Second, Andrew was suddenly and unexpectedly faced with an eye affliction that would plague him the rest of his life. At first, the headaches, dizziness, and shakiness made him moody and melancholy. He wondered if he could endure it much longer. Yet, learning how to cope, and in his words, "press through," was life-changing.

Third, Andrew developed oratory and recitation skills that at first attempt left him somewhat embarrassed by his performance. But he studied the techniques taught in his classes and learned from two master speakers – Dr. Nott and Dr. Lewis. He gained confidence so that when he left Union, he had a sense of direction for his life. A third career opportunity was now opened to him, aside from farming and teaching.

In the summer of 1851, Andrew Poppleton boarded a coach in New York and headed for Michigan. He was going home, a changed man. While fighting through challenging days of illness and loneliness, he had come to a momentous decision – he would pursue a career in the law.

Reading While in Union College

	Pitkin's, Civil & Political History 2vol.	No. of Vols
1.	First six Canto's of Don Juan. R.	
2.	Typee and "Fahaway" By Herman Melville.	1
3.	Salathiel. By Rev. Geo. Croly.	2.
4.	Hyperion. By Longfellow.	2.
5.	Brougham's British Statesman	2.
6.	Calderon the Courtier By Bulwer	1.
7.	England and the English " "	2.
8.	Bryants, Poems	1.
9.	The Pathfinder By Cooper.	2.
10.	Oliver Twist By Dickens (Boz)	1.
11.	Cronicles of Gotham By Paulding.	1.
12.	Charles Philips Speeches	1.
13	Blackstone's Commentaries, 4 Vol. 3	2.
14	Manfred. Marino Faliero. Sardanapalus. Mazeppa. Corsair. Lara. The Island. Parasina. Childe Harold. R Cain. Prisoner of Chillon — Goldsmith's Traveller.	
15	Life of John Randolph By Garland	2.
16	Life of Aaron Burr By Mathew L. Davis.	2.
17	Life of Goldsmith. By Irving	1.
18	Hammond's Political History of New York	2.
19	Kent's Commentaries	4.
20	Beecher's Lectures to Young Men.	1.
	Paradise Lost — The Minstrel — Deserted Village	
21.	Dicken's Notes on America	1.
22	David Copperfield. By Dicken's	1.
23	Bancroft's United States	3.

Fig 4. Reading List, Union College
Courtesy of A. J. Poppleton III. Personal Collection

3

A Ferry Boat to Omaha City

Andrew Poppleton arrived home from New York with a college degree, determined to repay his father for the money spent on his college education. The total cost for three years at Michigan University exceeded $300.00, in addition to a fee of $1.00 per week for room and board. Union College cost nearly the same amount.[41]

Early in September 1851, Andrew signed a nine-month contract for $300.00 to teach Latin and Greek at his alma mater, Romeo Academy. On January 18, 1852, half-way through his teaching assignment, he made a final entry in his college journal:

> I cannot justify occasionally taking up my pen to assimilate the heavy weight of life which is dragging through my hands. I have now been over four months a dweller in the village of Romeo and during that time I can now sincerely say that I have never so little enjoyed existence as here ... I have done wrong in not carrying out my original intentions as to study and I now think my best course will be to fall back from the follies which I have been insensibly drawn into and trade the rare luck for glory. I have seen a momentary weakness which has directed me from my original path, and I ought now to break away from its dominion and observe my former intentions in respect to my destiny in life. It is hard to chase oneself down, but it is wise. The spirit it willing, but the flesh is weak. Yet, one will face it.[42]

Andrew fulfilled his contract obligations with Principal Charles Palmer in April 1852, but due to the school's financial crisis, he received only $100.00, one-third of the amount promised him. Most importantly, his year of teaching at Romeo Academy convinced him it was time to pursue a career in the law seriously.

In the 1850s, there were only a few law schools in the country. Most aspiring young men followed the path of 'reading the law' in an attorney's office. In April 1852, Andrew began his formal period of reading the law under the mentorship of C. I. & E.C. Walker in Detroit, two distinguished leaders in the Michigan Bar Association.[43] Six months later, he appeared before the Michigan Supreme Court for his public examination and was admitted to the Bar on October 22, 1852.[44]

An Ardent Devotion to the Law

Near the end of his final year at Union College, Andrew made a journal entry on June 26, 1851, reflecting "on the best policy for a lawyer to pursue in respect to" a variety of subjects, such as religion, politics, and ethics.[45] He expressed remorse that "no profession is cursed with so much chicanery and dishonesty than lawyers."[46] Consequently, he believed lawyers needed to practice their profession with integrity and unquestionable honesty, even to their financial disadvantage, rather than gain riches through dishonest means. Andrew wrote of his admiration for Jefferson, Madison, Webster and other well-known lawyers, and then offered advice to anyone who would consider a law career:

> No man can succeed in the law (in the true sense of the phrase) without unfailing energy, unceasing perseverance and unyielding fussing, and in addition, he must nourish an ardent devotion to, and an earnest concentration upon the subject at hand.[47]

Internship With John W. Fowler

To be an effective trial lawyer, Andrew understood he needed to hone the oratorical skills he acquired at Union College, so he applied for an internship in the law office of John W. Fowler in Poughkeepsie, New York. Fowler had a reputation as "an orator of extraordinary power," well-known in New York.[48] From October 1852 to April 1853, Andrew concentrated on improving his speaking skills under Fowler's guidance. Years later, attorney James M. Woolworth described Fowler's skills and teaching method as vigorous, direct and effective:

> He not only gave instruction in the exercises of declamation but taught his pupils to think upon their feet; to prepare themselves by abundant study, and then express themselves at a moment's notice in the presence of others and under the direction of his critical skill. Timid, hesitating, ineffective and disconnected speech was, under his training, developed into direct, strong, vigorous, and impressive delivery, not after the pattern of his own style, but according to the natural modes of the pupil, when trained and cultivated. He never had a more apt and enthusiastic scholar than Mr. Poppleton.[49]

Cargill, Poppleton & Chase Law Firm

In April 1853, after Andrew completed his six-month internship with John Fowler, he moved back to Detroit to join two friends in forming the law firm of Cargill, Poppleton & Chase. He later wrote that the firm dissolved 18 months later because it "proved to be top heavy, too many partners and too little business."[50] Like many young men of his day, he looked to the West to begin a new life.

Going West to Council Bluffs

Andrew noticed an article in the *New York Tribune* containing a letter that forecasted a great city sprouting up on the western side of the Missouri River, across from Council Bluffs, Iowa. He wrote, "the influence of this letter really moved me from point to point westward of Chicago with a view of settling there myself if my judgment should approve upon seeing it."[51]

On October 1, 1854, Andrew left home in Michigan on a train heading to Davenport, Iowa, by way of Chicago. He heard that an important celebration had taken place the previous February commemorating completion of the Chicago & Rock Island Railroad which connected the East Coast by rail to the Mississippi River. Upon arriving in Davenport, he "found everybody talking about Des

Moines. Upon reaching Des Moines, I found the tide still setting further west to Council Bluffs."[52]

Andrew heard that leaders of the Chicago & Rock Island Railroad were discussing a possible expansion of the railroad west to the Pacific Ocean. Henry Farnam had spearheaded construction to Rock Island, Iowa. Thomas C. Durant had raised the capital to build it, while Peter Dey and Grenville Dodge performed the preliminary surveying and engineering work. These men began to promote a new town across the Missouri River from Council Bluffs called Omaha City. Historian Dee Brown described their promotion efforts:

> Out of a rude collection of ramshackle dwellings, livery stables, fur-trading posts, and grog shops, they created a town to ensure that the railroad from the East would be logically impelled to cross the Missouri at that point and continue toward the Western Sea. On land taken from the ten clans of the Omaha Nation of Indians, the new town was named for that disposed tribe, a precedent in railroad building that would continue across the West for another generation.[53]

A Ferry Boat to Omaha City

Andrew Poppleton arrived in Council Bluffs, Iowa, on October 13, 1854, five days after he left Des Moines on a Western Stagecoach. It was so significant to him that he wrote in his memoirs forty years later the exact time of his arrival, "seven o'clock in the evening," and the day of the week, "Friday."[54] He would never forget this day – it was the beginning of a new life.

The next morning, October 14, 1854, at 8:00 a.m., Andrew walked from his boarding house in Council Bluffs to the Missouri River. There, he boarded a ferry boat to the new city. He wondered if what he read in the New York newspaper article was true or only hyperbole:

> Early in the day I crossed the river, and along a narrow path cut by some stalwart man through the tall, rank prairie grass, I wended my way in search of the post-office. At length I found an old pioneer seated apparently in solitary rumination upon a piece of hewn timber, and I inquired of him for the post-office. He replied that he was the postmaster and would examine the office for my letter. Thereupon, he removed from his head a hat, to say the least of it, somewhat veteran in appearance, and drew from its cavernous depths the coveted letters. On that day the wolves and the Omahas were almost undisputed lords of the soil, and the entire postal system was conducted in the crown of this venerable hat![55]

By noon, he reached the high point of the city, present-day 20th, & Capitol Avenue, and he saw that "the *New York Tribune's* correspondent had not exaggerated the eligibility of the location."[56] Yet, in spite of the favorableness of the location for future development, Andrew wrote he was "depressed in spirits."[57] He could not envision making a living as a lawyer because "at that time there were perhaps twenty people on the site of the present city, but there was no government, no courts, no laws. For legal work it seemed an unpromising field."[58]

Fig 5. Postmaster A.D. Jones, with Hat for Post Office 1854-1855
Courtesy Douglas County Historical Society

Historical Note: Council Bluffs and Nebraska Ferry Company
Poppleton's ferry boat ride was part of the vision of businessmen in Council Bluffs led by William D. Brown, Dr. Enos Lowe, S.S. Bayliss, and others, who organized the *Council Bluffs and Nebraska Ferry Company* predicting there would be a sizable increase in ferrying goods and passengers across the Missouri River. They hoped to convince East Coast promoters that Council Bluffs would be a natural connecting point for a transcontinental railroad between the two coasts, especially if the new city – Omaha, would become the capital of the Nebraska Territory. A.D. Jones, Omaha's first surveyor and postmaster, later described the first organized ferry company crossing:

> The laying out of a town on the western bank of the Missouri River was first suggested by myself to a ferryman named William D. Brown whom I assisted to run a ferry between what is now Omaha and Council Bluffs, Iowa. He took a claim on the east bank of the river and put on the stream a flat ferry boat to be propelled by oars ....A company was then organized to run a steam ferry across the river and at my suggestion, included the laying out of a town on the west bank where Omaha now stands. The newly organized company crossed the river and walked around the proposed townsite. About the middle of November 1853, Thomas and William Allen, with myself, crossed the river in an old leaky scow; one of us rowed, another steered, while the third bailed the water out to

> keep the boat from sinking, with much difficulty we finally made a landing on the western shore ...We gathered wood and brush, made a fire, ate what corn bread we had in our pockets for our supper then laid down for the night with fallen logs for pillows. We did not sleep much, however, for it grew quite cold and we were obliged to take turns in hunting fuel for the fire we kept burning for warmth the entire night ... In the morning, we marked out our claims, then started for our boats. We found the river full of floating ice which made re-crossing the stream an exceedingly difficult and even dangerous task ... Thus, we were the first regular claims laid out where the future city of Omaha destined to stand.[59]

Chance Meeting with Old Classmate

Andrew's disappointment about the size of Omaha, compared to what he read in the *New York Tribune*, drove his decision to continue west to California. By 3:00 p.m. on that Saturday afternoon, he re-crossed the Missouri River from Omaha to Council Bluffs, exhausted and hungry, having not eaten anything all day. He later described an extraordinary meeting that happened next:

> I saw coming toward me a double team loaded with lumber and driven by a single person. What was my astonishment upon approaching him closely to recognize A.J. Hanscom. We had been fellow students at Romeo Academy [in Michigan] during the first months of my residence there, but from that time he had disappeared from my view. In the meantime, he had served in the Mexican War, been employed upon the Lakes, had married, drifted to Council Bluffs engaged first in farming and then in merchandise, and now as he told me had make a claim adjoining Omaha and was building a dwelling house thereon.[60]

Andrew's spirits were immediately lifted after Hanscom told him he was giving up his business operations in Council Bluffs having "made a claim adjoining Omaha and was building a dwelling house thereon."[61] He was genuinely happy for his friend's new life, but expressed to Hanscom, "My view of the discouraging outlook for me as a lawyer who must earn his living."[62] Hanscom tried to convince Poppleton that he was indeed fortunate to have come to the site of this future important city in the newly organized Nebraska Territory:

> He [Hanscom] went on to say that the Territorial officers had just arrived at Bellevue; that a Territorial organization would be immediately made; that an election for members of the legislative assembly would soon be called; that there was already more or less contention about claims and boundaries, and that he thought if I remained and established myself immediately in Omaha, that I could secure a good claim and earn something in claim disputes; that both of us could get elected to the Legislature and that I would be sure to earn enough to carry me through until spring.[63]

Fig 6. Andrew J. Hanson
Courtesy Douglas County Historical Society

Profile: Andrew Jackson Hanscom (1828-1907)

Andrew Jackson Hanscom was born in Detroit, Michigan on February 23, 1828. He attended Romeo Academy with Poppleton, then enrolled in Antioch College in Ohio. He fought in the Mexican War as a first lieutenant, and Thomas B. Cuming [future Nebraska governor] served under him as a private. Hanscom married Catherine A. Young in 1848 in Detroit and "read the law" in the office of Hunt & McCabe. In 1849, he moved to Council Bluffs. Investing heavily in real estate in Omaha, he helped found the Omaha Township Claim Club. In 1855, he was elected first Speaker of the House of Representatives in the Nebraska Territorial Legislature working alongside Poppleton to secure Omaha as territorial capital. He served on the committee that wrote the constitution for the State of Nebraska and helped incorporate Omaha's first street railway line. He also served on the Omaha School Board and City Council. In 1872, he and James Megeath donated 72 acres of land to the city for a park, later named Hanscom Park on Hanscom Boulevard, in his honor. He died in New York City on September 11, 1907, but was buried in Prospect Hill Cemetery, Omaha.

Called A.J.

Andrew Poppleton was 24, single, unemployed, and had no prospect for gainful employment as a lawyer. His first experience in practicing law failed. He left his family and friends in Michigan, searching for a new life out west. He became disheartened as he walked along the empty dirt roads of Omaha. Soon, a chance encounter with an old high school classmate changed his thinking. Hanscom's arguments and encouraging words made sense to him, so he "decided to act upon them and remain at least until the following spring."[64]

At this time, he began to sign his name, "A.J. Poppleton." His friends called him "A.J." for the rest of his life.

4

Omaha City in 1854

It was 1854, a pivotal year for a nation, territory, and city. A.J. Poppleton and other early settlers could now build on land in the newly founded Omaha City. The passage of the Kansas-Nebraska Act earlier in the year, together with the signing of a treaty with the Omaha Tribe to cede their land, opened the door for settlement in the new city.[65]

Poppleton Selects a Place to Live

On Monday, October 17, 1854, A.J. Poppleton took a ferry boat from Council Bluffs to Omaha City. He sought a place to build a home and a law office. Years later, he wrote: "I selected a lot on which to locate my habitation and immediately commenced the erection of what I called an office thereon."[66] He secured his lot "from the Council Bluffs and Nebraska Ferry Co. I paid 'White Cow,' the Omaha chief, ten dollars for peace and the privilege of occupying my lot."[67]

Historical Note: Omaha Tribe Cedes Land

The land of the new Omaha City had been owned and occupied by the Omaha Tribe for nearly 200 years. In March 1854, the tribe signed a treaty with the federal government in which it was agreed "The Omaha Indians cede to the United States all their lands west of the Missouri River and south of a line drawn due west from a point in the center of the main channel of said Missouri River due east of where the Ayoway River disembogues out of the bluffs, to the western boundary of the Omaha country, and forever relinquish all right and title to the country south of said line."[68]In exchange for this vast portion of their ancestral land, the U.S. Government agreed to resettle the tribe on land in the northeastern corner of present-day Nebraska. Jesse Lowe, one of the early settlers and Omaha's first mayor, proposed the name "Omaha" in honor of the tribe, meaning "upstream people" (u-ma-ha).[69]

Home and Law Office Built

O.D. Richardson, an acquaintance of A.J. Poppleton's from Michigan, saw him in Council Bluffs and asked if he could live with him for the Winter months before moving west in the Spring. For both men, Omaha City was only intended to be a stopping place for the Winter. The two men moved into their new home within 10 days of breaking ground. A.J. described the construction process:

> This so-called office was situated on Lot 4 in Block 133 of the original survey of the Council Bluffs and Nebraska Ferry Company, fronting 66 feet on Tenth Street and about 155 feet south of the southeast corner of Farnam and Tenth

Streets, standing on the rear of the lot. It was about ten by fourteen feet and consisted of a light framework of cottonwood scantling, covered at the sides, and ends with cottonwood slabs standing upright and nailed to the framework. The roof was of cottonwood boards, one door in front and a small window at the side of the door, and a small window in the rear of the structure, were the only openings. During the Fall we covered the whole exterior with sod, with our own hands, making if not an attractive, a very habitable structure. We remained in it during the winter and found it as comfortable as any house in town.[70]

Fig 7. Origen D. Richardson
Courtesy Douglas County Historical Society

Profile: Origen D. Richardson (1795-1876)

Born in Woodstock, Vermont, on July 20, 1795, Richardson served in the War of 1812. After being admitted to the Vermont Bar in 1824, he moved to Michigan to practice law. He served as prosecuting attorney for Oakland County, Michigan, from 1830 to 1836 and was elected to the state legislature. He served as Michigan's lieutenant governor for four years. He moved to Omaha in 1854 and was elected with Poppleton to the first territorial legislature. In 1855, the two men drafted Nebraska's first Code of Law. Richardson died November 29, 1876, followed by his wife Sarah three days later. Both were buried in Prospect Hill Cemetery. Poppleton paid tribute to his close friend and partner, saying, "Governor Richardson was a clear and logical thinker, with the additional gift of a pleasing and effective style of speech; yet his chief power lay in the vigor and conclusiveness of his argument."[71]

Historian Alfred T. Andreas described the living arrangements and division of housekeeping duties between Poppleton and Richardson after moving into their new home and opening the door of the first law office in Omaha:

> The office occupied by this firm consisted of a little board shanty about ten feet square, situated at the base of the bluff ... This interior structure subserved the firm for general purposes, for in this they transacted all their legal business, cooked, ate, and slept. The members of the firm were more than expounders of Blackstone and Kent, for they changed turns as cook, and Poppleton was chambermaid.[72]

Poppleton Attends Early Church Service

In the same month he built his home and law office, A.J. attended one of the first religious services in Omaha. Rev. Isaac Cooper, a Methodist clergyman from Council Bluffs, was invited by A.D. Jones, postmaster and surveyor, to preside at a Sabbath service for the benefit of the Omaha City residents. Historian Andreas described the service:

> At that time there was no hall in the village, and the congregation was obliged to rely upon the generosity of some family who would grant the privilege of meeting in their residence Alexander Davis had put up a small one-story frame dwelling on a rise of ground near the corner of Seventh and Jones Streets, which contained a room of about sixteen feet square, and as this was the most commodious for the purpose, it was secured. The improvised auditorium was entered through the rear kitchen door, and the audience numbered less than twenty worshipers, principal among whom were Mr. Davis, A.D. Jones, A.J. Poppleton and others. Mr. Cooper took his position in the southwest corner of the room and commenced the services by giving out the hymn which was sung to the tune of "Old Hundred." A.D. Jones acting as chorister. This was followed by the sermon, the text of which is forgotten. No collection was taken up, but the sermon was listened to with rapt attention and elicited highly commendable encomiums.[73]

First Settlers

A.J. Poppleton and O.D. Richardson were among the early settlers in Omaha City. The first settler was William D. Brown in 1850, followed by the Lowe brothers from North Carolina.

Historical Note: First Settlers of Omaha

Historian Alfred Sorenson identified the first 18 settlers:

1. William D. Brown (June 3, 1850)
2. Enos Lowe (June 25, 1853)
3. Jesse Lowe (July 3, 1853)
4. Hadley D. Johnson (October 1853)
5. A.D. Jones (November 1853)
6. C.H. Downs (April 23, 1854)
7. Addison R. Gilmore (May 24, 1854)
8. William P. Snowden (July 11, 1854)
9. O.B. Selden (September 23, 1854)
10. J.W. Paddock (September 24, 1854)
11. William Gray (September 1854)
12. O.D. Richardson (September 1854)
13. John Withnell (October 1854)
14. S.E. Rogers (October 1854)
15. A.J. Poppleton (October 13, 1854)
16. Loren Miller (October 19, 1854)
17. Dr.George L.Miller (October 19, 1854)
18. James G. Megeath (November 1854)[74]

Historian James Savage added 23 more men who came before 1855: Lyman Richardson, Thomas Swift, Patrick Swift, John M. Thayer, P.G. Peterson, Maurice Dee, Michael Dee, Dennis Dee, John Riley, Tim Sullivan, James Ferry, George Armstrong, Alexander Davis, Thomas Davis, John Davis, Experience Estabrook, Thomas O'Connor, William Rogers, John Kenneally, A.B. More, Thomas Barry, Joseph Mannien, and Timothy Kelley.[74]

Now, with his home built and law office opened in a sparsely populated new town, A.J. Poppleton wondered if he could make enough money to finance his move to California in the Spring. Within a few weeks, he heard that a legislative body would be elected and laws enacted to create a governing structure for the new city and territory. He could now envision exciting days ahead. Omaha City could become a good place to live and work.

5

The First Territorial Legislature

In January 1855, A.J. Poppleton and his Michigan friends, A.J. Hanscom, Origen D. Richardson, and Thomas B. Cuming became a political quartet. They either went to school in Michigan or lived near each other for a time. Together, they assumed leadership roles during the exciting days of organizing a government in the new Nebraska Territory.

Historical Note: Nebraska Territory

The Kansas-Nebraska Act of 1854 created the Nebraska Territory covering 350,000 square miles. It extended from the Missouri River on the east, to the Rocky Mountains on the west, between the fortieth and forty-ninth parallels.[75] It was called "the mother of states," as future states North Dakota, South Dakota, and parts of Colorado, Idaho, Montana, and Wyoming were carved out, leaving Nebraska at the time of statehood in 1867, with over 75,000 square miles.[76]

Territorial Officers Appointed

In August 1854, President Franklin Pierce appointed Francis Burt, age 47, of Pendleton, South Carolina, to be the first governor of the Nebraska Territory. Active in state democratic politics, he was a delegate to the 1832 South Carolina Nullification Convention and voted for the resolution that nullified a congressional act.[77] He had served as a state assemblyman, a state treasurer, and third auditor of the U. S. Treasury Department.[78] On September 11, 1854, Francis Burt left South Carolina with his son Armistead and a few close friends. The governor-elect stopped in St. Louis due to a sharp intestinal attack. He arrived in Bellevue on October 8, 1854, and immediately moved into the Presbyterian Mission House a very sick man He was sworn in as governor by Chief Justice Ferguson on October 16, 1854, two days before he died from pneumonia.[79] Burt was in Nebraska only 10 days. Armistead took his father's body back to South Carolina.

Historical Note: Francis Burt's Arduous Journey to Nebraska

On September 22, 1902, Dr. Armistead Burt wrote a letter to the editor of the *Illustrated History of Nebraska* describing the journey to Nebraska: "From Pendleton to Athens, Georgia, in his own conveyance; ... to Nashville, Tennessee, by rail; from Nashville to Louisville, Kentucky, by stagecoach;...to St. Louis by boat; then up the river by boat to St. Joseph, the river being so low that the boat could not go higher, and the governor, being anxious to reach the end of the journey, hired a hack and traveled to Nebraska City, which then contained one house, where we lodged one night. Next morning, he hired a two-horse wagon from the only citizen of the city, and traveled to Bellevue, reaching there I think, the same evening."[80]

Acting Governor Cuming Issues First Proclamations

President Pierce appointed Mark W. Izard of Arkansas to succeed Burt as governor. Because Izard couldn't travel to Omaha for another three months, Thomas B. Cuming, the first secretary of the territory, became acting governor. Immediately, Cuming issued the first official proclamation of the territorial government, paying tribute to Francis Burt:

> It has seemed good to an all-wise Providence to remove from the Territory by the hand of death, its Chief Magistrate, Governor Francis Burt. He departed this life this morning, at the Mission House in Bellevue, after an illness protracted since his arrival ... As a mark of respect and affection for the lamented and distinguished executive, and as a sign of the public sorrow, the national colors within the territory will be draped in mourning, and the Territorial officers will wear crape upon the left arm for thirty days from date.[81]

Cuming appointed an official escort to accompany Armistead with his father's body back to South Carolina and ordered that they each be paid $2.00 per diem from the territory's contingency fund.[82]

Thomas Cuming was suddenly faced with the obligation to begin the process of organizing a legislative body for the new territory. At the age of 25, Cuming and his wife Marguerite Murphy Cuming, had arrived in Omaha City only a few days earlier. Attorney James M. Woolworth, author of the first history of Nebraska, described the challenges facing the young acting governor:

> He might, indeed, have declined to assume the responsibility of his position, under the plea of waiting for instruction from Washington ... But here were already thousands of American citizens, without government, without laws, on the wide, wild prairies, without even the moral restraints of society ... The difficulties of his position were great ... The history of the settlement of Nebraska is the reverse of that of all other territories. It was not a gradual filling up ... all poured in together ... Every point along the Missouri at which the wildest imagination could see any advantages for a town was taken up. The Governor, under the organic act, appoints and directs at what place the first legislature should hold it session. Each town site sought, by every possible means, to secure to itself the advantage of this provision. Every approach to the officer charged with this power was filled up. He [Cuming] was plied, pressed, begged, assailed, threatened ... But Governor Cuming acted promptly.[83]

In his second proclamation, Governor Cuming called for a census of all residents living in the territory. It was completed on November 20, 1854, and identified 2,732 settlers. Cuming then announced that the first general election for members of the territorial legislature would take place on December 12, 1854. He followed the "organic act" governing the organization of the territory, *The Kansas-Nebraska Act of 1854,* which required, "The legislative assembly shall consist of a

Council and House of Representatives. The Council shall consist of thirteen members, and the House of twenty-six members."[84]

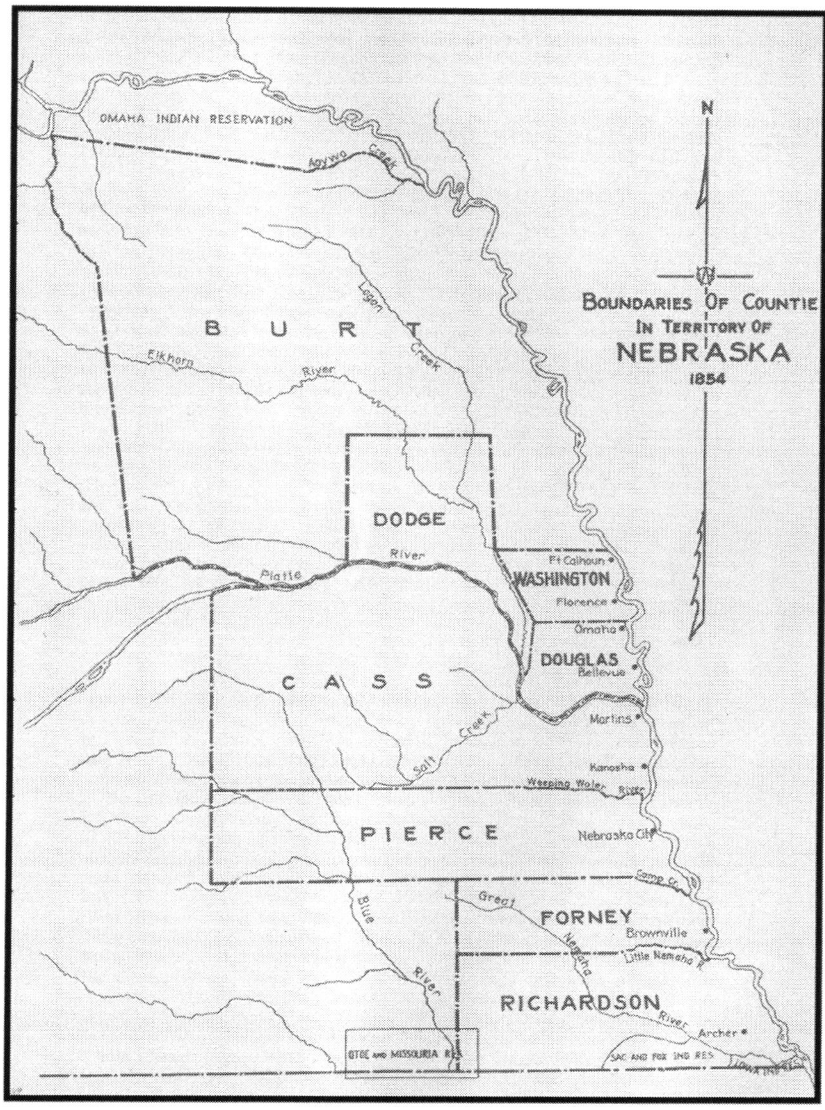

Fig 8. Boundaries of First Counties in Nebraska Territory
Courtesy of Nebraska State Historical Society

Historical Note: Results of First Census

As a result of the census, and under the organic law, Governor Cuming divided the Nebraska Territory into eight Counties: four counties north of the Platte River consisting of Douglas (which included present day Sarpy), Burt, Washington, and Dodge; and four counties south of the Platte River including Cass, Pierce (now Otoe), Richardson, and Forney (now Nemaha).[85]

Governor Cuming apportioned 18 members to the four counties south of the Platte: (six in the Council and twelve in the House. He then apportioned 21 members to the four counties north of the Platte (seven in the Council and fourteen in the House). This was even though the census listed more residents living south of the Platte than north.[86]

Douglas County, based upon election results, was allocated eight representatives to serve in the House of Representatives: A.J. Poppleton (Michigan), A.J. Hanscom (Michigan), William Clancy (Michigan), Alfred D. Goyer (Michigan), William N. Byers (Ohio), Fleming Davidson (Virginia), Thomas Davis (England),) and Robert Whitted (Tennessee); and four members to serve in the Council: O. D. Richardson (Michigan), Samuel E. Rogers (Kentucky), A.D. Jones (Pennsylvania) and Taylor G. Goodwill (Connecticut).[87]

Poppleton Elected Member of First Legislature

Just two months after arriving in Omaha City, A. J. Poppleton, age 24, was elected to represent Douglas County in the House of Representatives. A few weeks earlier his friend A.J. Hanscom assured Poppleton that his educational and legal background would serve him well for leadership roles in the new legislature:

> The training which he had enjoyed fitted him for these new duties. He had acquaintance with the methods and rules governing deliberative bodies; he is able to deliver himself of his views of every question, no matter how unexpectedly it was presented. He had a keen enjoyment of the excitements and contentions of unorganized conditions of a new society.[88]

Acting Governor Cuming then issued Certificates of Election to A.J. Poppleton and the other elected men as members of the first territorial legislature.

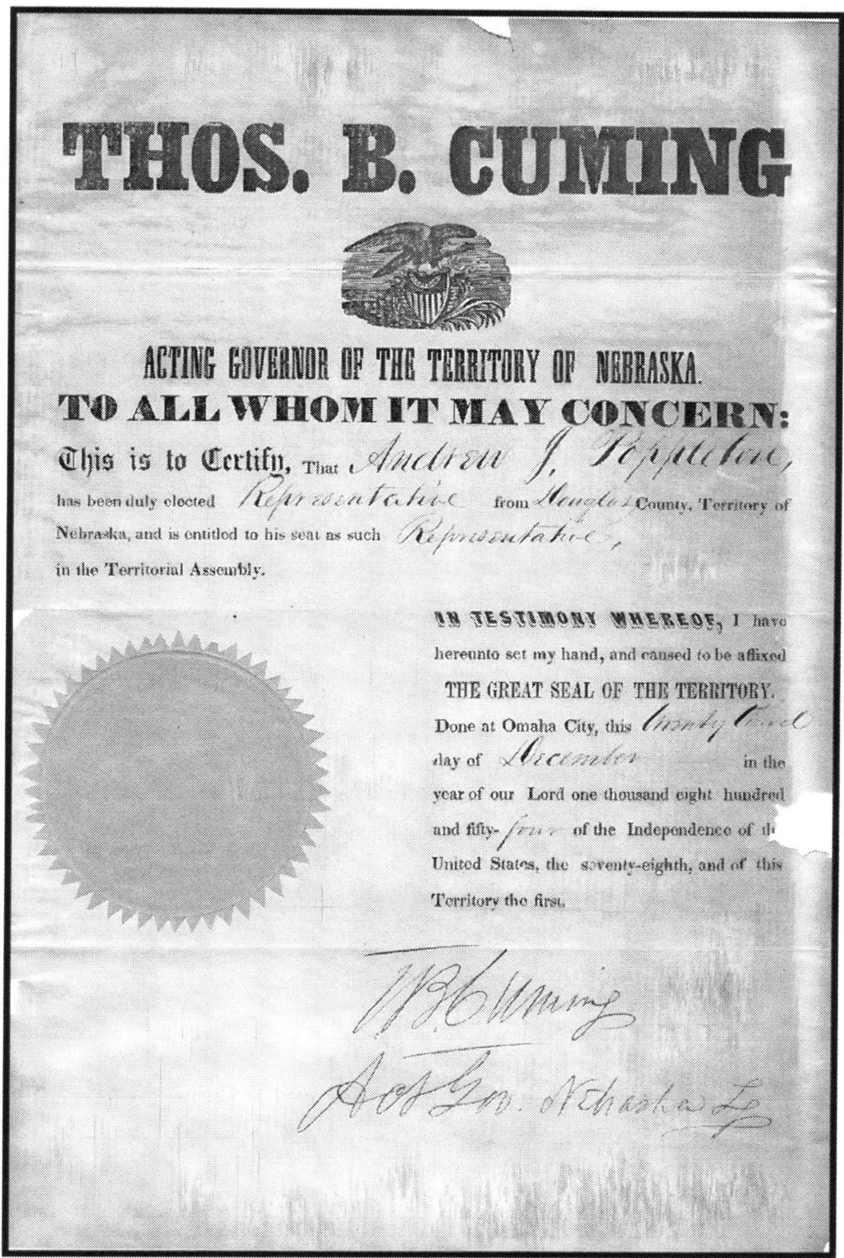

THOS. B. CUMING

ACTING GOVERNOR OF THE TERRITORY OF NEBRASKA.

TO ALL WHOM IT MAY CONCERN:

This is to Certify, That Andrew J. Poppleton, has been duly elected Representative from Douglas County, Territory of Nebraska, and is entitled to his seat as such Representative, in the Territorial Assembly.

IN TESTIMONY WHEREOF, I have hereunto set my hand, and caused to be affixed THE GREAT SEAL OF THE TERRITORY. Done at Omaha City, this twenty third day of December in the year of our Lord one thousand eight hundred and fifty-four of the Independence of th United States, the seventy-eighth, and of this Territory the first.

T. B. Cuming
Act Gov. Nebraska Ty

Fig 9. Certificate of Election
Courtesy A.J. Poppleton III Personal Collection

The First Session

Poppleton and Richardson walked the short distance from their law office on 10th & Farnam Street to the site of the territorial legislature on 9th & Harney Street. Historian James Olson described the scene:

> In accordance with Cuming's call, the first legislature assembled in Omaha on January 16, 1855. The Capitol, a two-story brick building, thirty-three by seventy-five feet, fronting east on Ninth Street between Farnam and Douglas, provided by the Council Bluffs and Nebraska Ferry Company. The House of Representatives met on the first floor, and the Council, or upper house, on the second. Both chambers were fitted out with school desks, and each desk was shared by two members. The windows were curtained with red and green calico.[89]

The Council elected Joseph L. Sharp, president, and Dr. George Miller, clerk. The House of Representatives elected Andrew J. Hanscom, speaker, and Joseph W. Paddock, clerk. After Cuming handed out the Certificates of Election, J. Sterling Morton and Stephen Decatur of Bellevue contested the certification of A.J. Poppleton and William Clancy to represent Douglas County.

Cuming had divided Douglas County into two precincts, Omaha City and Bellevue. This was the contention. If instead Cuming had divided Douglas County into two separate legislative districts, Morton would have been elected from the Bellevue District but Decatur would not have been elected. Poppleton received the highest number of votes cast in either precinct. The election results showed all candidates from the Omaha City Precinct received more votes than any man from the Bellevue Precinct:[90]

Omaha City Precinct:	**Bellevue Precinct:**
Poppleton, 202	Morton, 91
Byers, 202	Watson, 89
Whitted, 202	Smith, 88
Hanscom, 202	Holloway, 88
Davis, 200	Bennet, 87
Davidson, 200	Decatur, 82
Goyer, 198	Mitchell, 78
Clancy, 184	Strickland, 78

Morton and Decatur were allowed to enter the House even though they had not received certificates of election; but they were ineligible to make a motion. So, James H. Decker, representing Pierce County [later re-named Otoe County], an ally of Morton and Decatur, made a motion on their behalf. He asked that a committee be appointed to examine their claims and the right of the governor to issue certificates of election to Poppleton and Clancy. The dissenting men were angered at Governor Cuming because he had included Bellevue with Omaha City into one single legislative district. They argued that because Bellevue was the oldest settlement in the territory, as well as the third largest in population, after Omaha

City and Nebraska City, it should be separated from Omaha City and made its own legislative district. This ill-feeling festered in this first session.

The *Nebraska Palladium,* a Bellevue newspaper, sympathetic to the dissenting men from Bellevue, was vocal in its criticism of Governor Cuming's decisions, writing on January 31, 1855:

> Governor Cuming's appointees having the majority and being reluctant to have their claims investigated, yesterday they made it a rule of the House that Cuming's certificates were the only evidence which had a right to come before the House in the matter!!! And this in Nebraska and enacted by the very men who are so loud in their praises of popular sovereignty! Oh! Shame! Where is thy blush?[91]

A.J. Poppleton immediately made a motion to counter Decker's motion and asked the committee to examine only the validity of the certificates issued by Governor Cuming, not their claims. Poppleton based his argument upon the "organic law" of the territory which authorized the governor to decide these initial issues of organization of the legislature, saying that the certificates of election were conclusive and final and could be appealed only to the governor, and not to the assembly. Poppleton's motion was adopted by a vote of 13-12.[92] The committee issued its report declaring, "After considering the evidence of each party, your committee are of the opinion that A.J. Poppleton is entitled to a seat in the House according to the organic laws and rules adopted by this House."[93]

Historical Note: Organic Law of the Nebraska Territory

The term "organic law" referred to the *Kansas-Nebraska Act of 1854*, by which Congress created the Nebraska Territory. Section 4. mandated that "Previous to the first election, the Governor shall cause a census to be taken by such person and in such mode as the Governor shall designate and appoint ... And the first election shall be held at such time and places, and be conducted in such manner, both as to the persons who shall superintend such election and the returns thereof, as the governor shall appoint and direct; and he shall at the same time declare the number of members of the Council and House of Representatives to which each of the counties or districts shall be entitled under this act.[94]

A.J. Poppleton's powerful leadership in this first important debate in the House's seating of its members was highlighted by historian Judge James W. Savage:

It was loudly claimed on the part of the opponents of Omaha, that this basis of representation was forced and partial, and that the South Platte territory contained a larger population and was entitled to a larger representation than the northern portion of the Territory ... Under these circumstances, various persons not holding the Governor's election certificates applied for admission to the first session of the Legislature ... When it became the business of the legislature to pass upon these cases of contested seats, the legislators who favored Omaha as the permanent capital, under the leadership of Mr. Poppleton, took the ground that under the organic act the Governor's certificates of election were conclusive, and put it out of the power of the Legislature to seat any who were unable to exhibit such evidence of their election.[95]

Fig 10. Thomas B. Cuming
Courtesy Nebraska State Historical Society

Profile: Thomas Barney Cuming (1827-1858)

Thomas Cuming was born in Rochester, New York on December 25, 1827. His father was rector of St. Luke's Episcopal Church. Thomas' mother died when he was a small child, so his grieving father transferred to a new parish in Grand Rapids, Michigan, and left Thomas behind to be raised by his father's brother, a Presbyterian minister. At 13, Thomas went to live with his father in Michigan. Three years later he graduated from Michigan University and gave the commencement address in Greek. He taught school, and then served in the Mexican War under command of A.J. Hanscom. Afterwards, he became a geologist and then a telegrapher in St. Louis. He was hired as a reporter for *The Dispatach* newspaper in nearby Keokuk, Iowa. In 1853, he married Marguerite Carelton Murphy, a Catholic, and moved a year later to Omaha City as the newly appointed Secretary of the Nebraska Territory. He was one of the initial vestrymen at Trinity Episcopal Cathedral. He served two terms as acting governor, until his sudden death from a lingering disease on March 23, 1858, at age 30. He eventually was buried in the Holy Sepulchre cemetery, Omaha, next to his wife. A Nebraska county is named in his honor, as is a street in Omaha, located appropriately between Izard and Burt Streets.[96]

After the legislative committee ruled in favor of the members certified by Governor Cuming, the House moved to the next order of business, which was just as contentious and combative—the selection of a site for the territorial capitol. Poppleton and the Michigan quartet would again lead the fight on this issue, which would prove pivotal in the growth and development of Omaha.

6

Bludgeons, Brickbats, Pistols and the Grand Ball

The members of the first territorial legislature faced a second issue that divided the members into two camps: the location for the territorial capitol. The pro-Omaha City faction was led by Poppleton, Hanscom and Latham in the House, and Richardson and Goodwill in the Council. The anti-Omaha City faction was led by Decker, Cowles and Maddox. The debate began with the anti-Omaha City men alleging that deceased Governor Francis Burt preferred Bellevue as the site of the capitol and therefore the legislature should honor his wishes.

Dr. Armistead Burt, son of Francis Burt, in a letter to the editor of the *Illustrated History of Nebraska* dated September 22, 1902, related his father's wishes to locate the first session of the legislature in Bellevue, but stated that his father did not express a preference yet for a permanent location of the capitol:

> The governor's intention was to convene the first legislature at Bellevue; I think the Rev. Mr. Hamilton had offered the Mission House for the purpose. As to locating the capitol, I remember hearing him say he intended to choose a place that would, he hoped, be permanently the capitol of the state. He intended to make Nebraska his home.[97]

After Burt died, negotiations failed to find a suitable site on the grounds of the Mission House in Bellevue for the capitol building at an acceptable cost to satisfy Governor Cuming. So, in the first joint meeting of the legislature, Governor Cuming promoted Omaha City as the natural site for the capitol. He hoped to generate national support for Council Bluffs and Omaha City to be designated as the eastern terminus of the proposed transcontinental railroad. In his message to the legislature, Cuming argued that "the valley of the Platte is on the nearest and most direct continuous line from the commercial metropolis of the east by railroad and the great lakes; that it is fitted by nature for an easy grade; and that it is central and convenient to the great majority of grain-growing states.[98]

Poppleton and Hanscom Lead Fight in the House for Omaha City

Following Governor Cuming's message, Representative Latham of Cass County rose in the House to make a motion to locate the capitol in Omaha City. Poppleton described the scene that took place in the House chamber, crediting Cuming, Hanscom, Richardson, and himself for locating the capitol in Omaha:

> The first session of the legislature was an eventful and critical period for Omaha. The capitol was to be located, and this was universally regarded as deciding the fate of several projected cities. Nebraska City, Plattsmouth, Bellevue, and Omaha were the principal contestants. When I was elected to the legislature, of course all realized the importance of the session upon our peculiar interests, for, in the meantime, I, with others, had taken claims and

> become as much interested in the town as my means would permit. The struggle that resulted in the location of the capitol at Omaha was long and close. Of the Territorial officials, Acting Governor T.B. Cuming was unquestionably entitled to the greatest credit for this result. Of the members of the two houses of the legislature, while the entire delegation in such body did their best, it cannot be denied that A.J. Hanscom, A.J. Poppleton, and O.D. Richardson, member of the council, were especially conspicuous in that contest.[99]

Bludgeons, Brickbats and Pistols

The passions in the House chamber that day could be described as ferocious because of the intensity on both sides of the debate. The *Omaha Daily Herald* on January 14, 1867 reported that the members had brought with them into the room bludgeons, brick-bats, and pistols. Fortunately, these intimidating weapons were not used:

> Hanscom and Poppleton carried the art of winking to its highest perfection in those days. The latter was always first recognized by Speaker Hanscom when he wanted the floor. The Speaker was always very particular about keeping order. Any refractory member, opposed to Omaha, who refused to take his seat when so ordered by him, was forcibly notified that if he didn't sit down, he would get knocked down. The result was usually satisfactory to the Speaker. The excitement over the capital question was, at times, very great. The lobbies, we remember, were once crowded with the respective parties to the contest, armed with bludgeons, brick-bats, and pistols. A fight was thought to be imminent, but it did not occur.[100]

Finally, on the fifth ballot, by a vote of 14-11 in the House and 7-6 in the Council, Omaha City was selected as the first capital of the Nebraska Territory. Governor Cuming signed the bill into law on January 31, 1855.[101]

Parliamentary Skill of Poppleton and Hanscom

Dr. George Miller, Omaha's first physician and founder of the *Omaha Daily Herald*, was a lifelong friend of A.J. Poppleton. Nevertheless, he gave a frank assessment of the "parliamentary fence and skill" Hanscom and Poppleton asserted to win the vote in the debate to make Omaha City the capital:

> Speaker Hanscom was a great power in that struggle, upon which the existence of Omaha actually depended. Poppleton on the floor was more than a match for all comers; this was certainly so in debate and parliamentary fence and skill. He was eloquent of speech and masterful in both attack and defense. But as a presiding officer in a legislature, Hanscom was simply a genius. He could murder Jefferson's Manual and then mutilate the corpse when any exigency

demanded it with an audacity that appalled the opposition ... But the speaker was always insistent upon parliamentary order.[102]

James M. Woolworth, author of the first history of Nebraska in 1857, and later elected President of the American Bar Association in 1896, described the historical significance of this vote:

> In less than one week, the exciting questions were all disposed of: Omaha City was made the permanent seat of government; and the Territory saved from the sad scenes which Kansas has witnessed, to a course of unexampled peace and prosperity. What this Territory now is, she owes to the executive energy which, in her very first attempt at government, sustained and protected the law, against lawless violence. The wide contrast which Nebraska presents to her twin-sister Kansas, is due to this and no other cause. She has enjoyed now nearly three years of successful, safe government. None of the turbulence of the frontier, none of the outrages of heated strife, have disgraced her; no anarchy, no public demoralization has afflicted her; and to-day she offers to the emigrant a home guarded by law, and the promise of large rewards to his honest labor.[103]

Fig 11. First Territorial Capitol, 9th & Harney Street.
Courtesy Douglas County Historical Society

J. Sterling Morton, who felt he had been wrongly denied a seat in the House, was appointed the first clerk of the Nebraska Territorial Supreme Court. Years later he wrote admiringly of the influence of Poppleton and Richardson exerted in the capital debate:

> Richardson no doubt planned, formed, and shaped more statutes than any other member of either house, not excepting A.J. Poppleton, who was the most capable, industrious, and painstaking member of the House committee on the judiciary, the superior of any lawyer then in Nebraska, and the peer, perhaps, of any who have since practiced in the courts of this state. In those days, Mr. Poppleton was almost passionately fond of public speaking, for which he was well equipped with an unusual share of personal magnetism, reasoning power, and a plausible and persuasive address.[104]

During the same session, the legislature selected the highest bluff situated near Capitol Avenue at 20th Street as the site of a permanent building to house the judicial courts and territorial government offices. This second capitol building was completed in January 1858.[105]

The First Governor's Ball

On a cold evening in January 1855, A.J. Poppleton and several members of the legislature, as well as leading citizens of Omaha City and their wives, gathered for dinner at the newly constructed "City Hotel" at 484 10th Street on the southwest corner between Farnam and Harney Streets. The gathering, called "The Grand Ball," was held to celebrate the arrival of Mark W. Izard, second territorial governor. Historian A.J. Hall described the food, drink, dance, and women's apparel:

> Perhaps the whole affair was as ludicrous as any such could well be. The rooms had a slight coat of what was then called plaster, composed of a frozen mixture of mud and ice; and a very thin coating at that. The floor was rough and unplaned, very trying to dancers and not altogether safe for those who preferred the upright position. It had been scrubbed for the occasion, and as the night was dreadfully cold, and the heating apparatus failed entirely to diffuse any warmth, water froze upon the floor and could not be melted. Rough cotton-wood boards were ranged around the room as substitutes for chairs. The supper came off about midnight and consisted of coffee with brown sugar and no milk, sandwiches of a somewhat peculiar size, and dried apple pie. The sandwiches were very thick and made of brown bread and bacon. The room was so intensely cold that notwithstanding a lavish use of green cottonwood, the ladies danced with heavy shawls on, wore thick hoods at supper, and water froze in the tumblers before it could be drank. Dr. Miller, A.D. Jones, A.J. Poppleton, Joseph W. Paddock, and others of our well-known citizens may well remember this occasion.[106]

A.J. Poppleton and O.D. Richardson were single men and came to the dance unescorted. Nine women attended the ball, identified only as wives of important men in the city: Mrs. George Miller, Mrs. Thomas Cuming; Mrs. Fenner Ferguson; Mrs. J. Sterling Morton; Mrs. C.B. Smith; Mrs. Fleming Davidson; Mrs. A.J. Hanscom; Mrs. A.D. Jones; and Mrs. S.E. Rogers.

Music was provided by a lone fiddler who sat on a barrel in a corner of the room, never leaving the safety of his seat. A few women decided not to dance at all, and of those who did dance, several fell flat to the floor due to the icy conditions. Governor Izard journeyed from his home in Arkansas as the guest of honor. As he was unaccustomed to the cold January evenings in Omaha City, he gave a short speech, thanked everyone for their support, and left for warmer environs.[107]

Fig 12. The First Governor's Ball
Courtesy Douglas County Historical Society

Poppleton Helps Draft Nebraska's First Code of Law

A third issue faced by the members of this first legislative session was to create a code of civil and criminal laws for the territory. The members appointed A.J. Poppleton and J. D. Thompson to represent the House, and O.D. Richardson and J. L. Sharp to represent the Council. The committee was instructed to present their draft at the beginning of the next session in December.

A.J. Poppleton had demonstrated his leadership role in the first session of the legislature, fighting to secure Omaha City as the territorial capital, in the presence of 'bludgeons, brick-bats and pistols," and would draft the first code of laws for the territory.

7

1855: First Trials and July Fourth Celebration

Until a judicial system was created, no courts could be established or justice administered for the people of the new Nebraska Territory. The *Kansas-Nebraska Act of 1854* vested judicial power in a supreme court, three district courts, and various probate courts.

Congress authorized the president to appoint the first three justices to the Nebraska Supreme Court. President Franklin Pierce appointed Fenner Ferguson of Michigan as the first chief justice of the Nebraska Supreme Court, and Edward R. Hardin of Georgia and James Bradley of Indiana as associate justices.[108]

Congress authorized the governor to designate the initial counties that would become part of each district and assign one supreme court justice to preside over each district. The following were the initial designations made by Governor Cuming on December 20, 1854, reaffirmed at the first legislative session:

- 1st Judicial District: Dodge and Douglas Counties. Fenner Ferguson, presiding judge.
- 2nd Judicial District: All counties South of Platte River. Edward Hardin, presiding judge.
- 3rd Judicial District: Burt and Washington Counties. James Bradley, presiding judge.[109]

First Lawyers Admitted to Practice Before the Courts

On February 19, 1855, the first session of the Territorial Supreme Court was held in Omaha at the Capitol building. Seventeen men were admitted to practice law in the territory: A.J. Poppleton, O.D. Richardson, A.J. Hanscom, Samuel E. Rogers, A.D. Jones, Joseph D. Thompson, Joseph L. Sharp, William Corfield, Adam V. Larimer, Hiram P. Bennet, John L. Sherman, Isaac L. Gibbs, A.C. Ford, John M. Lathan, Silas A. Strickland, William Kempton, and Benjamin P. Rankin. Chief Justice Ferguson presided over the swearing-in ceremony and gave the following remarks:

> Gentlemen, we welcome you as officers of the court. It will be our desire to cultivate the most friendly understanding with the members of the bar. We shall expect to derive much assistance in the discharge of our duties from your industry and application in your professional labor ... We wish to discourage a loose and hap-hazard sort of practice. We hope to see the members of our territorial bar take a high stand for their learning, their courtesy, and sense of honor.[110]

First Civil Lawsuit Tried in Nebraska Territory

As the first session of the territorial legislature ended, Poppleton resumed his law practice in hope that it would grow sufficiently so he could remain in Omaha City. Soon he represented a client in the first lawsuit tried in the territory. In early winter 1855, John Pentecost entered Poppleton's office with a matter that would jump-start his law practice and convince him to remain in Omaha City. In his memoirs, he wrote:

> At the close of the session of the legislature, my occupation seemed to be at an end. It was no part of my purpose or ambition to engage in or subsist by politics or political preferment. I had never lost sight of the Law, and in its practice lay the path of my ambition. For a few days I felt somewhat depressed and then came employment in the shape of the first lawsuit ever tried in Nebraska, after which I was never idle in my profession. This was the suit of John Pentecost against F.M. Woods. It involved a claim situated on a tributary of Saddle Creek as I remember and not far from the present site of Elmwood Park, in fact I think a portion of it is now comprised in the park. My client was Pentecost; Governor Richardson represented Woods. A full day was spent in the trial and my client was successful. It took place in the room occupied by the House of Representatives in what was then called the State House, in which the legislature had convened.[111]

Within a few weeks of the first civil trial, Poppleton was asked to represent a well-known surgeon in the first murder trial held in Omaha City. He would handle many criminal trials over the years, but none would be more important to his career than this one.

First Murder Trial in Nebraska Territory

On April 20, 1855, Dr. Charles A. Henry was accused and arrested for killing George Hollister over a boundary line dispute in Bellevue.[112] A mob threatened to lynch Henry, so Omaha's Sheriff P.G. Peterson transferred him to his own home on 10th & Farnam Street. At the time, there was no formal place of incarceration. The sheriff occupied the rear of his home, while the front portion was rented out to a saloon and gambling hall.[113]

Dr. Henry retained A.J. Poppleton to defend him. A.J. asked O.P. Mason to act as his co-counsel because Mason had been a friend of Dr. Henry from their earlier days in Ohio. Dr. Henry pled not guilty to the charge claiming he acted in self-defense. The first grand jury ever empaneled in Omaha City failed to indict Dr. Henry, but First District Court Judge Fenner Ferguson ordered a second grand jury to reconvene due to the seriousness of the charge, along with his own personal examination of the evidence.[114]

At this time there was an outbreak of cholera among some government soldiers heading up the Missouri River to Fort Pierre, Dakota Territory. Dr. George Miller, the only other physician in town, agreed to go to the fort and tend the sick soldiers. He was absent from Omaha City the rest of the summer. Dr. Henry was the only doctor remaining in town, so the judge allowed him to practice during the day, provided he was accompanied by the Sheriff and kept in shackles. At night, he was returned to confinement in the sheriff's home jail.[115]

Poppleton and Mason argued that the facts did not warrant the charge of murder. Their argument proved successful as the second grand jury also failed to indict. Judge Ferguson discharged Dr. Henry from custody, and he returned to being an active citizen, later building and managing the first drugstore in Omaha.[116]

As a result of his success in the Pentecost and Henry trials, A.J. Poppleton's reputation as a competent lawyer was secure.

Omaha's 1855 Fourth of July Celebration

While A.J. Poppleton was heavily engaged in legal work throughout the region, the citizens of Omaha City held a three-day festival to celebrate Independence Day. The previous year, a few early settlers to Omaha City, along with friends from Council Bluffs, celebrated the Fourth of July with a small picnic near the town's highest bluff. The 1855 celebration would be much grander.

The *Omaha Bee News* asked Caroline Sears Poppleton fifty years later to describe the 1855 festivities. At the time of the celebration, Caroline Sears was single, 20 years old, and lived in Council Bluffs with her family. Caroline described what Omaha City looked like in July 1855:

> The city had not then arrived at the first anniversary of its existence and was a scattered settlement of small houses built with few exceptions of cottonwood, lined, and partitioned with white muslin, and situated at magnificent distances apart from each other. There were no trees except along the various creeks which wound their way through the town, and sunshine was as free as air. Only a few streets were sufficiently defined to be recognizable – Farnam, Harney, and perhaps Douglas, with their cross streets. Pavements were unknown. Sidewalks were a luxury exceedingly rare, and upon occasions there were seas of mud, both deep and unavoidable, which an old settler could possibly have forgotten.[117]

Caroline praised the people she met at the celebration. Together, they would forge lasting friendships and make this new and exciting city their home for years to come:

> [Omaha] had a population of several hundred people, which consisted largely of healthy, ambitious young men, who were but beginners in the world's work and entire strangers to each other. There were among them a few men of years and experience, but most of them were here to make their first independent start in life and to grow up with the country ... What strong and enduring friendships were formed in those days, friends who shared each other's every joy and sorrow, and whose companionship and loving kindness were to be lifelong. Gray heads were rarely seen then and there were few children. It was a community of vigorous young manhood and womanhood, whose strong characteristics and wise intelligence have left their indelible impress upon the city and state.[118]

According to Caroline, the 1855 July Fourth celebration was a great success. She described the food which came from a large barbecue pit located on Harney Street, open all day for everyone to enjoy. Drinks were plentiful. Speeches ended with toasts to the health of those present and hope for the future growth and prosperity of the city. Caroline added a personal note while watching the festivities:

> I remember sitting on the upper plaza of the Douglas House with Mrs. Murphy, the dear mother of Mrs. Thomas B. Cuming, and we watched the people going about in the progress of the celebration. As I recall the young men who participated in the exercises of the day, I see before me Governor Cuming, Dr. Miller, A.J. Poppleton, J.W. Paddock, Sterrit Curran, A.H. Bishop, H.C. Purple, and many others who I have not mentioned who were among the earliest settlers of Omaha.[119]

The highlight for Caroline was "the grand ball in the evening," which lasted until daylight. However, before the dancing could begin, the guests had to wait to cross the Missouri River based on the ferry boat's unorthodox schedule:

> The day passed off happily, but the great feature, after all, was the grand ball in the evening, at the Douglas House, which stood on the corner of Thirteenth and Harney Streets. Invitations had been extended outside of the city and the two pretty daughters of Dr. Glover and DeSoto, and the few young men and women of Bellevue and Council Bluffs responded with joyous alacrity to the call. The little steam ferry boat, which made its regular trips during the day, landing sometimes at the foot of Farnam Street and at other times somewhere else, was always 'laid up' at an early hour. Consequently, the expected guests from across the river had to come early and couldn't go home till morning.[120]

Once the guests arrived for the evening festivities, and after the barbecue pit was eaten dry and the speeches concluded, Caroline described her favorite activity – dancing:

> The dancing was in the dining room of the hotel, and all of Omaha society was there, its youth and beauty, fair women, and brave men. There were pretty toilets, like their wearers, of the latest importations from the east. And if there was any lack of conventionality in the surroundings, it was not permitted to interfere with anyone's enjoyment ... A row of benches around the room furnished ample accommodation for spectators and friends. They all gave themselves up to the pleasure of the occasion, and the hours were chased with flying feet, close to the dawn.[121]

With little sleep, 'a few untiring young people,' Caroline Sears and A.J. Poppleton among them, decided to take the party out of town for a picnic the next morning:

> The festivities were supplemented the next day with a delightful picnic at "Paddock's Grove." A party of eight drove out, forded the Papillion [creek] and spent the day under the trees. The sun had sunk behind the hills long before the city was reached on their return. Of course, the little ferry boat was "laid up," and it was the morning of the third day, before the final echoes died away in the distance, of the great celebration of Omaha's first Fourth of July.[122]

December 1855

In December 1855, Omaha City had grown to almost 200 inhabitants.[123] Although A.J. Poppleton had been a member of the committee that drafted the first Code of Laws for the Nebraska Territory, he was not a member of the second session of the legislature that adopted the committee's draft that same month.[124]

A.J.'s thoughts and heart had crossed the Missouri River to Council Bluffs. There, he would soon marry the most significant person in his life, Caroline Laura Sears.

8

"The Most Fortunate Day of My Life"

A.J. Poppleton called his wedding day the most fortunate day of his life:

> For me the most fortunate day of my life was that which brought the health and strength and sunshine of her nature into my own darker and more desponding life. Looking back nearly forty years, I can see very plainly that without her, my life might have become largely valueless and useless.[125]

He wrote these words as reminiscences four years before his death. The reflections expressed his great love for his beloved wife, Caroline, whom he said made life worthwhile.

Caroline Sears Poppleton's Diary

Caroline Laura Sears was born in Canton, St. Lawrence County, New York on May 11, 1835. Her father, Leonard Sears, born in Windsor, Vermont May 1802 was a descendant of William Brewster, who led the Pilgrims to America on the Mayflower in 1620. Caroline's mother, Delia Foote, born in Canton, New York November 1812, married Leonard Sears in Canton on September 16, 1827. They had eleven children.[126]

For nearly fifty years, Caroline Sears Poppleton kept a diary of important happenings in her life. She called her writings, *Diary of Events,* because the entries were not daily, and many times there were considerable breaks between entries. The first entry, dated May 2, 1854, gave a brief description of her family's move from New York to Council Bluffs:

> Leonard Sears and his wife Delia Foote Sears, my father and mother, with eight of their children, of which I was their oldest [living child], left Canton, St. Lawrence County, New York and took a propeller this same day for Chicago ... and arrived at Council Bluffs on June 10, 1854. Rented the Bohemian House on Broadway.[127]

The Omaha Excelsior published an interview with Caroline, who shared her memories of her family's journey to Council Bluffs, the many modes of transportation required, and the unforeseen delays before arriving at their destination:

> On May 1, 1854, they left Ogdensburg, N.Y. in a "propeller," a passenger and freight boat much used for lake navigation in those days before the enlargement of the Weiland canal, and which steamed or sailed according to the variableness of the winds. It carried them up the St. Lawrence River past the "Thousands Islands," through the canal and the Great Lakes, touching at Detroit,

> Milwaukee, and other points on the way, until at last after fourteen days of delightful travel, they reached Chicago, a city at that time of about 40,000 people. From there they had their only bit of land travel, 100 miles by rail to LaSalle, where they took a steamer down the Illinois and Mississippi rivers to St. Louis. Here they had a wait of ten days which was very enjoyable. It was spent on the steamer Genoa, which was about to make its first trip up the Missouri River and had been chartered by the American Fur Company for the Yellowstone. It was a new boat, well equipped and everything pleasant ... At last, the steamer started on it way. It reached Council Bluffs on the 10th day of June, and it made its landing almost directly opposite this city, which at that time had neither name nor habitation. It was a point, however, which was well known as one of the gateways of the great overland emigration route to Utah and Pacific coast, and Council Bluffs, or Kanesville, had for several years been an important outfitting station.[128]

A year after arriving in Council Bluffs, Caroline's family moved from the Bohemian House on Broadway into the Pacific House Hotel which her parents managed until 1856.

Dancing in Council Bluffs

On December 8, 1854, Caroline wrote a four-page letter to her cousin "Lib" who was living in New York. She shared the happiness she felt in her new life in Council Bluffs, and the dances she attended. She teased her cousin about the cold days of New York versus the warm, beautiful climate of Council Bluffs. At the end of the letter, Caroline sent her love and wrote of her longing to see her aunts, uncles, and cousins again. In an excerpt from this letter, she shared her favorite pastime - dancing:

> My Dear Lib: Council Bluffs city Dec 8, 1854
>
> I am very far from being homesick – this is a beautiful climate and country – if you could be here now Lib – I am sure you would never wish to spend another fall and winter in New York. We are having such a delightful fall and winter – neither snow nor rain and the streets as dry as in summer – such a thing as a shawl I have not thought of and have not worn my double shawl more than four or five times. I often imagine you all muffled up to your eyes in cloaks and furs ... If you are fond of dancing this is just the place for you for it is the only amusement we have here, and plenty of it. I have never participated in it however until the last two - I attended them and enjoyed them very much – the first at the Pacific House a three-story brick hotel and last Tuesday evening the same company met at the Atlantic House a little story and a half log hotel – I went with Mr. [J.W.] Paddock, and I can tell you we had a deal of fun ... I cannot realize that I am so far away from all my friends – but – I hope to see them again before time has made many changes. You must give all my love to all your folks – mother sends love too.
>
> Your friend and cuz, Carrie Sears[129]

Engagement and Marriage

On June 10, 1855, Caroline made a matter-of-fact entry in her diary: "Became engaged to Mr. A.J. Poppleton of Birmingham, Michigan who came to Omaha, October 13, 1854 - member of the first legislature."[130] Six months later, Caroline wrote: "December 2nd, 1855, we were married in Council Bluffs and crossed the river the next morning to Omaha, our home ever since at old Douglas House, 13th & Harney."[131]

Rev. George G. Rice officiated the marriage ceremony for Caroline, age 20, and A.J. age 25. Family friends, Mr. & Mrs. W.A. Robinson, acted as witnesses. In addition to her parents, Caroline's surviving siblings also attended the wedding: Delia Louise Sears, age 4; Millard Filmore Sears, age 7; Joseph Leonard Sears, age 9; Mary Rust Sears, age 11; Stillman Foote Sears, age 13; and Charles West Sears, age 18. A.J.'s parents were unable to attend due to the difficulty of traveling such a long distance in winter. In his memoirs, A.J. wrote of his deep love for Caroline:

> [Caroline] has been my stay and support and anchor in every worthy purpose and achievement, and in the darkness which now enshrouds me, her light shines with undiminished radiance. From this union have been born four children: Elizabeth E., Mary Zada, William S. and Mary D. Mary Zada died at the age of three years; my children have been a great support and comfort to me.[132]

First Years of Marriage

Mr. and Mrs. Poppleton began their life together in a one-room apartment in the newly opened Douglas House, on the southwest corner of 13th & Harney Street. It was Omaha's first regular hotel. C.B. Smith, then private secretary to acting Governor Thomas B. Cuming, leased an apartment and offered its use to the Poppletons while he and his wife were on a trip east. Caroline shared what their early months of marriage were like in an interview with the *Omaha Bee News*:

> The first three months we boarded at the old Douglas House on Thirteenth Street, after which I had hoped the new hotel would be named. Then we began housekeeping in one room in the brick building built by Jesse Lowe, the site since occupied by the old United States National Bank building at Twelfth and Farnam Streets. Mr. Poppleton's office was in the front, which was also partly occupied by J.W. Paddock, who was not married and often breakfasted with us. Across the hall was the bank of the Western Fire and Marine Insurance company, organized in 1855. The building was filled with offices and the rest of the block was used by the Indians to receive their yearly annuities. The room which we used was the home of C.B. Smith, the private secretary of Governor T.B. Cuming, and his wife kindly offered it to us with its furniture while they were away on a visit to the east. There we cooked, ate, slept, and entertained our visitors for another three months. I well remember having Mr. & Mrs. W. N. Byers to dinner with us, who afterward became a partner with Mr. Poppleton in loans and real estate. In May, we moved into our own home, with orchard and

garden, on the corner of Capitol Avenue and Fifteenth Street, where we lived for ten years.[133]

In the letter Caroline wrote to her cousin 'Lib' on December 8, 1854, she spoke of dancing with J.W. Paddock, who served with Poppleton in the first session of the legislature. He could have introduced Caroline to A.J., or they could have all met at the dances in Council Bluffs that Caroline loved so much.

Fig 13. Joseph W. Paddock.
Courtesy Douglas County Historical Society

Profile: Joseph W. Paddock (1825-1895)

J.W. Paddock was born in Matena, New York on April 27, 1825. He came to Omaha City on September 24, 1854, three months after Caroline arrived in Council Bluffs and one month before A.J. arrived in Omaha City. Historian Judge James Savage wrote of Paddock's near-death experience: "In January 1855, while crossing the Missouri river on the ice, he stepped into an air-hole and would undoubtedly have drowned but for the fact that he was holding under his right arm a buffalo robe rolled up in a long bundle, and this, catching on the ice, held him until assistance could be given." He had a distinguished career in local politics, serving as the first clerk of the first session of the territorial House of Representatives, as the first clerk of the First District Court held in Omaha, as a member of the Omaha City Council, as a member of the Douglas County Board of Commissioners, and as general claim agent for the Union Pacific Railroad. In 1858, he went back to Canton, New York, and married Susie A. Mack. They returned to Omaha and had two children. He died January 20, 1895, and was buried in Prospect Hill Cemetery, Omaha.[134]

Caroline made no more entries in her diary until May 1858, two months after her husband had been elected Omaha's second mayor. She devoted the three years between their marriage and his election to raising Elizabeth and supporting A.J. in his growing law practice and political activities.

Birth of First Child - Libby

Caroline gave birth to their first child, Elizabeth Ellen Poppleton, known in the family as "Libby", on September 10, 1856. The baby was named in honor of Caroline's two sisters who had died so young. Caroline's Diary noted: "Father and mother Poppleton made their first visit during this month, also my own mother."[135]

Fig 14. A. J. Poppleton (1856)
Courtesy of A.J. Poppleton III Personal Collection

Fig 15. Caroline and Libby Poppleton (1856)
Courtesy of A.J. Poppleton III Personal Collection

Caroline's Cousin Visits the Poppletons

In the early months of Caroline's pregnancy, her first cousin Mary Rockwood Powers came to visit her on the way to California. Mary's husband was a surgeon who left his practice and family in Wisconsin to go to the gold fields near San Francisco. Mary left her job teaching school and boarded an overland coach on April 8, 1856, headed for Omaha City. She did not want to leave her job or her widowed mother and friends to make the long arduous trip across such a long distance, especially with three children under the age of seven. But her husband insisted they join him in California.

On May 23, 1856, Mary Powers arrived in Council Bluffs and walked to the Pacific House Hotel expecting to see her aunt and uncle, Leonard and Delia Sears, Caroline's parents. Mary was disappointed when she was told they no longer managed the hotel, but had moved 60 miles away to a small village outside of Onawa, Iowa. Mary arranged for a room and bath for herself and the children because they had been on the road for nearly seven weeks. The next morning, they took a ferry boat to Omaha City.

Mary and her children walked from the ferry landing to A.J. and Caroline Poppleton's home at 15th & Capitol Avenue. A.J. was out of town on legal business, but Caroline greeted her cousin with open arms and prepared a large meal of fresh bread, jellies, pickles, and dried apples for her family. Caroline's mother, Delia Sears, traveled from Onawa, Iowa, to join them. Mary wrote in her journal that the three women had a marvelous reunion, laughing about old times while doing laundry, cooking meals, and playing with the children.[136]

In the meantime, Dr. Powers arrived in Omaha to meet his family and help with the journey to California. He purchased a wagon and four horses along with three sacks of flour, 100 pounds of bacon, 50 pounds of sugar, 55 pounds of coffee, eight pounds of candles, and nine bars of soap. On June 1, 1856, Mary and her children bid goodbye to Caroline and Delia Sears and headed west to California.

By the time Mary Powers and her family reached the Rocky Mountains, their food and supplies were running low, and three of their horses had died. In contrast to the eight happy and fun-filled days spent with the Poppleton family in Omaha City, the Powers family faced a fearful struggle trying to survive. Five months after leaving Omaha City, they arrived in San Leandro, California. The following Spring, Mary gave birth to her second set of twins, but they both died within six months.

In May 1858, less than two years after she left Caroline in Omaha City, Mary Powers died at the age of 32. In the years before the transcontinental railroad was built, the journey across the Great Plains to California was especially difficult and dangerous for a young mother with small children. It often ended in tragedy.

Caroline and Mary never met again.[137]

9

The Gathering Under the Lone Tree

A. J. Poppleton's law practice in the mid-1850's was by necessity general in nature, yet he soon gained a reputation as an expert in real estate matters, especially claim disputes. He later wrote of the significance of his land claim litigation:

> In March 1857 when the government surveys were completed and the United States Land Office opened at Omaha, contests in the land office and litigation in the courts following these contests became the staple litigation in which I was engaged until 1863, when my work for the Union Pacific Railway Company first began.[138]

The skills he gained as a trial lawyer were noted by fellow attorney and historian James M. Woolworth: "Mr. Poppleton threw himself into the controversies in which he was engaged with all the zeal, energy, and powers of which he was capable. The whole thing was a school in which the skill and the power of the orator and lawyer were trained." [139]

The Omaha Township Claim Association (Claim Club)

In the early days of Omaha City, land disputes frequently arose among rival claimants over the same land. For example, one person would base a claim by hammering a stake in the ground, even if he had not yet built a home. Another person would base a claim by satisfying the guidelines set forth in the U.S. Preemption Act of 1841, which included building "a residence of the claimant, and paying the federal government $1.25 per acre."[140]

The federal government did not open a land office in Omaha City until 1857, to provide a legal process for filing a claim. Consequently, the disputing parties would settle their differences by litigation, or by fisticuffs. Regardless, the entire process of laying claim to a tract of land could be contentious and confusing. To fill the gap in the legal system until the government could open a land office, a group of settlers met on July 22, 1854 "under a large elm known as the 'lone tree' which stood on the bank of the river at the landing of the ferry boat."[141] There they formed *The Omaha Township Claim Association*, a claim club modeled after similar clubs in Iowa and other territories. The initial chair was Samuel A. Lewis, and M.C. Gaylord acted as secretary. A.D. Jones was elected Judge of the Association with the responsibility of arbitrating disputes between rival claimants. He was called "judge" for the rest of his life, but never served as a judge in any established court of law.

Fig 16. A.D. Jones
Courtesy of the Bostwick-Frohardt Collection
owned by KM3TV and on permanent loan to the Durham Museum, Omaha.

Profile: Alfred D. Jones (1814-1902)

Alfred D. Jones was born in Philadelphia on January 13, 1814. He held a variety of jobs before arriving in Omaha in 1853: bricklayer, plasterer, merchant, teacher, and surveyor. He was active in Iowa politics and served as Clerk of the Court in Des Moines. Along with his friends Thomas and William Allen, he "marked" the first claims in Omaha City and built his home. Earlier he had surveyed the city of Des Moines, Iowa, so he was qualified to conduct the first survey of Omaha with William D. Brown. He served as Omaha's first postmaster, storing the mail in his stovepipe hat until he could deliver it to the proper recipient. He was a member of Omaha's first city council in1854; a member of the first Council in the territorial legislature in 1855, and speaker of the House in 1861. He never practiced law although he was a member of the Douglas County Bar. He helped create the Odd Fellows Lodge and served as its Grand Master. A street in Omaha is named in his honor. He died on August 30, 1902, age 88, and was buried with his wife Sophronia Reeves Jones in Forest Lawn Cemetery, Omaha.

Within a year, A,J. Poppleton became a member of the claim club along with many of the leading businessmen and civic leaders of the city, including A.J. Hanscom, Thomas B. Cuming, Dr. George L. Miller, Enos Lowe, Jesse Lowe, Joseph Barker, O.D. Richardson, John Redick, James M. Woolworth, and Byron Reed.[142]

Club Adopts Claim Laws

The members of the Association adopted a constitution and a set of claim laws including:

Section 1. Be it enacted by the Omaha Township Claim Association, that we unite ourselves under the above title for mutual protections in holding claims upon the public lands in the territory of Nebraska and be governed by these claim laws.

Section 2. That all persons who have families to support or who are acting for themselves will have protection from this association, providing they become a member of it and act in conjunction with the majority of its members.

Section 3. No person can become a member unless he resides in Nebraska territory or disclaims a residence elsewhere.

Section 4. All claims must be marked, staked, and blazed so the lines can be traced, and the quantity known by persons accustomed to tracing lines.

Section 5. No person will be protected in holding more than three hundred and twenty acres of land, but that may be in two separate parcels to suit the convenience of the holder.

Section 8. All differences respecting claims if they cannot be settled amicably between the proper claimants, shall be settled by arbitrators, each claimant shall select one arbitrator and those selected shall choose a third.[143]

Quitclaim Deeds were to handle all transactions. M.C. Gaylord recorded all such deeds and claim disputes. As a final resort, the parties could enter litigation, as was done in *Baker v. Morton,* 79 U.S. 150 (1870).[144]

Poppleton Files His First Land Claim

Following the newly adopted claim club laws, A.J. Poppleton submitted his first land claim on January 10, 1855, in the Office of the Recorder for Douglas County, Nebraska Territory. William B. Roger, the recorder, filed it two days later:

> Omaha City, N.T. Jan 10th, 1855
> This certifies that I claim the following described tract of land situated about four miles West of Omaha City on the Little Papio Creek, to wit: beginning at S.E. corner of O.D. & L. Richardson's claim, then running thence S. 43 degrees W. 65.00 chains, thence S.36.45 E. 39.30 chains and thence N. 43 degrees E. 65.00 chains, thence N 36.45 degrees West to place of beginning, containing 320 acres more or less, bounded on the North by O.D. & L. Richardson, West by McDonough and others, South by Lanly and East by staked lines. Said claim was made by me on the 10th day of January 1855. The corners and extension lines are well staked, and the stakes plainly marked. A. J. Poppleton

Attached to the claim was a diagram completed by surveyor, William N. Byers, with his signature, date, and certification.[145] Similar claim clubs were started in other towns in the territory, including Plattsmouth, Bellevue, and Elkhorn. Disputes then arose between these clubs over lands bordering their townships. In the Spring of 1856, representatives from the various claims clubs met to establish rules for handling border disputes between these towns. A.J. Poppleton attended the meeting and helped to draft resolutions to address the issue. [146] Yet, despite these rules, disputing claimants sometimes took matters into their own hands.

Historical Note: Enforcement of Claim Club Rules – Jacob S. Shull Case
Historian Alfred Sorenson wrote that a club could be arbitrary in its decisions, and some members could be cruel in the application of club rules. Sorenson told the story of Jacob S. Shull, who had squatted on what he believed to be a piece of government land, so he claimed the right to settle upon and improve it under the federal pre-emption law, but he was driven off his claim by an armed mob who set fire to his buildings and destroyed everything on the land. For two days he hid under the counter of J. J. Brown & Brothers store. His family later recovered the land at the end of a lawsuit.[147]

Historians of the day discussed the effectiveness of these claim clubs. Judge James Savage wrote in 1894 that "the good of many was secured by these organizations, though in some instances injustice may have been done the few."[148] Alfred Sorensen wrote in 1870:

> The rules of these clubs were the only security of the settler prior to the land sales, and hence much can be said in their favor, notwithstanding there were some abuses – an inevitable result whenever men take the law into their own hands. Claim-jumping was considered the highest crime in those days – horse stealing coming next in importance. Claim clubs were a necessity as long as squatter titles existed, but as soon as government title to land could be obtained, there was no further use for such organization and accordingly the Omaha claim club, as well as all other similar associations in Nebraska, disbanded in 1857.[149]

Poppleton & Byers Partnership Formed

In February 1856, three months after their marriage, the Poppletons moved into a one-room apartment in a building built by Jesse Lowe on 12th & Farnam Street. A.J. moved his law office to the front of the building. His office-sharing arrangement with O.D. Richardson ended amicably a few months earlier, as Richardson found his calling in legislative affairs for a few years, while Poppleton focused on building his law practice and specializing in matters pertaining to real estate. So, for that reason he formed a partnership with William D. Byers:

ADVERTISEMENTS.

A. J. POPPLETON. WILLIAM N. BYERS.

POPPLETON & BYERS,

ATTORNEYS AT LAW, NOTARIES PUBLIC, LAND COLLECTION, AND GENERAL BUSINESS AGENTS,

OMAHA, N. T.

LAND WARRANTS BOUGHT AND SOLD—LANDS ENTERED ON TIME.

Special attention given to the selection and entry of lands for settlers and others desiring choice locations.

Lands, town-lots, and all kinds of real estate bought and sold; taxes paid, and investments made for distant dealers.

Plots of all the lands in the *Omaha Land District* can be seen at our office, and copies obtained on application.

Complete abstracts of entries, and transfers of real estate, kept posted, and information furnished.

City and town plots surveyed, plotted and lithographed in good style on short notice.

REFERENCES:

M. W. Izard, Governor of Nebraska.
Col. J. A. Parker, Register, Omaha Land Office.
Col. A. R. Gilmore, Receiver, " "
Dr. Enos Lowe, Receiver, Council Bluffs.
Messrs. Greene, Weare and Benton, Bankers, Council Bluffs.
Hon. Joseph Williams, Muscatine, Iowa.
Col. S. R. Curtis, M. C., Keokuk, Iowa.
Hon. Charles E. Stuart, U. S. Senator.
H. N. Walker, Esq., President of Mich. Insurance Bank, Detroit, Mich.
H. H. Brown, Esq., Cashier of Penn Bank, Detroit, Mich.
John Thompson, Esq., Banker, 2 Wall-street, New York.
John C. Beale, Esq., cor. Wall and Water-streets, New York.
M. B. Bateham, Columbus, Ohio.

1

Fig 17. Poppleton & Byers Advertisement
Nebraska in 1857, James M. Woolworth

New Name for Omaha City

At the end of the third session of the territorial legislature, a bill was passed to "incorporate the Town of Omaha City," and officially change the name to the "City of Omaha." It was signed into law by Governor Mark Izard, February 2, 1857."[150]

The new law required that city officials be elected on the first Monday in March 1857. Jesse Lowe was elected Omaha's first mayor. He came to Council Bluffs in 1853 to work for his brother, Dr. Enos Lowe, who was serving as the treasurer for Council Bluffs. One day in 1853, Jesse Lowe looked across the Missouri River and pointed to what is now Omaha and predicted it would someday be a great city.[151]

Fig. 18. Jesse Lowe
Courtesy of Douglas County Historical Society

Profile: Jesse Lowe (1814-1868)

Jesse Lowe was born in Raleigh, North Carolina on March 11, 1814. He attended Bloomington College in Indiana and studied law before enlisting in the Army during the Mexican War, serving as a paymaster. In July 1853, he crossed the Missouri River and staked out one of the first claims in Omaha City on 160 acres near present-day 39th & Cuming Street which he called "Oak Grove Farm." He is credited with giving Omaha its name. As one of the founders of the Omaha Claim Club, he became active in the real estate business, building one of the first homes and one of the first banking houses in the city. He died on April 3, 1868, age 54, and was buried in Forest Lawn Cemetery along with his wife Sophia Hoppin. He may be the only Mayor in the city's history to have been buried in three cemeteries because of land transactions: Cedar Hill, Prospect Hill, and finally Forest Lawn.

Poppleton Elected to Fourth Session of the Legislature 1857-1858

As the days of the claim clubs ended, and Omaha had its first elected officials, the controversy over the location of the territorial capitol remaining in Omaha City once again came to the forefront. Although Poppleton was reluctant to set aside his growing law practice, he was elected to represent Douglas County in the House of Representatives for the fourth session, 1857-58.

His debating skills and expertise in parliamentary procedures would be needed in the battle ahead. He understood what was at stake for the future growth and development of Omaha, and was willing and ready to join the fight.

10

The Brawl in the House

A. J. Poppleton described the fourth session of the territorial legislature as "the most fruitful perhaps ever held in Nebraska."[152] Yet, during the fourth session, many controversies arose which he wrote "resulted in a portion of the members withdrawing from the lawful body in session in Omaha, seeking to establish themselves at Florence as the lawful legislative body."[153] The withdrawing members who sought to establish themselves as a legislative body in Florence brought out passion and vitriol in all the members. What began as a verbal brawl, developed into a physical brawl, and ended with Poppleton's election as speaker of the House of Representatives.

The Fourth Session of the Territorial Legislature

The session began on December 8, 1857, and ended on January 16, 1858. James H. Decker of Otoe County (formerly Pierce County) was elected speaker of the House, and Dr. George L. Miller of Douglas County was elected president of the Council. Forty-eight members were elected to serve in this session, 13 in the Council and 35 in the House. Governor Mark W. Izard had resigned and returned home to Arkansas a few months earlier so, for the second time in two years, Thomas B. Cuming became acting Governor.

The issue of re-locating the capitol from Omaha City to a town south of the Platte River dominated the debate during the month of December. Ironically, J. Sterling Morton, a strong opponent two years earlier on naming Omaha City the capitol, switched sides, and worked alongside Poppleton on this issue.[154]

Multiple tactics were employed by various members to sway votes during the debate: attempting to buy votes, filibustering into the night, filing multiple minor motions to delay the vote and sowing confusion. Verbal threats were heard in the hall, and some carried over to nearby saloons where members adjourned to eat or drink. Schemes were plotted for no other purpose than to simply counteract the other side's plan of attack. Historian Alfred Sorenson said, "[A] knock-down was no unusual thing as the war of words generally resulted in a set-to at fisticuffs. The persuasive revolver also played an important part at times in the spirited debate."[155]

Fighting Erupts

John C. Turk, age 26, Receiver of Public Moneys in the Dakota Land District, was present in the House of Representatives, representing Dakota County. He was seated near the speaker's stand on January 7, 1858, the day the mounting agitation finally erupted. Acting as chairman of the fourth session that morning was Dr. W.R. Thrall, a physician age 28, representing Douglas County. In his sworn testimony, John C. Turk described what occurred that day:

> Mr. Clayes of Douglas County had the floor. Mr. Decker, the Speaker, was promenading the floor with his cap on, conferring with the members with the view of taking the chair by force, as it was understood at that time. A message from the Council was announced: Mr. Poppleton got up and read from the rules of the House, having first inquired whether the Council was in session, and being answered that it was not, made the remark that no message could be received. Mr. Speaker Decker marched up to the stand took hold the gavel in the hands of Dr. Thrall, said he was Speaker of the House, and declared it adjourned, remarking soon after that he would hear the message from the Council or die right there; he asked Dr. Thrall to give up the chair; the doctor refused.[156]

Poppleton correctly followed parliamentary rules written in Thomas Jefferson's *Manual of Parliamentary Practice* Section XLVIL which said: "Messages between Houses are to be sent only while both Houses are sitting."[157] Nevertheless, the action of some turned physical, and the yelling and commotion in the hall intensified. Mr. Turk testified what happened next:

> Mr. Decker drew the gavel in a threatening manner in his right hand, and with his left took hold of the Speaker's chair, and endeavored to force Mr. Thrall forcibly out; at that stage of the proceedings Mr. Murphy caught hold of his right arm and the gavel, pulled him down on the floor of the House; about that time Mr. Paddock also caught hold of him; there was a great deal of confusion; a number of members rushed forward, and Mr. Hanscom rushed in, took Mr. Decker out of the hands of Murphey and Paddock, and rolled him under the table, after which Dr. Thrall succeeded in restoring order; Mr. Clayes proceeded with his remarks.[158]

Mr. Turk and other members testified that A.J. Hanscom, former speaker of the House, rushed into the hall. Hanscom was not a member of this session, but as an ex-member he was allowed to be present in the hall under the rules of the House. Turk said he believed Hanscom wanted to protect Mr. Decker from possible harm by Murphy and Paddock, both representatives of Douglas County. Mr. Turk concluded his testimony with these words:

> Mr. Speaker Decker and others who were acting with him endeavored to interrupt the business of the Committee by remarks, sneers and threats; Mr. Decker had his cap on at the time; treated the Chairman and Committee with contempt; promenading around the hall and whistling, and when ordered to take off his cap and desist by the Chairman, he refused; soon after, Mr. Decker and his friends withdrew.[159]

Fig 19. Brawl in the 1857 Legislature
Courtesy of Douglas County Historical Society

Poppleton played an important role after Speaker Decker and his supporters left the hall, according to Dr. W. R. Thrall:

> The Speaker having left the House, Mr. Poppleton nominated Mr. Morton Speaker *pro-tem*, and put the motion, which was carried, and thereafter Mr. Morton took the chair, and received the report of the committee, which was adopted, and then, upon motion, the House adjourned. On the morning of the 8th of January, the House assembled as usual. Mr. Decker in the chair. After prayer by the Chaplain, Mr. Donelan of Cass County sprang to his feet and moved that the House adjourn to meet in Florence tomorrow, the 9th at 10 o'clock a.m., which, being seconded by Mr. Cooper, I think, the Speaker put in a hurried manner, and declared it carried, whereupon he, with twenty-one other members, took their hats and left the hall. During the confusion of leaving, Mr. Morton nominated Mr. Poppleton Speaker *pro-tem,* which being seconded and carried, Mr. Poppleton took the chair. The remaining members continued in their seats and have assembled and adjourned from day to day regularly ever since up to the present time, doing little or no business, except to appoint a committee to investigate the matter in reference to which I am now testifying.[160]

Seceding Members Move to Florence

Following the withdrawal of Mr. Decker and the other 21 seceding members to Florence, a small town six miles north of Omaha, they applied to acting Governor Thomas B. Cuming requesting he order all the journals and documents of the legislature be sent to them in Florence, because they were the majority of the elected members. On January 9th, 1858, Cuming issued the following response:

> The General Assembly of the Territory is now in session according to law at Omaha City, the seat of government, where the executive office is required to be kept, and where the public documents and records must be preserved. The communication furnished by you is not from that body, but was sent from the town of Florence to which place a portion of the members of each House have adjourned. My convictions, under the law and facts are clear – that no act of such recusant members can be legal. Under such circumstances, any communication from them as a legislative body will not require the official attention from this department.
>
> Respectfully, T.B. Cuming, Acting Governor of Nebraska.[161]

Two days later on January 11, 1858, William A. Richardson of Illinois, the third newly appointed governor of the Nebraska Territory, arrived in Omaha. He was immediately thrust into the controversy. The withdrawing members of the legislature sitting in Florence, presented him with a similar application to which the new governor agreed with Thomas Cuming in upholding Omaha as the official seat of government. Governor Richardson issued the following statement:

> I need scarcely add, gentlemen, that no one regrets so sincerely as I do the necessity which compels me, upon the first assumption of the duties of my office, to differ with a majority of the members of the Legislative Assembly; nothing but a conviction so clear as to leave no doubt upon my mind would induce me to take upon myself so great a responsibility, but when the line of duty is so plainly marked, I should be faithless to the trust confided in me if I should for a moment falter or hesitate. I have the honor to be, gentlemen,
>
> Your obedient servant, W.A. Richardson.[162]

War of Words

The controversy was not over. Both sides published articles defending their respective points of view. An extra addition of the *Omaha Nebraskan*, January 8th, 1858, carried the following banner headlines – all in capital letters:

BORDER RUFFIANISM IN NEBRASKA!
KANSAS OUTDONE !!
BOLD ATTEMPT AT REVOLUTION !!!
SPEAKER DECKER HEADING THE REVOLUTION !!!![163]

On January 9, 1858, the withdrawing members sitting in Florence, published the following proclamation for general circulation among the people of Omaha City:

> TO THE PEOPLE OF NEBRASKA – FELLOW CITIZENS:
> The General Assembly of the Nebraska Territory is no longer able to discharge its legitimate functions at the Omaha seat of government. Owing to the organized combination of a minority of its members aided by an Omaha mob and encouraged by the Omaha Executive, they have been compelled to adjourn their present session to the nearest place of safety. They accordingly assemble today at Florence. The sovereign power of legislation for this Territory is now exercised alone at this place. Omaha can boast of having driven the Legislature from the seat of government. It now has become a question as to the right of the people to rule![164]

On September 16, 1858, *The Omaha Times* carried a front-page editorial and caption, "The Capitol Its Location and Removal:"

> The location of the seat of Government is always attended with more or less difficulty, and more generally, with much dissatisfaction. It is not possible to please all. The location of the Capitol of this Territory at Omaha, was not an exception to the general rule, nor would it have been if located at any other place. It is not to be expected that we can all see eye to eye in temporal, anymore than we can in spiritual matters; men differ in this as we do in everything: but is there to be no end to our difference on a question of policy in regard to where the seat of Government it to be located?[165]

Poppleton's Leadership Prevails

The decisions of acting Governor Cuming and succeeding Governor Richardson stood with the duly-elected members of the legislature in Omaha. A likely reason A.J. Poppleton's statement that this fourth session was "the most fruitful perhaps, ever held in Nebraska" could be that parliamentary rule had prevailed and that the issue was never again fought with such anger and hostile debate.

When Nebraska became a state in 1867, the capitol was moved to Lincoln with little opposition from the Omaha delegation. By that time, the leaders of Omaha had achieved their goal of Omaha being designated the eastern terminus of the Union Pacific Railroad Company.

11

Mayor of Omaha

The election for mayor in 1858 was held two months after the raucous fourth session of the territorial legislature adjourned. The voters were grateful to A.J. Poppleton for his role in retaining Omaha as the territorial capital, so they elected him the second Mayor of Omaha.

Death of Thomas B. Cuming

Shortly after Poppleton was elected mayor, his close friend and strong ally in the early legislative fights, Thomas B. Cuming, died at his home from a lingering disease on March 23, 1858. He was 30 years old. His funeral was one of the largest attended in the early days of Omaha. James M. Woolworth gave the funeral oration recounting Cuming's courageous leadership in the early days of territorial organization:

> What a work was that for a man of twenty-five, but how nobly did Cuming do it! Those factious jealousies and contests, so common and so bitter in new countries, rent the territory into numerous and distracted parties; and when the young governor took one step in the direction of organization, he found arrayed against him the combined opposition of all parts of the territory, save this city alone. When he convened the legislature assembly here all the fury of excited passion, burst upon him. Any other man would have stood appalled before it; would have retreated before its threats; would have compromised with its turbulence. To do so however, was to give up the peaceful organization of a territory, consecrated in the midst of national excitement to popular sovereignty; to give up all law and order. He did not waver.[166]

Thirty-six years later, historian Judge James W. Savage agreed with Woolworth's sentiments: "Light Artillery and the Council Bluffs Guards, with muffled drums, shrouded colors, trailed arms, and heavy hearts, participated in the obsequies. No more gifted person has ever lived in Nebraska."[167]

Cuming may be the only Nebraska Governor buried in three different cemeteries in a span of 57 years. In 1858, he was first buried in a small cemetery that was sold in 1872, so his body was re-interred at Prospect Hill cemetery. After his wife Marguerite died in 1915, her nephews buried her in Holy Sepulchre Catholic cemetery and moved his body for the last time so the couple could be buried together. They had been married for only five years when Thomas died. They had no children and Marguerite never re-married.[168][169]

Historical Note: Lifelong Friendship

Caroline Poppleton and Marguerite Cuming remained lifelong friends until their deaths. When Marguerite Cuming died on February 12, 1915, the *Omaha Bee News* included in her obituary quotes from both women describing how they first met. Marguerite Cuming said: "I first met Miss Caroline Sears, a tall, graceful, dignified girl, with a quantity of dark hair. A popular belle, now Mrs. Poppleton."[170] Caroline Poppleton said: "I remember very well on New Year's Day 1856; a large party drove to Governor and Mrs. Cuming's cottage. Mrs. Murphy, mother of Mrs. Cuming, had made some of her famous old Virginia eggnog. The rooms were filled with people, many members of the first legislature being there, and a jolly time was enjoyed by all. For the eggs with which to concoct this particular eggnog tradition says $1.00 apiece was paid by Governor Cuming."[171]

Poppleton Struck Down by Illness

In April 1858, A.J. and Caroline were exhausted, so they traveled to Michigan to visit his siblings and parents.[172] He was drained from all the fighting and tumult of the fourth session of the legislature, and the excitement of his election as mayor. The grief at the untimely death of his friend Thomas Cuming added to the emotional strain for both A.J. and Caroline. They needed rest.

After they returned to Omaha to resume their hectic lives, A.J. was struck down in July with an illness that later forced him to resign as mayor. In his memoirs, he explained what happened:

> In July 1858, I was stricken with a sudden and painful illness, from which I did not recover sufficiently to resume the practice of my profession until March 1860. I had been elected mayor of the city in the Spring of 1858, which office I had been compelled to resign in that October, following on account of my sickness.[173]

Caroline Poppleton described a few more details in her Diary: "Mr. Poppleton was elected Mayor of Omaha in March 1858. Suffered a stroke of facial paralysis from a cold, which also caused an abscess on his hips, resulting in a long illness. Resigned his Mayorship."[174]

James M. Woolworth described the impact of the illness on his close friend and colleague.:

> In 1858, Mr. Poppleton was mayor of the city of Omaha, being the second person to hold that office. In the following spring, after exposure in a severe storm, he suffered an attack of facial paralysis, which was followed by a protracted and dangerous illness. Upon his recovery, the use of one of his limbs was greatly impaired, and he never recovered its strength.

He was absent from the life of the city for about eighteen months and returned to it with a vigor greatly reduced. Gradually, he recovered his position at the Bar and enjoyed for many years a large measure of health and strength. He was, however, always obliged to exercise the greatest care of himself, and his habits largely upon that account have been very abstemious. During the time his strength was impaired, he cultivated his love of literature and engaged in the study of the best political and philosophical works.[175]

Historical Note: Stroke or Guillain-Barré Syndrome (GBS)?

The *Frontiers in Neurology* journal, published by the National Institutes of Health (NIH), in an article entitled *Early-Onset Guillain-Barre Syndrome Mimicking Stroke* (2021) may suggest A.J. Poppleton did not suffer a stroke as doctors in 1858 suspected.[176] The NIH website defines GBS as"a neurological disorder in which a person's immune system mistakenly attacks part of their peripheral nervous system."[177] The 2021 article recommends "neuroimaging for diagnosis." Of course, the disease was unknown in 1858, and diagnostic imaging was unavailable. However, symptoms of GBS are very similar to those experienced by Poppleton and include paralysis on both sides of the body – both arms and legs, muscle weakness, uncoordinated movements, numbness, muscle aches, pains, blurred vision, eyelid droop, double vision, inability to move the eyes and trouble with facial movements, involving speaking, chewing, or swallowing. It often begins with a viral infection, then a sudden and rapid onset of weakness that can start with the face. Recovery is slow and typically takes six to twelve weeks but can take up to three years. Present research suggests only about ten percent do not recover.[178] *Note:* Many of the GBS symptoms described today fit the descriptions recorded by those attending Poppleton during his illness in 1858 after he developed a cold virus. It seems more plausible than a stroke because he had no other signs of cardiovascular disease reported during the rest of his life.

Birth of Mary Zada Poppleton

While A.J. continued to recover in Omaha, Caroline gave birth to their second child, Mary Zada Poppleton on April 4, 1859, in their home on 15th & Capitol Avenue. Three months after the birth of Mary Zada, and one year after A.J. was struck down with his illness, Caroline wrote that her husband's recovery was progressing sufficiently to allow the family, with his doctor, to travel once again to his parents' home in Michigan for further recuperation and rest:

> Mr. Poppleton was taken on a boat, accompanied by his wife and two children, Elizabeth and Zada, and accompanied by his physician Doctor Jonelle, to his father's home in Birmingham, Michigan, by river to St. Louis and Alton [Illinois], and across by rail.[179]

12

Abraham Lincoln Impacts Poppleton's Life

It was nearly a year since A.J. Poppleton suffered a debilitating illness, forcing him to vacate his office as Mayor of Omaha. He had been recuperating with his family in Michigan since June 1859.[180]

While the Poppleton family was in Michigan, Abraham Lincoln, an attorney from Springfield, Illinois arrived in Council Bluffs on Friday August 12, 1859. He had spoken the day before in St. Joseph, Missouri on the issue of slavery. The magnitude of Lincoln's three-day visit to Council Bluffs reverberated around the region, and would significantly impact A.J. Poppleton's future law career and the development of Omaha.

Lincoln came to Council Bluffs to investigate some parcels of land offered him as collateral for a loan requested by Norman Judd, a fellow attorney in Springfield who had come upon financial difficulty. While in Council Bluffs, Lincoln met with William Pusey, an old friend from Springfield who operated the "Banking House of Officer & Pusey."[181] On Saturday, Lincoln delivered a passionate speech on slavery at the Council Bluffs Concert Hall. His debating performance against Senator Stephen A. Douglas in "the Lincoln-Douglas debates" the previous year, gave him prominence everywhere he spoke.[182]

At that time, Abraham Lincoln's law practice was heavily engaged in trial work for several railroads. He always held a keen interest in the potential benefits of a transcontinental railroad. In 1831, during his first campaign for elected office at the age of 22, Lincoln wrote: "No other improvement that reason will justify us in hoping for, can equal in utility the railroad. It is a never-failing source of communication between places of business remotely situated from each other."[183]

On Sunday August 14, 1859, Lincoln asked his friend Pusey if there was anyone in town who could discuss possible routes for the proposed transcontinental railroad. Pusey pointed to railroad surveyor Grenville Dodge who happened to be standing on the front porch of the Pacific House Hotel. Dodge wrote of his meeting with Lincoln:

> He sought me out, and on the porch of the Pacific Hotel, for two hours, he engaged me in conversation about what I knew of the country west of the Missouri River, and greatly impressed me by the great interest he displayed in the work in which I was engaged. He stated that there was nothing more important before the nation at that time than the building of the railroad to the Pacific Coast ... This interview was of the greatest importance to me. It was a milestone in my life, and Mr. Lincoln never forgot it.[184]

Profile: Grenville M. Dodge (1831-1916)

Grenville Mellen Dodge was born in Danvers, Massachusetts on April 12, 1831. After graduating from Norwich University in 1851 with a degree in civil engineering, he worked as a surveyor for the Illinois Central Railroad and the Chicago & Rock Island Railroad. During the Civil War, he served as Colonel of the 4th Iowa Volunteer Infantry Regiment and was wounded several times. General U.S. Grant appointed him chief intelligence officer during the Vicksburg campaign to develop an intelligence-gathering network. He left the Army in 1866 with the rank of Major General and became chief engineer for the Union Pacific Company. From 1867-1869 he represented Iowa's 5th congressional district in the U.S. House of Representatives. Dodge had a distinguished career in the fields of real estate and banking and authored multiple books and articles. On April 27, 1897, he served as Grand Marshall for the dedication of General Grant's Tomb in New York City. He died on January 3, 1916, and was buried in Walnut Hill Cemetery, Council Bluffs near his wife Ruth Anne Browne Dodge. The Dodge House and Museum in Council Bluffs preserves his historical impact on Omaha-Council Bluffs and the Union Pacific Railroad.

In 1853, Dodge performed extensive exploration and surveying work in the region west of the Missouri River. He did so on behalf of Henry Farnam, Thomas C. Durant, and Peter A. Dey, who constructed the Chicago & Rock Island Railroad, with the primary goal to extend the railroad from Davenport-Rock Island through Iowa to Council Bluffs. Their plan was to build a bridge over the Missouri River to Omaha, creating a direct path to the Pacific coast, following the 42nd parallel, also known as 'The Great Platte Valley Route.'[185]

In the early 1850's, Congress ordered surveys of possible routes to the Pacific Coast including the northern-most route along the 49th parallel west from St. Paul to Seattle, and the southern-most route along the 32nd parallel west from New Orleans to San Diego, as well as other routes in between.[186] Interestingly, the Great Platte Valley route favored by Dodge had few supporters in the Senate. However, when Abraham Lincoln was elected President in November 1860, Jefferson Davis and most of the other southern senators who favored various southern routes resigned from Congress. Then the Civil War came, and discussion of a transcontinental railroad halted.

Edward Creighton Builds 'The Singing Wires'

At the same time, a discussion was taking place in Congress regarding the building of a transcontinental railroad, Edward Creighton promoted the idea of building a telegraph line between the Missouri River and the West Coast. He built the first line from St. Louis to Omaha and then approached Western Union to support the project. In 1860, Congress enacted the *Pacific Telegraph Act* and awarded the contract to Western Union, which then organized the Pacific Telegraph Company of Nebraska to build a line from Omaha to Salt Lake City. Edward

Creighton was hired to supervise the construction. Despite all the logistical challenges, he was able to complete the project on time. This new means of instant communication over what was commonly referred to as 'the singing wires' made Omaha the initial point of the Pacific telegraph. It also contributed to the argument that Omaha should be the eastern starting point of a transcontinental railroad heading west across the 42nd parallel to the Pacific.[187]

Poppleton Returns Home From Michigan

In November 1859, three months after Lincoln's historic visit to Council Bluffs, Caroline wrote in her Diary that the family returned to Omaha from visiting A.J.'s family in Michigan "by rail to St. Joseph, Mo. and by stage to Council Bluffs, crossed the river partly by dug-out [canoe]. Moved into the offices on Farnam St."[188] In the winter of 1860, eighteen months after the onset of his illness, Poppleton gradually resumed his law practice. He was now 30 and an experienced trial attorney. His work sometimes took him to other cities and states. During one time away from home, Caroline wrote a long letter to him. She affectionally called him "my good husband," wondering where he was, how he was doing, and telling him how much she and their two children, Elizabeth ("Libby"), age four, and Zada, nearly 18 months, missed him terribly:[189]

My Dear Good Husband: Omaha, Sept 27, 1860

Mr. Armstrong told me yesterday, he thought you would be at Nebraska City on the 1st and so I am going to try and write you this letter – I would like to know where you are tonight. I can imagine what you are doing for it is about eight o'clock & you are probably before a crowd discussing this great question of "who shall be the next delegate to congress," which I hope will interest you again to this extent ... It is very quiet here, nothing particular going on. Gov. Richardson's wife and daughter started today for Michigan. I was aware she said she would visit at your father's before she returned and asked if I had any message to send which I had not – only that we seem well and doing well ... I was so disappointed when Geo [George Lake] came back from the office with no letters for me – you must know how much a letter helps to pass off this time - I feel almost as if I had lost you and couldn't wait more patiently for a few days - but it is lonely – I don't find it so common every day, but once in a while, when the children happen to be quiet and I am sitting at work with busy thoughts and fusing's, I'd give almost anything to see this door open and my good husband walking in - I think he would get one welcoming kiss at last –It isn't home without you, everything seems out of joint.

I can't keep house without someone to work for, whose comfort and happiness I care more for than my own. There have been two letters come from you since you left – one from Leavenworth [Kansas] and one from Council Bluffs. Now – so my dear husband, write from Nebraska City if possible one of your good, long, loving letters – such as I always delight to receive from you and almost reconcile one to an occasional emotion and some good saying – With a thousand kisses and best wishes of your loving wife,

Carrie

Death of Mary Zada Poppleton

On November 15, 1862, Caroline shared in her Diary the tragic news that "Little Zada died after a short illness of typhoid fever, 15th & Cap. Ave."[190] Mary Zada was only three and a half years old. After a funeral service and burial in Prospect Hill cemetery, A.J. and Caroline donated a stained-glass window of St. James the Minor in her memory, that was prominently placed in the sanctuary of Trinity Episcopal Cathedral. The window still shines forth in the church today.

After some time alone with their personal grief over the loss of Mary Zada, A.J. resumed his practice to defend a retired judge accused of murder in one of the most notorious criminal cases in Omaha's early history.

Judge Tator Murder Trial

Cyrus H. Tator left his practice as a probate court judge in Kansas to form a partnership with Isaac H. Neff. In 1860, they began operating a dry-goods business between Denver and Omaha. In early June 1863, they were seen camping north of Omaha. Then on June 19th, Neff's body was discovered laying in a body of water in an area known as Sulphur Springs. Two of the three wagons Neff and Tator brought to Omaha were found near his body. Neff's body could not be positively identified for a few days due to decomposition.

One week later, Cyrus H. Tator was arrested near Schuyler, Nebraska, and formally charged with theft of stolen goods and murder. Trial was held in the Douglas County courtroom presided over by Judge William Kellogg. George B. Lake and Charles H. Brown appeared as co-counsel for the prosecution. A.J. Poppleton appeared as counsel for the defendant Tator. He asked William A. Little to act as his co-counsel, because Little was an acquaintance of the defendant.[191]

The prosecution's main witness was Herber P. Kimball who testified he had purchased some livestock from Tator but declined Tator's offer to sell him any wagons. He further testified he saw Tator leave town with one wagon loaded with trade goods belonging to Neff, who had disappeared.[192]

The sheriff found a large sum of money in Tator's possession at the time of his arrest, and one wagon. The prosecution argued the money must have been gained by Tator's fraudulent sale of Neff's property. Poppleton argued the evidence against his client was circumstantial, and there was no direct proof that Tator had robbed or killed Neff. Tator maintained his innocence and denied all charges throughout the trial. Poppleton spoke of Tator's character as a man of good reputation who had been a probate court judge in Kansas and a former member of the Kansas legislature. Despite Poppleton's best efforts, Tator was convicted of theft and murder and sentenced to death. Poppleton's appeal to the Nebraska Supreme Court was denied.[193]

On August 28, 1863, Cyrus H. Tator, age 29, was hanged on gallows built near the site of where Neff's body was found. Forty soldiers, the sheriff, and Rev. Thomas B. Lemon, a Methodist minister, escorted Tator from the jailhouse to the gallows. Hundreds of spectators lined the streets. Tator gave a 30-minute prepared speech declaring his innocence right up to the moment of his hanging. He was the first court-adjudicated person hanged in Douglas County. His body was buried in an unmarked grave in Prospect Hill Cemetery, Omaha.[194]

Fig. 20. Hanging of Cyrus Tator 1863.
Copyright Omaha World Herald

President Lincoln's 1863 Executive Order

On November 17, 1863, three months after the conclusion of the Judge Tator trial, President Abraham Lincoln issued an Executive Order selecting the route for the transcontinental railroad. It would symbolize the unity of the nation during the third year of the Civil War, following union victories at Gettysburg and Vicksburg, and ultimately link the Atlantic and Pacific coasts:

> I, Abraham Lincoln, President of the United States, do hereby fix so much of the western boundary of the State of Iowa as lies between the north and south boundaries of the United States township within which the city of Omaha is situated, as the point from which the line of railroad and telegraph in that section mentioned shall be constructed.[195]

Lincoln's executive order was based upon authority given him by the *Pacific Railroad Act* of 1862, whereby Congress authorized the construction of a railroad across the 42nd parallel (the Great Platte Valley route) and gave Lincoln the right to select its eastern terminus. Prior to issuing the order and selecting the terminus site, Lincoln called General Grenville Dodge to the White House. Lincoln wanted to confirm the advice Dodge gave him when they met on the porch of the Pacific House Hotel in Council Bluffs, August 1859.[196] Dodge confirmed his advice, and Lincoln issued his order.

Omaha's Groundbreaking Celebration

Peter A. Dey, chief engineer for the Union Pacific, received a telegram notifying him of President Lincoln's executive order. He quickly formed a committee of prominent citizens to organize a celebration. The committee included A.J. Poppleton, Edward Creighton, Enos Lowe, Jesse Lowe, Augustus Kountze, and Ezra Millard, among others. A.J. Hanscom was appointed chair.[197]

On December 2, 1863, at 2:00 p.m., nearly 1000 people gathered on a sunny day for a groundbreaking celebration near 7th & Davenport Street in Omaha.[198] Governor Saunders presided over the event which began with a prayer by Rev. Thomas B. Lemon, followed by speeches from the governor, Omaha Mayor B.E.B. Kennedy, Council Bluffs Mayor Palmer, George Francis Train, and A.J. Poppleton.[199]

The first spadefuls of earth were ceremoniously removed by the governor and the two mayors. Salutes fired by cannon on the Nebraska side of the river were soon answered by cannon fired from the Iowa shore. Governor Saunders then read a message from Colonel John Hay, private secretary to President Lincoln.[200] The *Omaha Daily Bee,* June 19, 1904, recalled that historic day by publishing an interview with Edward Rosewater, its editor. Rosewater spoke of the speeches he heard, and the impact Poppleton's address had on him and on the audience:

> After [George Francis] Train had gotten through amidst uproarious applause, a man with a very florid [ruddy] face, whom I had noticed frequently walking about the streets in a red woolen shirt and who I had always taken for a butcher, climbed on the tail end of a wagon, got into the box, and delivered a speech that eclipsed all other speakers and simply paralyzed everybody. I was dumbfounded and asked a bystander "who is this man?" "Why, Andrew J. Poppleton, said he."[201]

Peter A. Dey introduced A. J. Poppleton. The eloquent and captivating words A.J. spoke that day and Dey's reaction to him, would change the course of A.J.'s life for the next 24 years:

Poppleton's Speech at the Celebration

FELLOW CITIZENS OF OMAHA AND COUNCIL BLUFFS:
On the 13th of October 1854, about 7 o'clock in the evening, I was set down by the Western Stage company at yonder city of Council Bluffs. At the rising of the sun on the following morning, I climbed to the summit of one of the bluffs, which overlook that prosperous and enterprising town, and took one long and lingering look across the Missouri at the beautiful site on which now sits, in the full vigor of business, social and religious life, the youthful but thriving and this day jubilant city of Omaha ...

To-day at least 4,000 radiant faces gladden our streets, and the postal service, sheltered by a costly edifice, strikes its Briarean arms towards the north, the south, the east and the west, penetrating regions then unexplored and unknown and bearing the symbols of values then hidden in the mountains and beneath the streams, of which the world in its wildest vagaries had never dreamed.

Then it took sixty days for New York and California to communicate with each other. Today, San Francisco and New York, sitting upon the shores of the oceans, 3,000 miles asunder, hold familiar converse. Iron and steam and lighting are daily weaving their destinies more closely with each other and ours with theirs, as the inter-oceanic city, whose commerce, trade, and treasures leave the last great navigable stream in their migration from the Atlantic to the Pacific seaboard.

It is natural, therefore, that you should lift up your hearts and rejoice. And though we have watched for nine long years, during which our fortunes have been, like Antonio's treasures, 'mostly in expectancy,' we at last press the cup in full fruition to our lips. The lines have indeed 'fallen to us in pleasant places,' and, as I look upon the smiling faces before me, I seem to read in their happy expression the words of the pious poet:

'This is the day we long have sought,
and mourned because we found it not.'

All this, however, is but the personal significance of this great national enterprise to us. To us it means prosperity. To the nation and all its people, it bears a significance well expressed in a telegram received from Governor Yates, of Illinois, which I am requested to read:

St. Nicholas Hotel, New York, December 1, 1863.
Committee of Arrangements, Union Pacific Railroad:

To Major-General John A. Dix, President of the Union Pacific Railroad Company:

Sirs: I have regarded the enterprise of building the Union Pacific railroad as of the utmost national importance. While in Congress, when opportunity offered, I urged the necessity, and it is with peculiar pleasure that I learn that the building of the road, so long delayed, is to become a verity. When completed it will be an enduring monument of the enterprise and patriotism of our common country, firmly uniting the two extremes of the nation, and rendering them indissoluble for all time to come.

I am, respectfully yours, Richard Yates

I esteem myself fortunate in there being allowed to give expression to this concourse, the greeting of the state of Illinois, through its chief executive officer. In this hour of sanguinary struggles, when that great and union-loving state, through that most trusted fortunate chieftain, General Ulysses S. Grant, is hurling its victorious sons in the very vitals of the so-called confederacy, she still finds time to turn aside for one brief moment and wish us God-speed in this wonderful work upon which we now enter. When those iron bands with which we hope to gird the continent shall stretch from sea to sea, they stand perpetual hostages against the terrible calamities of national estrangement, disruption, and dismemberment.

The act of Congress establishing this great enterprise, should have been entitled 'An act to promote the preservation of the union, to prevent national dissolution, and bind together the Atlantic and Pacific coasts by an indissoluble covenant, to resist and repel foreign aggression.' There is not on all the Mississippi and its tributaries, a citizen so craven but that were the free navigation of that noble stream, from its source to its mouth, denied him, he would achieve it with the sword. So will this highway of the world be the common boon of every citizen, to be cherished and defended with special devotion.

Standing here, at the initiation of this stupendous enterprise, in this third year of our civil war, let us devoutly pray that the hour which witnesses its completion may behold a rebellion overthrown, a union restored, a constitution unimpaired, civil liberty and the pursuit of happiness the inalienable birthright of the weakest, the poorest and the lowliest citizen in all our borders. Then with full hearts and bounding pulses we may renew the strain:

Great God, we thank Thee for this goodly home
This bounteous birth-land of the free,
Where wanderers from afar may come
And breathe the air of liberty.
Still may it flowers untrampled spring,
Its harvest wave and cities rise –
And long 'till time shall fold his wing,
Remain earth's loveliest paradise.[202]

An Evening of Eating, Drinking and Dancing

After Poppleton's speech and the conclusion of the outdoor ceremony, the railroad company executives, along with Mayor B.E.B. Kennedy, hosted a lavish banquet and dance for approximately 150 guests at the Herndon House Hotel. Telegrams of congratulations were read from Brigham Young, Governor Stanford of California, U.S. Secretary of State William Seward, and other prominent national leaders. Supper was served at 1:30 a.m. and the guests thereafter returned to their homes knowing they had partaken in one of the most important days in Omaha's history.[203]

During the dinner, the attendees raised a toast to the vision of the city's early settlers. They realized that their dream of making Omaha the home of the transcontinental railroad had come true, and they believed that the benefits of this achievement would ensure the city's prosperity for generations to come.

Years later at the centennial celebration of the founding of Omaha, the *Omaha World Herald, 1954,* confirmed their vision came true:

> As rails were laid westward, Omaha's growth could almost be noted from month to month. The Union Pacific constructed car-and engine houses and machine shops, spending a quarter of a million dollars a month in the city. More new buildings went up rapidly, one brick block costing 100 thousand dollars.[204]

Poppleton's Career with the Union Pacific Begins

Shortly after Poppleton's speech, Peter A. Dey hired him as legal counsel for the UPRR. In his memoirs, A.J. wrote of the impact of his speech:

> It gave great satisfaction to Mr. Dey and other railway officials and to the people of Omaha and attracted general attention; portions of it were soon published in the *London Daily News.* A few days afterwards I was engaged by Mr. Dey on behalf of the road to attend to such legal business as might arise at Omaha for the Company ... Contests in the land office and litigation in the courts following these contests became the staple litigation in which I was engaged until 1863, when my work for the Union Pacific Railway Company first began.

> During the time that I was engaged in controversies over land titles, I laid the foundation of that knowledge of the law of public lands which enabled me to deal intelligently and successfully with innumerable small and some great litigations which sprang up when the Union Pacific Company proceeded to perfect the title to its land grant from the United States.[205]

Dodge's survey, Creighton's telegraph, Lincoln's executive order, and Poppleton's speech and work as the UPRR's general counsel, changed Omaha forever. Omaha railroad historian William Kratville confirmed the railroad's impact on Omaha:

> When you think Omaha, you think Union Pacific ...
> The big player on the Omaha-Council Bluffs scene has always been
> the Union Pacific ...
> Its name is synonymous with railroad history. [206]

13

"The Legal Career Which I Cherish"

In January 1864, A.J. Poppleton began working for the Union Pacific Railroad Company (UPRR) on a part-time hourly basis. He drafted the first general railroad law and acted as a lobbyist for the railroad that often took him to Washington D.C. In his memoirs, he described the type of legal work he did for the railroad:

> [I was] specially requested to prepare a general railroad law to be brought before the general [Nebraska Territorial] legislative assembly at its next session. This law I drafted. It was passed at the session of 1864, and it has remained practically unchanged from that day to this upon our statute books; with some additional provisions mainly prepared by myself in subsequent years, relating to sales, leases, consolidations and the mortgaging of railroads and railroad property. From this time until the Spring of 1869 very much of my time was occupied in advising and assisting railway officers, in acquiring right of way, depot and shop grounds in the city of Omaha, and in considering the vast variety of questions that constantly spring up in the inauguration and prosecution of great railway enterprises.[207]

In November 1865, after the first 15 miles of track were laid from Omaha, UPRR Vice-President Thomas C. Durant invited 20 well-known men, including Poppleton and General William T. Sherman, to accompany him on an inspection tour to Saling's Grove, the end of the track. The guests rode in flat cars with seats made of nail kegs. Historian Alfred Sorenson wrote, "It was an enthusiastic party, and as the commissary department was well supplied, the gentleman enjoyed themselves."[208]

In May 1866, Durant hired General Grenville Dodge to be the Chief Engineer for the UPRR. He was put in charge of bringing efficiency to the construction of the railroad across the Great Platte Valley route. Dodge immediately began laying out towns and building depots and shops to store supplies and materials. He hired key men to manage various components involved in this enormous task. UPRR historian Maury Klein wrote that Dodge hired A.J. to handle much of the legal work:

> The choice proved a wise one. Poppleton not only started the Union Pacific's legal department but remained its bulwark for two decades. His presence marked another important step toward the creation of an efficient organization.[209]

In the mid 1860's, A.J. Poppleton had a demanding part-time client in the Union Pacific, a thriving law practice, and a growing family. Caroline gave birth to William Sears Poppleton on April 7, 1866, at their home on 15th & Capital Avenue. The following December, the family moved into a new home near Fort Omaha.[210]

In his memoirs, A.J. wrote that "[M]y general practice, especially in the trial of heavy law and equity cases, was constantly increasing, and I think that at no period of my whole life have I ever been more completely absorbed in business; nor was I ever faster educated."[211]

Nebraska Granted Statehood

In March 1867, Nebraska became a state and the issue that had played such an important role in the first twelve years of the territorial legislature was finally resolved. The capital moved to Lincoln. By that time, Omaha had established itself as a growing and prosperous city for settlement and commercial development and had secured the permanent home of the UPRR, which A.J. believed was "the foundation stone upon which the present prosperity and growth of the city has been built."[212]

When the legislature was selecting a name for the new city after statehood was granted, the original name "Douglas" was dropped from consideration. Senator Stephen A. Douglas had been chiefly responsible for the passage of the Kansas-Nebraska Act of 1854. Historian Arthur C. Wakeley wrote that A.J. Poppleton was the first person to suggest Lincoln for the name of the new capital city:

> It is said that the Legislature of 1867 was about to adopt the name of "Central City" for the new capital, when Mr. Poppleton, although not a member, suggested that as Mr. Lincoln had supplanted Mr. Douglas in the thoughts and admiration of the American people, it would be a fitting recognition of his great services to the country to confer his name upon the new seat of government. The Legislature accepted the suggestion and named the capital "Lincoln." The first session of the legislature held there began on January 7, 1869.[213]

Poppleton Nominated for U.S. Senate and The Rock Bluffs Swindle

Despite his busy schedule, Poppleton remained an active member in the Democratic Party. According to Caroline's Diary of Events, the couple attended the 1864 National Democratic Convention in Chicago. Afterwards, their daughter Elizabeth accompanied them to Canton, New York, the city of Caroline's birth, to visit her family and friends.[214]

When Nebraska became a state in 1867, it was granted the right to select two men to represent it in the U.S. Senate. The Nebraska Democratic party caucus nominated A.J. Poppleton and J. Sterling Morton. The decision would be made by the state legislature, not by the citizens. It was not until the 17th Amendment to the U.S. Constitution was ratified by the states on April 8, 1913, that citizens were allowed to vote directly for their senators.[215] However, the citizens of the state could vote in their county of residence for the men to represent them in the state legislature.

The Republican party won a majority of votes and gained control of the new state legislature. The legislature then elected John M. Thayer and T. W. Tipton instead of Poppleton and Morton to be Nebraska's first two members of the U.S.

Senate. However, a controversy arose over the counting of ballots in Cass County. In his memoirs, Poppleton said that it was "then and long afterwards known as the 'Rock Bluffs Swindle'; namely by falsifying the count in the precinct of Rock Bluffs in Cass County. This changed the result of the election and gave the Republican party the requisite majority."[216]

The Ballot Box That Went to Lunch

A.J. Poppleton and his democratic party colleagues felt justified in calling the votes cast in Cass County, "the Rock Bluffs swindle" because something technically questionable had occurred. Nebraska historian Addison E. Sheldon wrote that the votes cast in the Rock Bluffs precinct were in favor of the Democrats over the Republicans by a margin of 107 to 49, enough to give the Democratic party a majority in Cass County and control of the legislature, which meant that Poppleton and Morton would have been elected to the U.S. Senate.[217] However, when the Cass County Clerk counted the votes at the end of the day, he learned that the Rock Bluffs precinct election officials had closed the door for lunch and taken the ballot box with them to a location one mile away. In the opinion of the Clerk, this broke the law, which required the ballot box to be visible to the voters the entire day, so he threw out all votes cast in Rock Bluffs, resulting in the Republicans winning a majority in Cass County and gaining control of the new state legislature.[218]

Fig 21. Rock Bluffs Precinct Location
Courtesy Nebraska State Historical Society

Poppleton Nominated for U.S. Congress

One year later in 1868, Poppleton was nominated by the Nebraska Democratic party caucus as its candidate for the U.S. House of Representatives, but he was defeated. A.J. reflected on his two defeats in the federal races with a positive perspective and sense of gratitude that he did not win:

> Looking back from this distance it is plain that my election to the Senate in '67 or to the Lower House in '68 would have been an unmixed calamity to me. It would have removed me from my profession and doubtless closed to me the legal career which I cherish as the best work of my life.[219]

14

"Safe in Mr. Poppleton's Hands"

In 1869, Webster Snyder, superintendent of railway operations for the Union Pacific Railroad Company (UPRR) asked A.J. Poppleton to go to Salt Lake City to be available for a possible legal struggle. The issue concerned the race to Promontory Summit between the Union Pacific and the Central Pacific railroads.

A.J. left Omaha March 18, 1869, and "reached Wahsatch by regular train," then "rode upon a caboose at the rear of a long trainload of timber ties," to Ogden and then "hired a team to Salt Lake City and spent a day in making the drive."[220] In his memoirs, A.J. described the legal issue at hand:

> In the race between the Central Pacific and the Union Pacific, each of which was authorized to build to a junction with the other and own the road to the point where the junction took place, the Union Pacific had graded its line as far west as Humboldt Wells, with the exception of some exceedingly heavy rock work at Promontory Summit, about seventy miles west of Ogden. The Central Pacific on the other hand had surveyed and partially graded its line to the head of Echo Canon about one hundred miles east of Ogden. Both companies were rapidly laying track and soon a junction of tracks would be reached.[221]

Poppleton, eager to demonstrate his ability to handle a crucial matter for the Company, described the type of work he faced when he arrived in Salt Lake City:

> Being engaged a considerable portion of the time in preparing affidavits and taking testimony to be used in case an application for an injunction should be necessary on our part or should be made on the part of the Central Pacific. These papers were prepared mainly in the tent of Major Bent, pitched near the summit of Promontory, a point where the lines of the two companies were less than three hundred feet apart, and where the roar of blasting explosions in the work each was prosecuting, was constant night and day.[222]

A few weeks later, he received a telegram from the UPRR office in Boston, informing him that the parties had settled their controversy. Poppleton said the agreed-upon settlement stipulated the following terms:

> The Union Pacific was to take and own the track to Promontory Summit, but that portion of it west of Ogden was to be leased to the Central Pacific; thus, admitting the Central Pacific to Ogden and placing it at equal advantage in respect to the trade and business of Salt Lake City and the great Salt Lake Valley.[223]

During Poppleton's stay in Salt Lake City, he attended the April 1869 conference of the Mormon community. It left a lasting impression on him. He particularly enjoyed the beautiful surroundings and the preaching of Brigham Young:

> I attended the April conference and saw from a thousand to fifteen hundred Mormon people in their great tabernacle, and there was not the slightest evidence in the dress or appearance of either men or women to indicate any close connection with the east. During the conference, I heard Brigham Young preach two sermons, so-called. One was upon temperance, and the other was devoted to discussion of the best crops to raise in Utah, the best grades of cattle and horses to import and raise, and generally how best to advance the property interests of Utah and its people. Both were discourses characterized by keen common sense, great shrewdness, good judgment and full of sound advice.[224]

Transcontinental Railroad Completed

On May 10, 1869, the transcontinental railroad was completed with a historic ceremony held at Promontory Summit, Utah, 50 miles from Ogden. Representatives from the Central Pacific and the Union Pacific symbolically drove the golden spike just before noon. The local telegraph operator wired the nation with a single word "DONE," and bells began to ring, canons fired, and fireworks lit the skies across the country. *The Deseret News* of Salt Lake City on May 19, 1869, reported:

> The Great Pacific Railroad is at once an imperishable monument of the genius, enterprise and wonderful vitality of this great nation. It is but yesterday, as it were, since the bloodiest war recorded in the pages of history, waged between the two sections of our nation, was brought to a close – a war which caused a million of lives and thousands of millions of treasure, - and yet, since then, this great work has been commenced and brought to a successful termination.[225]

Omaha Celebrates

The citizens of Omaha gathered at 20th & Capitol Avenue, the old 'Capitol Hill,' for a parade and fireworks spearheaded by Dr. George L. Miller. They celebrated the great event that everyone believed would ensure the city's future growth. Historian W.E. Broadfield described the celebration:

> Omaha was wreathed in flags ... Governor Saunders presided; he had been chairman of the initiatory ceremonies nearly six years before ... Cannon boomed, bands played, and speeches were made. It was a glorious day for Omaha. The ceremonies were concluded by the singing of the doxology ... In the evening the old Capitol building blazed with light, each of its windows illumined with candles. It was a fit ending of the old building, so soon to be

demolished in making way for the high school – within it walls Pacific railroads had been discussed for years.[226]

UPRR Business "Safe in Mr. Poppleton's Hands"

During the first five years of his part-time employment with the Union Pacific, A.J. Poppleton's fee was based on an hourly rate for specific services rendered. He later wrote that "my railway work together with the general practice which was also constantly growing had given me the largest income from my profession I had yet received."[227]

John Duff and C.S. Bushnell, directors of the UPRR, requested to meet with Poppleton in Omaha. They came from Boston to straighten out a problem in relation to some local timber contractors.[228] The meeting took place at the Cozzens House Hotel, July 1869.[229] At the end of the meeting, John Duff proposed to Poppleton a fixed salary, instead of an hourly rate to ensure he would give preference with his time to the Company and its growing business. They eventually settled on a salary, and Poppleton agreed to work for the railroad on a full-time basis. In his memoirs, he described his negotiations with Duff:

> He put the question what salary I would require. I knew the position of the legal business of this company better than these gentlemen knew it themselves, and I answered promptly, Twelve Thousand Dollars per year. Mr. Duff appeared to be somewhat astonished, but in a few moments, we had agreed upon Ten Thousand as the proper sum. My salary was afterwards raised to Twelve Thousand Dollars and continued at that sum until my resignation.[230]

As the full-time general counsel for the UPRR, Poppleton was put in charge of all legal matters from Chicago to the West Coast. Duff handed him a large packet which A.J. said contained "about a dozen summons and subpoenas served upon them that day involving litigation to the amount of nearly one million dollars and covering the whole line from Omaha to Utah."[231] Duff left Omaha and returned to Boston, while A.J. began responding to the summons and subpoenas.

A few days later, Poppleton received a telegram from Duff directing him to go immediately to Boston for an emergency meeting with Sidney Bartlett, national general counsel for the Company. The Wyoming Territorial Legislature had recently passed a law that allowed a single creditor to file a claim against the UPRR for non-payment of a debt and request the court to place the Company in receivership until the matter could be adjudicated.[232] This had the potential to be a financial disaster for the Company. Duff told Poppleton that such a case had just been filed in a Wyoming court.

Poppleton was surprised to receive the telegram so quickly after he met with Duff in Omaha. He wondered if Bartlett wanted to meet him in person to decide if he was able to handle such an important case. To make certain he made a good impression on Bartlett, Poppleton secured a copy of the *Application for Receivership* filed in a Wyoming court by creditor Davis & Associates against the UPRR. Davis was a supplier of ties and timber for the construction of tracks in Wyoming, and the Company had disputed part of Davis's submitted invoice. Poppleton drafted an *Answer* to the complaint during his three-day train ride to Boston.[233]

John Duff met Poppleton at the Boston train station and drove him in his horse and buggy to Bartlett's office. Poppleton described Bartlett as a no-nonsense lawyer, who by-passed any customary small talk and went right to the matter at hand. Bartlett asked him, "How do you propose to answer this bill?"[234] Poppleton took his draft of an *Answer* from his vest pocket and read it to Bartlett and Duff, and described what happened next:

> As I closed the reading which had been wholly uninterrupted, Mr. Bartlett rose from his chair, and turning to Mr. Duff and Mr. Ames said, "Gentlemen, I think this business, important as it is, is safe in Mr. Poppleton's hands." With very little further consultation, I returned to Omaha.[235]

A Case of Judicial Bribery

As soon as Poppleton arrived back in Omaha, he received a telegram notifying him that the hearing on Davis & Associates' Application for Receivership was scheduled to take place in Wyoming in a few days. So, he boarded the train to Cheyenne and appeared in court on behalf of the railroad. The hearing lasted three days. While he and the opposing attorneys were making their arguments in the courtroom, Poppleton was informed of an extraordinary allegation concerning the judge, and wrote how he responded to the allegation:

> I was reliably informed that there actually existed between the complainant and the Judge a contract under which the Judge was to receive five-thousand dollars for rendering a decision in his behalf. I set to work at once for a postponement of the decision. I finally succeeded in procuring a stipulation which postponed the decision twenty days. During those twenty days, we secured the disapproval by Congress of the (Wyoming) Territorial Act, thus nullifying it; and the Judge, upon intimations of knowledge of his situation, became so far intimidated that, at the expiration of the twenty days, he went to Cheyenne and decided the case in favor of the Railroad Company. This was the first experience I had ever had in fighting judicial bribes in a lawsuit.[236]

The Glaring Gap

As the celebrations ended in Promontory Summit and across the nation in May 1869, a glaring gap existed between the two coasts – the Missouri River. Passengers and freight riding the rails from the East Coast were forced to stop upon reaching Council Bluffs and take ferry boats across the river. Then, they were forced to re-board trains in Omaha in order to continue their journey west. Passengers and freight heading east faced the same difficulty upon arriving in Omaha.

There was no bridge.

15

The Bridge Connecting the Nation

A.J. and Caroline Poppleton moved into their newly built home on 19th & Dodge Street so he could shorten his commute time into downtown Omaha, as he entered full-time employment with the Union Pacific Railroad Company (UPRR). In 1870, the railroad moved their headquarters into the spacious 100-room Herndon House Hotel on 9th & Farnam Street. The hotel had been built in 1858 by a group of investors headed by Dr. George Miller and Lyman Richardson. The *Omaha Bee News* wrote that when the hotel was built, it was "destined to become the focal point from which the lines of industry, running in all directions, were to lead to the establishment of a modern, metropolitan city. It was the cornerstone of Omaha."[237]

Fig. 22. Union Pacific Railroad Co. Headquarters, Herndon House.
Courtesy of Douglas County Historical Society

Poppleton handled hundreds of cases on behalf of the railroad in courtrooms from Omaha to the west coast for the next 19 years. None was more important for the growth and development of Omaha than the bridge case that would connect Council Bluffs to Omaha.

A Rickety Old Ferry Boat

Once the transcontinental track was completed, the Union Pacific ran two freight trains and one passenger train daily from New York to Council Bluffs, and from Omaha to Promontory Summit. In the beginning, the average cost for first class one way was over $60.00, and second class nearly $27.00.[238] Passengers traveled about 1230 miles from New York City to Council Bluffs, in five days. In contrast, Poppleton said it took him five days just to travel some 300 miles from Davenport to Council Bluffs by stagecoach.[239] Transcontinental passengers faced many discomforts on their journey, including having to stop for food at eating houses near the stations. Historian Klein described the irritations for early travelers:

> The coaches were freezing in winter, stifling in summer. Open windows caught a rush of smoke and hot cinders from the engine. With few exceptions, the food at eating houses ranged from bad to awful, with the same fare of steak, fried potatoes, fried eggs, and tea for every meal."[240]

Passengers faced a bigger problem traveling east from Promontory to Omaha, and west from New York to Council Bluffs. Maury Klein explained:

> They [passengers] waited interminably to cross the Missouri in what one called "a rickety old ferry boat." Omaha was a mud hole or a dustbowl, its depot a swirl of confusion from which trains departed abruptly with no more warning than the shriek of a whistle and the cry of "All Aboard!" from the conductor leaving those caught by surprise to jump aboard moving cars.[241]

Fig 23. Transfer Ferries of the UPRR.
Irene for freight and *P.F. Geisse* for passengers on Council Bluffs side of Missouri River. Until the bridge was completed, passengers and freight ferried across to Omaha. Courtesy of Douglas County Historical Society.

Location of the Bridge

In his memoirs, A.J. Poppleton described the first issue the Union Pacific faced in addressing the rickety old steamboat ride across the Missouri River: "As the building of the Union Pacific Railroad progressed westward from the Missouri River, the necessity of a railway bridge across that stream became increasingly apparent. The first question arising in connection with the bridge was that of location."[242]

The UPRR searched for a location to bridge the Missouri River from the western shore of Council Bluffs to the eastern shore of Omaha. Historian Klein wrote that the engineers faced a difficult task:

> The Missouri River had to be bridged; a task as formidable as any that confronted the engineers in the West. At Omaha, the meandering river was four miles wide with an adjacent floodplain on which it rose as much as ten feet during the high-water season. The bedrock was covered with layers of sand, gravel, and silt deposited by a shifting, treacherous current ... the building of the bridge became a miniature version of the building of the road.[243]

Initially, the railway's engineers recommended a site south of Omaha known as *Child's Mill*.[244] Many Omaha business leaders strongly opposed this site, and instead supported a site closer to the city center, identified as *lower Omaha crossing No. 2* on the engineer's map.[245]

After much negotiation between the opposing interests, the UPRR Board of Directors agreed to the city's proposed center site, conditioned upon Douglas County agreeing to pay $250,000 of the construction costs. The County would issue 20-year coupon bonds to be held by a third-party trustee, who would pay installments to the railroad as work progressed.

Douglas County agreed, so the company began constructing the bridge at the *lower Omaha crossing No. 2*.[246] The chief engineer supervising the project was Theophilius E. Sickels, successor to Grenville Dodge, who resigned in January 1870.[247]

When the UPRR made sufficient progress, it requested a first installment payment. However, Douglas County refused to pay until the railroad contract had been amended by adding the following terms:

> Omaha should be made the eastern terminus of the railroad, and all passengers and freight transfers should be made on the west side of the river in Omaha, and the machine shops and general offices should be established and permanently remain in Omaha."[248]

The majority of the UPRR's board of directors refused Douglas County's additional conditions. Instead, they favored Council Bluffs as the terminus and site of its shops and facilities. Poppleton explained why the board favored Council Bluffs:

> Most of them had long and persistently favored the concentration of the terminal facilities and advantages at Council Bluffs, upon the east side of the river, on a large tract purchased at the instance of [director and financier] Sidney Dillon, and by him held as trustee for the Credit Mobilier of America and the Union Pacific Company.[249]

In January 1872, despite Douglas County not making payments, the UPRR completed construction of the bridge and signed a new contract agreeing to most of Douglas County's additional terms. Poppleton drafted the contract and credited UPRR acting President John Duff as the person who convinced the company's board of directors to agree. Poppleton was effusive in his praise of John Duff:

> I say without hesitation that the contract of January 1872 would never have been signed by any other president or acting president of the Union Pacific Company, and that it was very largely through his [Duff's] confidence in me and my influence over him that he was prevailed upon to enter into it. In doing so, in my opinion, he [Duff] rendered a greater service to the city than any other man connected with the Union Pacific Company, with the exception, possibly, of Thomas C. Durant, who was mainly instrumental in securing the eastern terminus of the road at Omaha.[250]

"The Most Beneficial to Omaha of Any Event in its History"

Poppleton worked arduously on the contract. It had great meaning for him because he believed the contract secured future growth with long-term benefits for Omaha. He wrote of its significance:

> This contract has been much criticized and reviled, but gave Omaha, the Union Pacific machine shops, the largest on the line, its business and financial headquarters, the concentration of all the telegraphic interests west of Chicago at this point, and concentrated in the collections and disbursements and other pecuniary interest, which in the year 1892, reached in gross earnings the sum of $46,000,000 and has preserved and maintained them to this day.
>
> From these advantages sprang thousands of others, difficult to enumerate, but two of which occur to me to be mentioned; the organization of the Pacific Express Company, which has become one of the largest express companies in the country, and the extension of the Missouri Pacific Road upon the west bank of the Missouri River from Kansas City to Omaha.
>
> I further believe that without this contract neither the Northwestern nor the Chicago, Burlington & Quincy would ever have concentrated at Omaha their extensive railway and business interests west of the Missouri River, represented by several thousand miles of railway.[251]

> I therefore put on record my belief that that contract, next to the location of the eastern terminus of the Union Pacific at Omaha by President Lincoln (moved and influenced by the solicitation of Mr. Durant as before mentioned), was the foundation stone upon which the present prosperity and growth of the city has been built.
>
> Had this contract never been made, it is my firm belief that all the interests above mentioned would have been concentrated east of the Missouri River, and that Council Bluffs would have contained by the census of 1890 not less than 150,000 people and that Omaha would have been a mere country town. In other words, the position of the two cities would have been completely reversed.[252]

Poppleton Praised for Piloting the Effort

Historian and Attorney James M. Woolworth wrote of the important role Poppleton played in settling this matter, pointing out an editorial written in the *Omaha Herald*:[253]

> By 1873, the fixing of the Union Pacific Company's terminal plant, offices, and equipment at Omaha was finally decided upon and settled. In regard to Mr. Poppleton's share in this result, the most beneficial to Omaha of any event in its history, the following words from *The Omaha Herald* of that time speak:
>
>> While we rejoice it is but proper that a few words should be said on behalf of the citizen to whom this people owe much for his intelligent, steady, and well directed efforts to bring about the results over which every man in Omaha is rejoicing. Andrew J. Poppleton is the one man who, more than any other, has piloted the people through these railroad complications to their present final settlement and security. We say this as a matter of sheer justice to Mr. Poppleton, without going into details to show how richly he deserved it.

The Terminus Controversy

Before the bridge project was completed, passengers and freight heading west had to de-board in Council Bluffs and then take a transfer steamboat to cross the Missouri River. Once in Omaha, they would re-board trains at the 20th Street Passenger Depot and continue their journey west. The burdensome procedure was reversed for east-bound trains. The bridge was supposed to solve the problem, but didn't.

The UPRR bridge opened for use in March 1872, at a final cost of $2,870,000. It had 11 cast-iron piers grounded into the bedrock. Each pier had two cylinders eight-feet wide filled with concrete and rubble. The piers were 250 feet apart, and 60 feet above the water.[254]

Fig 24. First UPPR Bridge between Omaha and Council Bluffs
Courtesy KMTV/Bostwick-Frohardt Photograph Collection, permanently housed at The Durham Museum, Omaha

A new problem arose. Some of the employees complained the contract benefited Omaha, not Council Bluffs, so they organized a separate business called *"The Bridge Transfer Company."* This new company required passengers and freight to deboard the train in Council Bluffs and reboard a distinct and separate train called a *"Transfer Train"* to cross the river on the new bridge. A toll was charged of 50 cents per passenger and $10.00 per freight car. The Bridge Transfer Company managed the transfer trains and kept a separate account of the bridge transfer earnings.

Because of the inconvenience and extra toll charges, a lawsuit was filed in early 1875 in the Circuit Court of the United States for the District of Iowa, *United States ex.rel. Hall et.al. v. Union Pacific Railroad Co.,* before Judges Dillon and Love. The Petitioners claimed that the UPRR was in violation of the congressional mandated duty to operate their regular trains over the bridge as one connected, continuous line.[255] The case was heard in the Spring of 1875. Poppleton and Woolworth represented the railroad. Judge John F. Dillon wrote the opinion that ruled in favor of the petitioners.

Poppleton immediately filed an appeal to the U.S. Supreme Court. Mr. Justice Strong delivered the Supreme Court's opinion that affirmed the lower court's decision in favor of the petitioners:

> Holding then, as we do, that the legal terminus of the railroad is fixed by law on the Iowa shore of the river, and that the bridge is a part of the railroad, there can be no doubt that the company is under obligation to operate and run the whole road, including the bridge, as one connected and continuous line. This is a duty expressly imposed by the Acts of 1862 and 1864 and recognized by that of 1871. What this means it is not difficult to understand. It is a requisition made for the convenience of the public. An arrangement, such as the company has made, by which freight and passengers destined for or beyond the eastern

terminus are stopped two or three miles from it and transferred to another train, and again transferred at the terminus, or by which freight and passengers going west from the eastern end of the line must be transferred at Omaha, breaks the road into two lines, and plainly is inconsistent with continuous operation of it as a whole.[256]

Overworked and Frustrated

These cases were among several that drew Poppleton to different parts of the country on the railroad's behalf. He became frustrated at being pulled in so many directions when he wanted more time with his family. In December of 1875, he planned to travel to New York to spend a few days before Christmas with Caroline and their daughter Libby, and then close up some railroad business in Washington D.C. He wrote a letter to Sidney Dillon, then president of the UPRR, to assure him that he would have things under control by the time he left Omaha for Christmas in New York:

> Sidney Dillon, President Omaha, Neb Dec 10, 1875
> Union Pacific Railroad Company
> 20 Nassau Street, New York
>
> Dear Sir:
> Your three telegrams of yesterday received. I hope Mr. Carr [President of the Kansas Pacific Railroad] will not call me to go to Denver between Dec 20 & January 8th as I have other arrangements which I am anxious to carry out. The Terminus case is to be submitted January 8th and on the 5th a case of the *United States v. the Pacific RR Co.* in Nebraska is to be heard before Judge Miller in Washington in which it will be urged by the U.S. Dist Atty that east of the 100th Meridian, the Union Pacific Land Grant is only 10 miles wide. This point is liable to be decided in that suit and we must be heard. The suit is pending here but is heard before Miller by arrangement between the parties. I wanted to leave here [Omaha] the 20th and 21st spend the holidays with my daughter, take some depositions in New York between the 25th & 31st and then close up the business in Washington & get back to here about January 10. The tax case, if advanced, may also be set down for about the same time. I have so arranged matters here that I can be away without injury to the Company matters, unless the Denver matter which I intended to put in motion before the 20th interferes.
>
> Yours Respectfully, A.J. Poppleton[257]

Caroline, with Mary Delia age two, and William age nine, joined A.J. on the trip to New York to spend Christmas with 19-year-old daughter Libby, a senior in college.

Fig 25. First UPRR Bridge, partially destroyed by April 4, 1877 tornado
temporarily repaired and used until rebuilt in 1886
Courtesy KMTV/Bostwick Frohardt Photograph Collection,
permanently housed at The Durham Museum, Omaha

16

The Case of the Kidnapped Judge

The kidnapped judge case was one of the most interesting cases that A.J. Poppleton handled in his 24 years as general counsel for the Union Pacific Railroad Company (UPRR). He discovered the West could be an untamed place with its own brand of justice.

"The Court Stolen Bodily by Masked Men"

Poppleton referred to "Mr. Carr and the Denver matter" in his, letter to Sidney Dillon, December 10, 1875, which he hoped would not prevent him and his family from spending Christmas with daughter Libby, in New York.[258] After A.J. returned to Omaha from New York in early 1876, he traveled to Colorado to deal with the matter. It turned out to be more problematic than expected.

"The Denver matter" began in 1872 when William Loveland, President of the Colorado Central Railway Company (CCRC), on behalf of its Board of Directors, purchased equipment from the UPRR via businessman Jay Gould, to build a connecting line between two towns in Colorado. The CCRC gave a mortgage on the property to secure bonds in the sum of $1,212,000 with coupons payable semiannually. By 1876, the CCRC was in default for failure to make required interest payments. At the time of the default, the UPRR owned more than a half interest in the CCRC.[259]

Poppleton's attempt to negotiate an amicable settlement with the CCRC was rebuffed, so he filed a pleading with the territorial district court requesting a third-party receiver be appointed to recover the company's property. Judge Amherst W. Stone approved Poppleton's pleading on August 12, 1876, and appointed David H. Moffat, a banker from Denver, as receiver. Because of the high value of the property, the judge adjourned the proceedings for a few days to allow the preparation of the receiver's bonds. Poppleton described the shenanigans that followed the adjournment:

> A day was fixed at Boulder City, Colorado, when the court would convene for the purpose of approving the receiver's bonds. On the morning of that day the receiver with his bondsmen and friends took the train for Boulder City; the Judge of the Court was also on the same train. A short distance from Boulder the train was stopped, a body of masked men appeared, took possession of the Judge, blindfolded him, and started in the direction of the mountains. The limit of the term of court would expire the following day, after which the bond could not be approved. The Judge was taken to the mountains, just how far or where has never been known; kept there for about three days, then placed in a carriage and after a long and tedious drive, the carriage stopped, he was directed to alight, his eyesight was released, and he found himself standing in front of the Alvord House in the city of Denver. Of course, these legal proceedings failed.[260]

On August 17, 1876, Judge Stone returned to his court and accepted the bond that receiver Moffat provided. Poppleton immediately filed a Writ of Assistance with the court requesting the judge order an officer to re-take possession of the company's property. Historian Robert G. Athearn quoted Poppleton's complaint in a letter to Sidney Dillon, President of the UPRR, written on August 26, 1876. Poppleton said the officer charged by the court to re-take possession of the property "has done nothing yet, and I think is surrounded by political influences to such an extent that I don't believe he will do anything. This State is too full of thieves for residents' property to have any chance except in the U.S. Courts."[261]

Poppleton was so upset by the proceedings that he even thought of filing for a change of venue, but the UPRR executives eventually consented to build 60 miles of track to connect two towns in Colorado to the main line, as the local group had initially demanded, in exchange for return of the stolen property. Poppleton wrote that masked men stole the court:

> Aside from this particular instance, my experience of Colorado Judges and of Colorado Justice has been entirely satisfactory, but this is the only instance in which I ever lost an important case by having the court stolen bodily by masked men and driven out of its jurisdiction into the Rocky Mountains.[262]

The Snowplow Case

Another fascinating case Poppleton handled for the UPRR demonstrated how his thorough pre-trial preparation, legal acumen, and oratorial skills made him a successful trial attorney. This was the first patent law case he ever litigated.

For years, the UPRR used a snowplow on its mountainous tracks in the Laramie plains of Wyoming and portions of the Rocky Mountains, built by I.H. Congdon, a master mechanic for the UPRR. But the railroad never patented his invention. In the meantime, Samuel Richards filed a lawsuit against the UPRR claiming he was the original inventor of the snowplow and owned a patent to prove prior use. Poppleton assumed personal responsibility to argue the case on behalf of the railroad. Attorney Shaw of Philadelphia represented the plaintiff. George Harding, a nationally known patent lawyer, assisted Shaw in the case.[263]

Poppleton realized a trial of this magnitude would require an expert investigator to assist him in gathering evidence necessary to win the lawsuit. At A.J.'s request, UPRR President Sidney Dillon hired Frederick E. Sickels, a New York engineer who had previously worked with Grenville Dodge. Sickles investigated the matter in the federal patent office in Washington D.C., and took testimony from engineers and inventors of other snowplow models to determine if Richards' snowplow was truly an original invention.[264]

On March 20, 1878, Sickels wrote a letter to Poppleton from Philadelphia, suggesting Poppleton file a continuance of the hearing for another month, in order to secure additional evidence and testimony. Sickels shared the results of his investigation:

> The value of the specifications of Daniel D. Stillwell [another patent holder] consists in the fact that it serves to explain the model we have already in the case ... The specifications of Joseph A. Gregg [another patent holder] serves to show that the idea of first lifting and then throwing the snow latterly is an old idea ... The patent of Samuel Richards proves that prior to the patent of Demary [another patent holder] the whole operation as claimed in the Demary patent had been fully described. The file wrapper and contents as certified by the [patent] office prove that Richard's specifications as sworn to by him insist that he first raised the snow and then moved it laterally. Since I have had these papers, I have met Mr. Richards in Mr. Shaw's office. The explanation he gave me is too long to insert here, but if he swears to his statement as he gave it to me, I can disprove it by the record of the patent office that I have ready here for his cross-examination when our counsel R.C. McMurthrie questions him. If you have not looked up the questions of uncertainty, I may save you some valuable time by giving a reference here – see *John M. Carr vs. John Rice Blatchford* vol 4 of 1868, page 200.[265]

The trial was held in the Iowa Circuit Court sitting at Keokuk, Iowa. Judge George Washington McCrary presided. Poppleton's strategy was to overwhelm the opposing side with depositions totaling nearly 1400 pages. He also entered into evidence "fifty-seven models of snowplows ... that comprised every known device for removing snow from a railway track ever resorted to, previous to that suit."[266]

Even though Poppleton was thoroughly prepared to argue the case, he wrote that he felt a heightened degree of anxiety when he entered the courtroom:

> My inexperience in this branch of the profession, and my natural distrust of my own powers in a wholly untried field so wrought upon me that during the night before I was to make my argument, I was unable to sleep a single moment. At nine o'clock the next morning the thermometer marked ninety-six degrees, and I felt extreme doubt whether I would be able to go on. However, at the appointed hour I commenced my argument, moving slowly at first and depending upon the glow of warmer work to arouse me to my full strength. After I had been on my feet about fifteen minutes, my strength came, my head cleared, and at half past twelve I had finished my argument and sat down with the conviction that the case was mine.[267]

Three-Hour Closing Argument

As A.J. Poppleton stood before the court, ready to deliver his closing argument, he decided to "throw aside all extraneous and other matter" and focus his attention on two points which he believed would succeed: "First, that the Richards' plow contained no invention. Secondly, if the court should differ with me upon that point, it was not novel but had been anticipated twenty-five years before and in constant use since."[268]

After Poppleton spoke for more than three hours, Judge McCrary took the case under advisement and adjourned the proceedings. A few days later, the judge dismissed the plaintiff's request for an injunction and damages against UPRR. No appeal was taken. Poppleton had won his first patent law case for the railroad.

From his days at Union College, A.J. Poppleton journaled his worries and concerns with complete candor. He didn't hide his emotions or dismiss his concerns, but instead described them as he experienced them.

In his memoirs, he gave us a window into some of the anxieties he faced during crucial times in his life, like the snowplow case, allowing us to further admire his fighting spirit in the challenges of life.

17

Leader of the Bar

The 1870s were extraordinary times for A.J. Poppleton. He was deeply involved in important litigation across the country on behalf of Union Pacific, yet he still found time and energy to support Omaha's legal community.

Omaha Law Library Association

In December 1871, A.J. Poppleton, John L. Webster, James W. Savage, Charles Manderson, B.E.B. Kennedy, and Eleazer Wakeley established the *Omaha Law Library Association* to support the growing number of lawyers and jurists working in Omaha. Wakeley was elected the first president. Poppleton was elected to the Board of Directors.[269] The library housed its collection in the Simpson building on 14th Street between Dodge and Douglas Streets. Judges could use the library at no charge. Lawyers living in Douglas County could use the library if they purchased at least one share of stock in the corporation at $100 per share and paid an annual fee of $15. Lawyers living outside Douglas County paid a $5 monthly fee. [270]

The library was open daily from 9 to Noon and reopened from 2 to 6 p.m. It was closed on Sundays. When court was in session, the library extended hours from 7:30 p.m. to 9 p.m.[271] In 1877, the year Poppleton was elected president of the association, the library catalogue contained 1,983 volumes of reports, including 70 U.S. Supreme Court Reports, 1,223 State Reports, four Insurance Reports, and 371 English Law Reports.[272]

Fig. 26. Judge Eleazer Wakeley
Courtesy Douglas County Historical Society

Profile: Eleazer Wakeley (1822-1912)

Wakeley was born in Homer, New York on June 15, 1822. He was admitted to the Ohio bar in 1844. Three years later, he moved to Wisconsin, and served in the territorial legislature where he helped draft its constitution in 1848. He married Sabina S. Comstock in 1854. They had five children. In 1857, President Franklin Pierce appointed Wakeley the first associate justice of the Third District of the Nebraska Territorial Supreme Court, which was the country's largest judicial district covering 350,000 square miles. He served briefly in the Civil War, receiving a medical discharge after the Battle of Fredericksburg in 1862 and then returned to practice law in Wisconsin until he moved back to Omaha in 1867. He served on the committee to draft the Nebraska constitution in 1871. Poppleton hired him in 1871 as assistant attorney for the UPRR, where he worked for seven years. Wakeley served as a Douglas County District Court Judge from 1883 to 1892. For one year in 1896, he was a member of the executive board of the Nebraska Historical Society. In 1900, he was elected president of the Nebraska State Bar Association. Wakeley was a member of the vestry of Trinity Episcopal Cathedral for 36 years, and chancellor of the diocese in 1910. On June 14, 1912, after working all day in his office, Wakeley at the age of 90, addressed the Omaha Bar Association at its annual dinner. The *Omaha Bee News* reported Wakeley's address: "Every faculty is retained in full strength, a remarkable vocabulary is at his command to express the profound thoughts of an active mind, the voice rings loud and clear." Five months later on November 21, 1912, Wakeley died in the home he had built in 1868 on the corner of 19th & California Street. He was buried in Prospect Hill cemetery. A street in Omaha is named in his honor. His son Arthur C. Wakeley (1855-1928), became a judge in the Douglas County District Court from 1917 to 1927, was president of the Omaha Bar Association in 1909, and was president of the Nebraska State Bar Association in 1918. He was supervising editor of *Omaha: The Gate City and Douglas County Nebraska* in 1917.

Omaha Bar Association (1875)

On August 10, 1875, A.J. Poppleton, Clinton Briggs,[273] James W. Savage, Experience Estabrook,[274] B.E.B. Kennedy, and Albert Swartzlander gathered in the Douglas County Court House to organize a county bar association.[275] Their purpose was "to maintain the honor and dignity of the profession of the law; to cultivate social intercourse among its members and to increase its usefulness in promoting the due administration of justice."[276] Initially, the six charter members called the organization the Douglas County Bar Association. They held the first meeting of the Board of Directors on the first Monday of October 1875, adopted a constitution and by-laws, and elected the following officers:

President:	Andrew J. Poppleton
Vice-President:	B.E.B. Kennedy
Treasurer:	James W. Savage
Secretary:	Albert Swartzlander [277]

Membership was open only to lawyers in good standing who resided, or practiced in Omaha, or other parts of Douglas County.[278] Thirty-four lawyers were admitted as members in the first year.[279] An initial subscription fee of $5.00 was required, with annual dues of $2.50.[280] The title page of the Association's first directory featured these words:

> It is upon the profession, therefore, that the trust devolves of preserving the law and its administration in its purity and integrity. They are to keep alive that noble *esprit du corps* which regards an indignity or reproach cast upon the bar as a wound upon the personal honor of every member who deserves the name of lawyer.[281]

In 1879, twenty-five years after its founding, the Omaha City Directory listed 59 active lawyers serving a population of 26,000 residents.[282] By 1888, the number of lawyers practicing in the City of Omaha had nearly doubled. Consequently, on December 1, 1888, members of the Douglas County Bar Association adopted a new constitution and changed the name to the Omaha Bar Association reflecting a new rule that only lawyers residing within the city limits of Omaha would be eligible for membership.[283] The first officers elected were:

President:	Andrew J. Poppleton
Vice-President:	Herbert J. Davis
Treasurer:	James W. Savage
Secretary:	Frank Irvine.[284]

No new subscription dues were required of the 106 members.[285] Annual dues were reduced to $2.00.[286] The Constitution stated:

> The object of this Association is to maintain the honor and dignity of the profession of the law; to promote a fraternal feeling among the members of the bar; and to aid in the due and expeditious dispatch of the business of the courts of justice.[287]

Nebraska State Bar Association (1876)

Five months after formation of the Douglas County Bar Association, on January 6, 1876, the Nebraska State Bar Association was established in Lincoln, Nebraska with the adoption of a Constitution and By-laws. As a charter member, A. J. Poppleton was issued a Certificate of Membership along with 83 other lawyers. S.H. Calhoun of Nebraska City was elected president, and James M. Woolworth of Omaha was elected one of the eight vice-presidents.[288]

The by-laws established four standing committees: Amendment of the Law, Judiciary, Legal Education, and Grievances. A.J. Poppleton was appointed to the Grievance Committee charged "with the hearing of all complaints against members of the Association, and also all complaints which may be made in matters affecting the legal profession, and the practice of law, and the administration of justice."[289] Annual dues were $2.00 payable in two installments."[290]

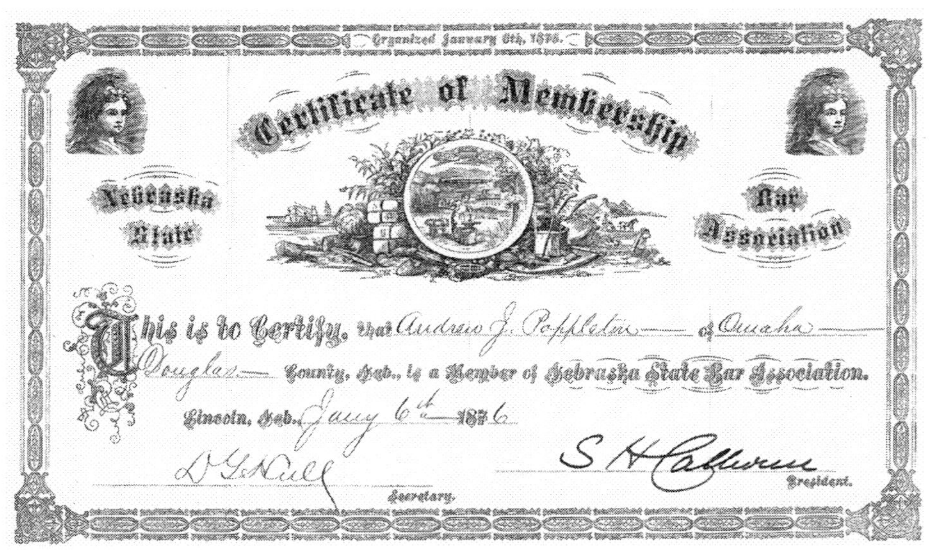

Organized January 6th, 1876.

Certificate of Membership

Nebraska State Bar Association

This is to Certify, that Andrew J. Poppleton of Omaha Douglas County, Neb., is a Member of Nebraska State Bar Association.

Lincoln, Neb., Jany 6th 1876

D G Hull
Secretary.

S H Calhoun
President.

Fig. 27. Nebraska Bar Association Membership (1876)
Courtesy A.J. Poppleton III Personal Collection

A.J. Poppleton's reputation as a respected trial attorney and supporter of the legal fraternity, prompted his fellow lawyers and jurists to honor him with leadership positions in these new associations. One hundred fifty years later, they are still important in the legal community.

Note: See *Chapter 17 Endnotes* for profiles of: Briggs, Davis, Estabrook, Kennedy, Irvine, Manderson, Savage, and Swartzlander.

18

Business Community Leader

A.J. Poppleton's leadership in the Omaha legal community resonated with the leading businessmen of the city. Both communities, legal and business, came together to ensure the continued growth and development of the city. Simultaneously, he represented the Barkers and a few other families in his private practice and served as legal counsel and member of the board of directors of a few of Omaha's most important companies, such as the Nebraska State Insurance Company and the First National Bank of Omaha.

Omaha Board of Trade

In 1865, business leaders formed the Omaha Board of Trade and elected Augustus Kountze the first President. However, the group disbanded after a few years. Fifty-eight individuals and companies re-established the organization on March 12, 1877, and elected its first officers:[291]

President:	A.J. Poppleton
First Vice-President:	James E. Boyd
Second Vice-President:	Elam Clark
Third Vice-President:	Samuel R. Johnson
Fourth Vice-President:	George W. Lininger
Treasurer:	C.C. Housel
Secretary:	W.C.B. Allen

The Board of Directors established seven committees to serve the organization: Livestock & Stockyards, Memorials, Transportation, Arbitration, Manufactures, Douglas County Lands, Government Meteorological.[292] The original members of the newly re-organized Board of Trade included: Fred Krug (Brewery), Herman Kountze (President First National Bank), E.W. Nash (Omaha Smelting Works), George A. Hoagland (Lumber), William A. Paxton (Livestock), S. H. Buffett (Groceries), Col. M.L. Luddington (Chief Quartermaster, Department of the Platte), Frank Murphy (President State Bank), Thomas Kimball (UPRR Executive), and John McCormick (President Omaha Elevator Co).[293]

President Poppleton's Address

On January 8, 1878, A.J. Poppleton, president of the Omaha Board of Trade, gave an address to the members at the conclusion of his term:

> With the origin of this body, the business interests of our city, for the first time, were represented by an organization which combined the indispensable and essential elements of success. It is popular in its character and prescribes no test of membership, except capacity, integrity and commercial honor ... It has no

> social aims ... It is purely a commercial, financial and business organization ... With the best energy and devotion of each and all its members, to advance and extend the commercial supremacy and importance of Omaha and the State.[294]

In the next portion of his address, Poppleton reviewed the history of commerce in Omaha over the prior 20 years and suggested areas of future growth and development:

> The history of Omaha naturally divides itself into three epochs. The first began with a period of purely speculative and fictitious activity and ended in the panic of 1857. The second began with the construction of the Union Pacific Railroad and developed into an exaggerated prosperity in which over-building and over-trading, receiving extraordinary stimulus from an enormous local expenditure of money, and reinforced by the wasteful and extravagant habits of life and business, engendered by the war and a depreciated and superabundant currency, ended in the panic of 1873. The third marks from about the spring of 1875. Since that time, beyond all controversy, the trade, manufactures and general financial and commercial prosperity of the city, has had a constant and yearly accelerated growth. The building record proves this ... A city of twenty to twenty-five thousand inhabitants cannot expend three-quarters of a million dollars in building - largely dwelling and business houses- in a single year, except in a state of sound and even robust commercial and financial health.[295]

Poppleton listed several projects which had been completed in Omaha the previous year. He then recommended actions that the city could take to achieve even greater financial, commercial and manufacturing success:

> We must remain unflagging in our efforts to maintain a standard of honor and credit which will challenge the implicit confidence of the money-centers of the world ... We must use our utmost efforts to establish, maintain and perpetuate an honest, economical and efficient city, county and state government ... Our city organization is needlessly cumbrous, inefficient and expensive ... The chief problem before this city is whether its great natural advantages, the high civic and business capacity of its people, can outrun the waste and deterioration, extravagance and inefficiency inherent in its government. I am not speaking of men, but of systems.[296]

Poppleton returned to a common theme he first proclaimed in an 1852 Address to the Agricultural Society of Oakland, Michigan at the age of 22; and re-stated a second time in his Address to the graduates of the University of Nebraska in 1877 - the importance of character:

Let us lift high that standard of honor which counts gain got by dishonesty, fraud, perfidy, infidelity to public or private trusts ... simply badges of infamy. So shall this community thrive and prosper, not only in material development, but in that higher and better intellectual and spiritual life, out of which it wrought the only imperishable and indestructible growth of this planet – Character.[297]

Fig. 28. First Annual Report of Board of Trade
UPRR Railroad Bridge & Downtown Omaha from Council Bluffs side of the Missouri River 1878. Courtesy A.J. Poppleton III Personal Collection

As a conclusion to his address, Poppleton touched on a subject well known in the community for many years, but seldom spoken out load - the tenuous relationship between Omaha and Council Bluffs. His final plea was for reconciliation between the cities:

> One other suggestion: In times past we have had many, and not always friendly, controversies with our Iowa neighbor, Council Bluffs. It is plain to me that points of difference are rapidly disappearing, and a common interest is rapidly bringing us together for common work. The mutual welfare of both, beyond all controversy, will be better advanced by cultivation of closer intercourse and friendship ... Harmonize the conflicting interests of the inhabitants of either bank of the Missouri, weld them into a common force, animate them by a common purpose, and their consolidated strength will rear the richest and largest city between the Mississippi and Pacific Ocean. Is not such an achievement worthy of the highest ambition of both?[298]

Creighton College

Poppleton and the other officers of the Board of Trade included in their 1878 Annual Report more than just facts and figures concerning the financial health of the city. Their report also contained statements of pride in the city's educational institutions, at all levels, including the newly built Creighton College located at 24th & California Street:

> A handsome brick building with stone facings, erected on an elevated site in the southwestern portion of the city, is one of the institutions of Omaha. It has just been completed at a cost of $55,000, which sum, with a further amount of $100,000 as a permanent endowment, was bequeathed for that purpose by the late Mrs. Edward Creighton. The school will be conducted under the supervision of the Jesuit Fathers, in charge of Father [Romanus] Shaffel and a competent corps of teachers. It is calculated to accommodate 480 pupils and will be a free school. The building is 54 x 126 feet, three stories and a basement.[299]

Creighton College held its first classes on September 2, 1878. One hundred twenty students attended the first term, and the teachers were one Jesuit priest, three Jesuit scholastics, a layman, and one woman.

Poppleton in the Forefront of Downtown Omaha Development

In 1880, Poppleton built a three-story brick building at 1001 Farnam Street, for wholesale and retail merchants, known as "The Poppleton Block." It was significant in Omaha architecture, noted in the 1982 application for inclusion in the National Register of Historic Places. Poppleton was identified in the application as a man in the forefront of commercial development in a thriving metropolitan community:

When A. J. Poppleton erected the three-story Italianate Poppleton Block in 1880, he was in the forefront of a trend toward new construction and changing land use in that section of downtown Omaha. The 1880s marked the beginning of the City's development as a metropolitan center for meatpacking, heavy industry, wholesaling, and retailing. Throughout his years in Omaha, Poppleton purchased a great deal of property and invested in various business enterprises. One of his first real estate acquisitions was the lot at 1001 Farnam, purchased for $1,500 in 1856. The lot contained a frame building, reputedly the fifth house built in Omaha, in which Poppleton opened a law office. Since Farnam Street was one of the main business streets in the city, the lot undoubtedly held commercial firms for the following decades until Poppleton erected his new building.[300]

In 1886, A.J. Poppleton constructed another building at 413-23 South 11th Street, which is now part of "The Old Market" area in downtown Omaha. Poppleton's building housed retail and wholesale merchants.[301]

Leadership

In organizing the Law Library Association, the Omaha Bar Association, and the Omaha Board of Trade, Poppleton incorporated these organizations with a governing structure founded on three principles: 1) a succinct written constitution and by-laws; 2) an annual rotation of officers to ensure new leadership; and 3) a straightforward purpose that encouraged members to act for the common good in a spirit of integrity and honor. Poppleton's formula was simple. It worked well in the 19th Century, and it is still working today because these organizations are still operating successfully 150 years later.

Fig 29. Creighton College 1879 (NW 20th & Dodge Streets)
Courtesy KMTV Bostwick-Frohardt Photograph Collection
Permanently Housed at The Durham Museum, Omaha

19

Clients: The Barker Family

A.J. Poppleton found little time for his private practice as his work for the Union Pacific Railroad Company grew in volume and complexity. Yet, over the years, he made time to represent a few families, including the Barkers, in various matters.

Reverend Joseph Barker Sr. was head of one of the families A.J. represented for several years. Rev. Barker was a Methodist preacher living in Yorkshire, England, near the ancestral home of Poppleton. He was a prolific writer and lecturer on behalf of the political reform movement known as the Chartists. His magazine, *The People*, had a circulation of over 20,000, and his outdoor lectures drew thousands. In 1848, at the same time he was elected to Parliament, the British authorities threatened him with arrest unless he stopped his political activities. So, Rev. Barker moved his family to America.[302]

In 1851, the Barker family left England to settle in Ohio. Upon hearing of the Kansas-Nebraska Act opening land for settlement, Rev. Barker and his 21-year-old son George headed west in 1856. Rev. Barker described their journey:[303]

> We reached Council Bluffs on April 1st, and the next day crossed over to Omaha City. At that time the city consisted of a few huts, two or three decent houses, a bank, the State House, a sawmill, and a few stores. The population would be about three or four hundred. The country round was one vast wild. It looked anything but inviting to the eye. But when you came to look at the soil, it was rich beyond all that we had ever conceived ... The site on which the infant city stands was the finest I ever saw.[304]

Shortly after his arrival in Omaha, Rev. Barker sent for the rest of his family. His wife Frances left Ohio with her son Joseph Barker Jr., age 25, and her daughter Mary Jane, age 22. Unfortunately, their journey was delayed because the steamboat carrying them to Omaha sank. They lost much of their property, including a significant portion of their family's library collection.[305]

Rev. Barker and his sons immediately focused on acquiring land for investment purposes, over 166 individual lots in less than three years. In addition, they purchased over 800 acres of land outside the city limits, a portion of which became their home. They called the area *Cold Creek,* which today would be located between 72nd and 90th Streets, Western to Maple.[306]

The Barker family were active members of Trinity Episcopal Cathedral at the same time as the Poppletons and many other early settlers. Joseph Barker Jr. was elected to the City Council in 1859, and he and his brother George were members of the Omaha Claim Club. The brothers were among the founders of the Omaha Gas Company and the National Bank of Commerce. As their involvement grew in many commercial ventures and real estate transactions, so did their need for Poppleton's legal services.

Fig 30. George, Mary Jane, and Joseph Barker Jr.
Courtesy Douglas County Historical Society

In 1860, Frances Barker's mother died, and the entire family moved back home to England to administer her estate. They stayed in England for the duration of the American Civil War. Prior to their departure from Omaha, they hired agents to manage their extensive real estate holdings, collect rents, make repairs, pay taxes, and defend their land against squatters.

Poppleton and the Case of Rudowsky v. Barker

In 1866, the Barker family received word from their agents in Omaha that they were losing part of their farmland to claim jumpers. To investigate the matter, Joseph Barker Jr. returned to Omaha on May 26, 1866, after a two-month journey from England. He immediately met with A.J. Poppleton, who informed him that the main land dispute was with Julius Rudowsky.

Rudowsky was a lumber merchant who had worked for the Barker family from the time when they purchased their farmland. Because the family owned more than the amount allowed by the government, 320 acres per person, in the Summer of 1857, Rev. Barker sold 120 acres to Rudowsky for $600.00. Rudowsky made a down payment of $100.00 and executed a Promissory Note for the balance. Rev. Barker told Rudowsky to file a pre-emption claim with the land office, which he did six weeks later. On September 11, 1857, George Barker re-purchased the same 120 acres from Rudowsky who signed a deed to George Barker in return for payment of $600.00 and cancellation of the promissory note as paid in full.[307]

In 1866, the case of *Rudowsky v. Barker* was filed in the Douglas County District Court at Docket G. No.143. Rudowsky claimed that the 1857 deed given to him by Rev. Barker was an absolute conveyance of title, and the payment from George Barker six weeks later was simply a cancellation of a mortgage debt. He claimed the

Barkers had defrauded him, saying he did not understand he had signed a deed of conveyance back to George Barker. C.A. Baldwin represented Julius Rudowsky, plaintiff; and A. J. Poppleton represented Joseph Barker Sr., defendant. [308] A year after he filed his lawsuit, Rudowsky was elected to the Omaha City Council, and re-elected in 1869.[309]

The Barker Letters

From the time Joseph Barker Jr. arrived back in Omaha in May 1866, he wrote letters to his family in England to keep them informed of the Rudowsky claim. Barker's letters shed light on his longtime relationship with A.J. Poppleton, offering a unique perspective from a client's point of view. Barker frequently expressed frustration in his letters with Poppleton's busyness and inability to meet with him to discuss his case. However, Barker understood Poppleton's workload for the railroad, plus his involvement in Nebraska Democratic party politics, took much of his time. Whenever Barker did get the chance to talk with Poppleton, Barker wrote that his time with him was limited. Nevertheless, Barker believed Poppleton's work was competent, and his fee was reasonable. The following excerpts from his letters cover the attorney-client relationship between Barker and Poppleton from 1866 to 1871:

Barker Letter to Family in England - May 26, 1866:
I just had a few minutes talk with Poppleton on Monday, but he was just going off for the week. I am to see him next week when he returns. He was walking about the street as firmly as any other man, and as stout as before his illness. He said he was attending to your case and had postponed it to October next. He thought there was little trouble but would go through the case when he returned. [He was] paid $40 as a retainer. He is the head lawyer. I have found your 120-acre patent [deed] at the Recorders office. It has lain there six years. The house on the farm is in good condition. The land is clean, and they have a fine crop of wheat on the hillside. Omaha has grown considerably. I think you may safely say that there are full twice as many stores and houses as when we left ... Well, I have told you all I can at present ... I like this place, climate, and people better than any other part of America. And if we have to be here, we can get along. One thing is certain, I must stay here awhile. When you are away people will try and attack your property.[310]

Barker Letter to Family in England - June 19, 1866:
I have not been able to see Poppleton again. He is very busy. He is the Railway's Solicitor. And just now he is busy with politics ... Poppleton is a Democratic candidate and will very likely be elected if the Democratic Party is strong enough ... They are all up to their eyes in political logrolling, as the newly elected legislature opens today.[311]

Barker Letter to Family in England - June 20, 1868:
I paid Mr. Poppleton the other day – he charged me twenty dollars – very reasonable in settlement in full to date - he says he thinks they will not attempt anymore. I thanked him.[312]

Barker Letter to Family in England - December 19, 1871:
Our suit with Rudowsky has been pending in Court all the past week and has kept us on the alert – today we learned it was put off-with many more - till next March ... And Poppleton desires to have you here as a principal witness if possible - to be able to put your testimony against Rudowsky's false swearing. So, my dear father you and Mary Jane must try and arrange to start for Omaha in February next ... Poppleton thinks it wisest to have you here.[313]

On March 28, 1872, Rev. Joseph Barker Sr. returned to Omaha with his daughter Mary Jane and his two sisters after his wife Frances had died the previous year.[314] On November 16, 1872, he gave a four-hour deposition. Rev. Barker, under oath, denied Rudowsky's claim and stated that Rudowsky understood what he was signing and had never taken possession of the 120 acres.[315] Despite numerous delays and proceedings, the Judge dismissed the case in favor of the Barker family on June 3, 1873.[316] Finally, after six years of on-off proceedings, Poppleton had successfully defended the case. The Barker family continued to retain him as their lawyer until his retirement. Rev. Barker died September 15, 1875, and was buried in Prospect Hill Cemetery, Omaha. His son Joseph Barker Jr. died July 4, 1896, at 65, at his home at 1505 S. 8th Street, Omaha. Funeral services were held at Trinity.

Historical Note: Omaha in 1868

The collection of over 2000 letters between the members of the Barker family in England and those in Omaha, includes numerous references to their collective love for Omaha, the beauty of the city and its endless opportunities for growth. On November 6, 1868, Joseph Barker Jr. walked up Capitol Hill to the high point of the city to gaze upon the city at night. Returning to his boarding house room, he wrote a long letter to his family in England:

> It was dark- no moon and rather cloudy - prairie fires, red and lurid were in the distance up and down the river on both sides and crawling over the Bluffs – the City at my feet was all alight dotted thickly over with lights - Farnam & Douglas were quite brilliant – all along the river and at the Railway works were lights and on the opposite shore – and stretching up all the way to Council Bluffs – where the lights of that City stretching two miles along the foot of the Bluffs shone out clear and bright and quite near. It looked like one vast City. I was surprised and struck by the appearance it made, the prairie fires surrounding it all and the lurid shadows reflected on the clouds made quite a picture ... C. Bluffs is steadily growing down towards the river and someday it will be one great City on both sides of the river with railroad and foot and carriage bridges connecting the two.[317]

Fig 31. Omaha 1870 looking East on Douglas Street
towards the Missouri River and Council Bluffs.
A view Joseph Barker Jr. likely gazed upon.
Courtesy Douglas County Historical Society

20

Commencement Speaker

A.J. Poppleton was highly esteemed for his eloquence and command of the English language, whether speaking in a courtroom, before the legislature, to university faculty and students, at ceremonial events, or before civic and cultural organizations. James M. Woolworth wrote that A.J. "possessed a full vocabulary, a glowing style, and elevated sentiments, as a perusal of his addresses will attest."[318]

Notable Addresses

Poppleton made many notable addresses in his career including at the presentation of colors to honor the soldiers leaving Omaha to fight for the Union Army in the Civil War, at the groundbreaking ceremony for the Union Pacific Railroad in 1863, at a fund-raising event for the citizens of Omaha to support families rendered destitute and homeless by the great Chicago fire of 1871, at the Nebraska Bar Association Annual Meeting in 1880, at the public memorial for Bishop Robert Clarkson of Trinity Episcopal Cathedral in 1884, at the laying of the cornerstone for the new Douglas County courthouse in 1885 and at the dedication of the Exposition Building in 1886.[319]

Ironically, one of the addresses that must have given him great satisfaction, was when he was asked to speak in Indianapolis at the 1878 National Convention of Beta Theta Pi, his beloved fraternity from college days at Michigan University. A few years after Poppleton left Michigan University because the administration had banned all Greek/Literary societies from campus, they rescinded their policy. But by that time Poppleton had already graduated from Union College and was pursuing a career in the law. Obviously, the national leadership of Beta Theta Pi had not forgotten his courageous actions on their behalf twenty-seven years earlier.

Poppleton generally followed the same structure in composing a major address. He began by expressing gratitude for the opportunity to speak, while at the same time saying he felt a sense of unworthiness for the task before him, showing his respect for the audience. The body of his talk often included references to historical events and characters, ancient and modern, with quotations from their writings. Interspersed were elevated sentiments of challenge and encouragement, and then a close with a verse or two of poetry he composed.

At the age of 22, A.J. Poppleton made his first public address before the Agricultural Society in his hometown of Oakland, Michigan, in 1852. His 38-page handwritten copy included a theme that he would frequently use over the next 40 years—the importance of character in the citizens of a community and the value of education in molding character. His parents had instilled in him the importance of education. He never forgot it. It was part of his heritage.

University of Nebraska Address (1877)

On June 27, 1877, A.J. Poppleton was asked to give the commencement address at the fifth annual graduation ceremonies of the University of Nebraska in Lincoln. His address was so powerful and well received that the University published it in a 21-page pamphlet for public distribution titled *Character: Development and Exaltation —The True End of Education.*

> I am painfully conscious that I am little fitted for the task before me. Twenty-five years of business life – absorbed in practical affairs, isolated from scholastic associations, down on one's knees with the muck rake, inhaling the foul atmosphere of Mammon until the pure ether bathing the mountain summits of learning has almost lost its exhilarating effect – constitute a slender title to audience upon an educational theme, at the state's intellectual center. Yet, as to none is liberty so dear as to those long girt about by prison walls, so I trust may I urge as my best warrant for the duty I have undertaken, an unconquerable longing to pause for a moment from the wearisome march upon the hot and dust-swept highway of business and revisit for once, at least, the green fields out of which I stepped with regrets and tears, now nearly thirty years ago.

Poppleton spoke of a major problem prevalent in society – the struggle of people trying to make ends meet for their families, and their frustration in never seeming to get ahead. So, how could they advance? His answer was always the same – education:

> Geography, mathematics, philosophy, languages, and all the technical learning of the schools, will leave one without the edge which will pierce or cut the problems with which men are confronted and surrounded, either in practical or intellectual life ... No teacher rises to the true dignity of his office who is not at the same time a leader and inspirer of the youthful mind. It is through this leadership and inspiration that the technical learning of the schools becomes effectual in the true purpose of education. And sad will be the day with this noble guide to the higher aims and purposes of life shall fail or falter in his high office.
>
> It being then the true end and aim of education to develop, strengthen, and exalt individual character; to mold for society a useful, upright and progressive member; to furnish to the state an intelligent and patriotic citizen; how shall it be accomplished? It may all be summed up in a single sentence. The welfare of the state rests upon the ballot; the purity of the ballot rests upon the intelligence, integrity, honor and patriotism of the citizen; the character of the citizen rests upon the schools in which he is taught, and the traditions by which they are guided, and the quality of the school is molded by the teacher.

Among the poets Poppleton admired the most, was Alexander Pope [1688-1744], who wrote *An Essay on Man* in 1733 which included a phrase that most university students in A.J.'s day would likely have memorized and tried to emulate: "*Act well your part: there all the honor lies.*"[320]

In the next part of his address, he laid out a roadmap for a quality educational system with a teaching faculty committed to uplifting the character of the students:

> As there is no royal road to learning, so there's no magnificent highway conducting to the perfection and exaltation of human character ... And so, the traits upon whose development the solid structure of a perfect character must rest, are homebred virtues:
>
> **Honor.** First of all, I would inculcate the sentiment of honor, that mysterious touchstone which tests all transactions, all motives, all aspirations – not by an external measure, but by the subtle perception of taint or stain upon one's own manhood. In all ages and every country under different names and customs and usages, it has been the solvent which has preserved the merely human impulses of men from a lower and deeper descent in the scale of existence.[321]
>
> **Courage, Fortitude, and Charity Are Akin to Honor.** By courage and fortitude, I do not mean that which dares or endures mere physical suffering; nor by charity do I designate mere benevolence in material things. I refer rather to that intellectual courage and fortitude which faces the results of conviction, once crystallized into opinion, without unflinching pluck, and endures all things in their vindication; and to that broader charity which mounts to the serene elevation of intellectual, political and religious toleration.[322]
>
> **Education Molds Character**. Let, then, the University go forward in the noble career to which every voice of the future calls it; patiently, steadfastly, persistently, deaf to calumny, and jealous of praise – but ever vigilant to detect abuses; abating neither heart nor hope; spurning not the wisdom and advice of others, but winnowing all carefully and then resting unmovably upon its own conviction, and executing its judgment without fear or favor, assured that its work will only cease when the state shall have been molded into the likeness of a perfect individual character; when honor, courage, fortitude, charity, patriotism, inflexibility shall have fused incongruous and diverse nativities, and lives, into a homogeneous and perfect commonwealth; when birth, and color, and sex, and creed, shall have been completely disenthralled; when strength shall have become the guardian and not the oppressor of weakness; when wealth shall have become the almoner and not the despoiler of poverty.[323]

The following year, at their commencement ceremonies, the University of Nebraska conferred upon A.J. Poppleton the honorary degree of "Doctor of Laws". He received numerous plaudits from friends and colleagues for his address, none of which he treasured more than the following handwritten letter from a member of the Nebraska Supreme Court:

Hon, A.J. Poppleton
Attorney at Law Omaha July 3, 1877

Dear Sir:
I want to say to you that I have read your address delivered before the University with a great deal of pleasure, such an address would have done no discredit to [Daniel] Webster at the zenith of his power. I am Truly Yours,

Samuel Maxwell
Judge of the Supreme Court of Nebraska

At the bottom of the letter which he sent on to his wife who was out of town, A.J. Poppleton wrote:

"My Dear Carrie:
What do you think of this? AJP"[324]

21

Missing Caroline and Libby

A.J. Poppleton's work for the Union Pacific Railroad often took him to Washington D.C. for weeks at a time. Whether he was appearing before a congressional committee, or arguing a case before the U.S. Supreme Court, he found it difficult to enjoy any lengthy time away from his wife.

When he was away from home for long periods of time, Caroline often traveled to the east coast to visit cousins in upstate New York, or to see their daughter Libby. By 1878, Libby had graduated from Vassar College and was teaching courses there on William Shakespeare and Thomas Carlyle. The following letter conveys A.J.'s affection and longing to be with Caroline and Libby:

My Dear Carrie: Washington D.C. January 25, 1878

I received your telegram this morning. It is plain to me that I am not likely to get away from here for many weeks to come unless some change in UP affairs takes place. There is hard work to do – Jay Gould [majority owner in UPRR] seems to rely upon me to be sure it is done and my things at home are of minimum consequence. So, much as I dislike it, I am setting my mind to stay. I know no news. The weather is not unpleasant & Washington seems full of strangers. Though aside from my work, it seems dull to me. When you come here, I think you can get a through train from Boston leaving there in the evening and arriving here about one o'clock the next day. Any other [schedule] will subject you to an inconvenient transfer at New York. The Boston people will no doubt give you the requisite information ... I have no doubt you will have a delicious visit with Libby. You seem to have dropped yourself into a cozy house in a strange city ... Give me a day or two notice when you are coming so I can make necessary arrangements. I don't think I am likely to go to New York- though I would like to for a few days. With a thousand kisses for yourself and Libby,

your good husband, A. J. Poppleton[325]

A.J. often addressed his letters to Caroline using her nickname, Carrie. When Caroline wrote back, she often called him "my good husband." So, he in turn would frequently sign his letters to her "your good husband." In every letter, A,J. always expressed his love for Caroline. Sometimes he included a poem clipped from a newspaper. In this January 25, 1878 letter, written 22 years after their marriage, A.J. slipped into the envelope an anonymous poem titled "Love Song." The words expressed his longing to be with Caroline, now and forever, in this life and the next:

LOVE SONG
She who sleeps upon my heart
Was the first to win it,
She who dreams upon my breast
Ever reigns within it.
She who kisses oft my lips
Wakes their warmest blessing.
She who rests within these arms
Feels their closest pressing.

Other days than these shall come
Days that may be dreary –
Other hours shall greet us yet,
Hours that may be weary;
Still this breast thy pillow;
Still these lips meet thine as oft
Billow meeteth billow.

Sleep then, on my happy heart,
Since thy love hath won it-
Dream, then on my loyal breast,
None but thou hast done it –
And when age our bloom shall change,
With its wintry weather,
May we, in the self-same grave,
Sleep and dream together.[326]
(anonymous)

The 1870s were fruitful years for A.J. and Caroline's family. Mary Delia was born on July 23, 1873, in their new home on 19th & Dodge; and Libby graduated with honors from Vassar College in June 1876.

Elizabeth "Libby" Poppleton

Ellen Elizabeth Poppleton, born on September 11, 1856, in Omaha, was known to family and friends as "Libby." She attended Brownell Hall, an all-girls boarding school opened in 1863 by Trinity Episcopal Cathedral.[327] The course of study in the school's circular dated September 17, 1867, listed a group of lecturers that included her father (biography course) and family friend James Woolworth (general history course). The curriculum included languages (Latin, French and German), sciences (astronomy, botany, geology, mineralogy, cartography, geography, chemistry), mathematics (algebra, geometry) the fine arts (music with piano, singing, drawing), in addition to courses in history (British, American, ancient, and general), literature, scripture, philosophy (moral and mental), composition and rhetoric, spelling and grammar.[328]

A.J. and Caroline valued higher education for their children and so they sent Libby to Vassar College in Poughkeepsie, New York, near where A.J. had attended Union College. Although it was over 1,000 miles from Omaha, Libby would be near her New York cousins.

Apparently, Libby took to college life with joyful rigor evidenced by the long weekly letters she wrote to her parents describing her course work and daily activities. One letter written in 1877, expressed the inspiration she felt to complete her manuscripts on two historical figures, William Shakespeare and Thomas Carlyle:

> Dear Papa and Momma: Sunday Night, Nov. 12, 1877
>
> This has been a long quiet day, and I have enjoyed every part of it. This morning, I began by doing a wholly unprecedented and inexcusable thing – deliberately planned not – to get down to breakfast till just as the others were coming up stairs – so I had a nice cozy time all by myself which was just what I needed – what I wanted. Then I came up here lightning fast and sat myself down in my rocking chair and proud of it – where I stayed till dinner time reading thru after dinner and all then started for church. You remember the afternoon service at Trinity. Phillip Brooks preached the most glorious sermon I ever heard in my life – that sounds exaggerating – but is certainly not. The text was "let every man prove his own work;" and the great thing he said gave me a real inspiration.[329]

Libby wrote that she was resolved "to expand my Carlyle into a more complete study."[330] In this same letter she shared a lecture she attended by Professor Raymond on *The Merchant of Venice* by William Shakespeare. Leaving Raymond's talk, she heard people say,

> How wonderfully he read it; whereas no one said what a glorious play that it was. Still, I believe that anyone who has not read the play nor heard of it, would have come away with the strongest impression, not of Shakespeare, but of Professor Raymond – so the moral of all that is that I propose to hold dramatic readings in connection with my lectures. The thought has been growing in my mind and I like it better and better.[331]

Libby ended her seventeen-page missive with these words: "Well, it is half past nine, I had no idea I was going to write back a long letter when I began. That sermon stirred me up and put me in the mood, so indirectly, you may thank Phillip Brooks for this volume. Goodnight and pleasant dreams,

with love and kisses to all, Libby."[332]

On February 9, 1878, A,J. replied to Libby's letter while still working in Washington D.C. on behalf of the Union Pacific. He offered some fatherly advice to his daughter regarding her manuscript on Thomas Carlyle, which he had failed to include in the letter he wrote to her the previous day:

My Dear Libby: Washington Feb 9, 1878

In writing to you yesterday, I failed to speak of one thing I intended on the printing of your "Carlyle." If you desire to complete it just as you want to, I would advise you to make a clear complete copy on good wide-ruled legal paper with the lines numbered, writing on only one side. If you submit it to Prof. B., he may make suggestions for corrections or changes you will accept. In this way your work will be in a numerical list. I would like to see it also and may make some suggestions you would think good. I wouldn't give a copy to anyone who does not write a clear, legible hand, which can be read nearly as easily. For such a copy ten dollars is not much out of the way. If she has the facilities she could make you a letter-press copy of her copy, which would be easily as useful as the original. I would like it copied as soon as I could get it done, leaving it to be printed when the criticism of it is finished. With a thousand kisses,

your affectionate papa, A.J. Poppleton.[333]

After graduation, Libby taught as an instructor in the Department of English at Vassar. In March 1878, Vassar offered her "Short Course in Shakespeare" on seven Thursdays from 3-4 p.m. at a cost of 50 cents.[334] For the next four years, she lectured nationwide on Carlyle.[335] In 1887, Vassar elected Libby as the first woman to its Board of Trustees, and she served in that position for 10 years.[336] Her love for Vassar and her work on behalf of its alumni association continued the rest of her life.[337]

When Libby returned to Omaha, she joined her sister Mary in performing for charitable events. Mary sang while Libby played the piano, mostly classical works by Bach and Beethoven. Libby served on boards of civic and cultural organizations that contributed to the growth and beauty of Omaha, following in her parents' footsteps until her death in 1936.

Fig. 32. Elizabeth "Libby" Poppleton (1856-1936)
Courtesy A.J. Poppleton III Personal Collection

Fire Destroys Poppleton Home

On January 2, 1879, Caroline made the following entry in her diary: "Our house on the hill was burned to the ground. Elizabeth and Bill both home for vacation."[338] The family lost many of their personal belongings and memorabilia in the fire.

Four months later, Poppleton became involved in what he described as one of the most important cases of his life - the trial of Chief Standing Bear.

22

Standing Bear's Attorney

In the early hours of April 4, 1879, A.J. Poppleton was already working at his desk in the Herndon House, the headquarters of the Union Pacific Railroad Company (UPRR), when an unexpected visitor knocked on his door. The visitor did not have an appointment and was not there to see Poppleton on railroad business. Thomas H. Tibbles, deputy editor of the *Omaha Daily Herald,* needed to talk to him on a matter of great urgency.[339]

Poppleton recently returned from a business trip on behalf of the UPRR and was very busy. In addition to his work for the railway, he served as legal counsel for the Omaha & Republican Valley Railroad, a subsidiary of the UPRR. He continued to lead and support various civic and cultural organizations in Omaha.

Fig. 33. Thomas H. Tibbles
Courtesy Nebraska State Historical Society,

Tibbles Meets with John L. Webster

Thomas Tibbles was determined to convince Poppleton to serve as co-counsel with John L. Webster to represent Chief Standing Bear and twenty-nine members of the Ponca tribe of Nebraska. The Poncas had been arrested by George Crook, Commanding General of the Department of the Platte, under orders from Washington D.C. The Poncas were imprisoned at Fort Omaha, charged with violating federal law by leaving Indian Territory without government permission. General Crook would be forced to return them to Indian Territory unless legal action could quickly be taken to stay his orders.

Tibbles had heard the Ponca story from General Crook and had interviewed Standing Bear and the other Ponca prisoners, so he knew that only a federal court would have jurisdiction and authority to stay the removal order. Tibbles and Webster attended the same school in Ohio, so Tibbles called on Webster two days before he met with Poppleton. Webster told Tibbles he would consider the case overnight. Tibbles later wrote that the 35-year-old Webster was established in Nebraska as "a hard student [of the law] and a man whose opinions commanded respect in the courts and outside."[340]

Fig. 34. General George Crook
Courtesy Douglas County Historical Society

When Tibbles returned the next morning, Webster told him he had serious concerns about getting involved in this unprecedented matter, one that would require a significant amount of time and energy, and of necessity be pro-bono. Yet, Webster told Tibbles that he would take the case on one condition, if A.J. Poppleton would assist him:

> This is a question of vast importance. A petition for such a writ [Habeas Corpus] must be based upon broad constitutional grounds, and the principles involved in it underlie all personal liberty. It is a question of the natural rights of men, such as was discussed by the fathers and founders of this government. I am not satisfied that a writ would hold on account of the peculiar relation of Indians to the government. They have always been treated as "wards," as incapable of making contracts, etc., but it will do no harm to try. It seems to me that there ought to be power somewhere to stop this inhuman cruelty, and if it does not reside in the courts where shall we find it? My services are at your disposal, but on account of the magnitude of the questions involved, I would like to have assistance. If Hon. A.J. Poppleton will assist me, I will go right to work and draw up the papers. I know of no lawyer in these United States, who can handle these underlying, fundamental questions of government and human liberty more ably than he.[341]

Tibbles agreed with Webster that Poppleton "was considered without a peer in the legal profession in the State, and that as an orator there were few in the whole country who could so entrance an audience."[342]

Poppleton Agrees to Take the Case

At his meeting with Poppleton, Tibbles laid out the facts of the case. In the spring of 1877, the tribe had been forcibly removed to Indian Territory, modern Oklahoma, even though the Poncas had never broken a treaty with the government, never taken up arms against the government, and were good neighbors to the white farmers living near them in the Niobrara River valley of Nebraska. Other facts included:

- The Ponca Tribe was the smallest tribe in the Great Plains, with only 710 members at the time of their removal. They were living as farmers in log cabins they built, with a gristmill, sawmill, blacksmith shop, school, and church in their villages. They were a peace-loving people who grew their own vegetables and crops but were defenseless against the military.

- In 1877, when the government moved the tribe to Indian Territory, against their will, to a land unsuitable for farming, the soldiers tore down all their homes and buildings, including their church and schoolhouse, without compensation.

- Nine Poncas died on the 500-mile journey to Indian Territory, including Chief Standing Bear's 22-year-old daughter, Prairie Flower. 158 men, women, and children died of disease and malnutrition in the following 18 months there.

- In December 1878, Chief Standing Bear's 16-year-old son, Bear Shield died of malaria. Before his death, he asked his parents to bury him in the ancestral burial grounds of the Ponca Tribe. Standing Bear and his wife Susette promised their son they would.

- On January 2, 1879, amid a fierce blizzard with howling winds, snow and ice, Chief Standing Bear led 29 members of his family on a quest for freedom. He carried the bones of Bear Shield with him. After 60 days of grueling travel, the Poncas arrived at the reservation of their cousins, the Omaha Tribe. Omaha Chief Joseph LaFlesche (Iron Eye), his daughter Susette LaFlesche (Inshta-theamba - Bright Eyes), and other members of the Omaha Tribe tended to the Poncas' bleeding feet and wounds, respiratory illnesses, and did whatever they could to comfort their broken hearts.

- In March 1879, the soldiers arrested the Poncas and marched them 100 miles to Fort Omaha, as prisoners.

After listening to Tibbles describe the facts of the Ponca plight, Poppleton agreed to take the case. He later explained his reasoning:

> I was requested to join Mr. J. L. Webster in an application for a habeas corpus to test the validity of the restraint of the liberty of Standing Bear for the purpose of removing him to Indian Territory. The question of whether the writ would lie on behalf of a tribal Indian and whether the United States had any lawful power by its soldiery to remove him were wholly new and of vast importance. Without fee or reward or any hope or promise of compensation, Mr. Webster and myself entered upon this work and espoused the cause of the Indians.[343]

The Great Writ

Poppleton and Webster understood the enormous challenge facing them because the U.S. Supreme Court had ruled in 1831 that Native Americans are "In a state of pupilage. Their relation to the United States resembles that of a ward to his guardian."[344] Therefore, they were not considered to be "persons" under the law with no "standing" to file an action in federal court. Poppleton and Webster believed a writ of habeas corpus was the only legal pleading capable of stopping General Crook from carrying out his orders to escort the Ponca prisoners back to Indian Territory.

The *Writ of Habeas Corpus* is a judicial order directing the person detaining a prisoner to "present the body" of the prisoner before the court, to test the legality of the imprisonment. It is called "The Great Writ" because it is the guardian of all other rights against the lawless action of the State. It was first established in 1215, when King John was forced by his barons to sign the Magna Carta at Runnymede, England. The U. S. Supreme Court stated in a 1963 ruling that:

> Although in form the Great Writ is simply a mode of procedure, its history is inextricably intertwined with the growth of fundamental rights of personal liberty. For its function has been to provide a prompt and efficacious remedy for whatever society deems to be intolerable restraints.[345]

Poppleton and Webster filed an application for a writ of habeas corpus in the District Court of the United States for the District of Nebraska on behalf of Standing Bear (Ma-Chu-Nah-Zha) and the other Ponca prisoners against General George Crook as Commanding Officer of the Department of the Platte of the United States Army. A hearing was held in the Federal Courtroom in Lincoln, Nebraska on April 8, 1879, before Judge Elmer S. Dundy. After listening to the lawyer's argument, Judge Dundy granted their application and issued the following Order:

> It being made to appear to the Court that the said Petitioners are detained without any legal authority. It is therefore ordered that a Writ of Habeas Corpus be allowed to issue on behalf of the said Petitioners directed to George Crook, a Brigadier General of the United States, commanding the Department of the Platte, returnable within ten days from the date of the service of said Writ upon him.[346]

Later that day, General Crook was served the writ by Ellis L. Bierbower, deputy United States Marshall. The writ blocked Crook from carrying out the order of removal issued by Carl Schurz, Secretary of the Interior. As a result, nothing more could be done until a formal hearing could be convened in federal court.

Fig. 35. Office of the Federal Court, Omaha, NE, 1879
Courtesy from The Bostwick-Frohardt Collection,
KM3TV on permanent loan to The Durham Museum, Omaha

The Trial

The case of *United States ex rel. Standing Bear v. George Crook* (5 Dill.453, 25 F. Cas. 695) was heard on the third floor of the Federal Courthouse in Omaha, Nebraska on Thursday morning, May 1, 1879, and concluded late in the evening of May 2, 1879.[347] Men and women of all ranks of society attended the trial. Many Americans across the nation followed the trial in their local newspaper thanks to the on-site reporting by Thomas Tibbles in the *Omaha Daily Herald*.

A Case of "Firsts"

This was an unprecedented situation for attorneys Poppleton and Webster, and for Judge Dundy, who was hearing a case previously reserved for white people since Native Americans were considered not to be persons or citizens in the eyes of the law. This would be the first time in American history that the writ of habeas corpus was applied to Native Americans, 664 years after the great charter of liberty, the Magna Carta, was signed.

Poppleton and Webster had to be creative and factual in their presentation to persuade the judge that he had legal authority to rule favorably on behalf of their clients. On the first day of the trial, Webster called Standing Bear as a witness. He became the first Native American to testify in a federal courtroom. The second day of the trial was reserved for the lawyers' closing arguments. Webster spoke for three hours, followed by District Attorney Genio Lambertson, who also spoke for three hours, then the court adjourned for dinner. After the court re-convened for a rare evening session, Judge Elmer Dundy directed A. J. Poppleton to deliver his closing argument, which lasted two hours.

Poppleton's Closing Argument

The *Omaha Daily Herald* allocated the largest number of columns for Poppleton's closing argument, compared to Webster and Lambertson's closing arguments combined. Thomas Tibbles reported on Poppleton's closing argument, saying that the audience in the courtroom "listened with breathless attention to every word ... From the very start it was a masterly speech, but the latter portion was intensely thrilling and powerful."[348] Poppleton began by saying:

> May it please the Court. I suppose it would be impossible for counsel under any circumstances to approach a case of this character without a feeling of oppression at its magnitude and the consequences involved in it ... it is intensified in this case by the fact that I am to appear here on behalf of a feeble remnant of a class of beings who seem, for two or three hundred years to have had no friends and to have never had any rights.[349]

Lambertson had argued against the application for a writ of habeas corpus, saying the Poncas were without any right to even be in federal court. Poppleton countered Lambertson by saying:

> I confess, I have been somewhat surprised as to the character of the argument made here. What it is in effect, is that these relators have no right whatever, not even the right of petition, not even the right to the protection of their liberty. What is the reason in that? ... Our government has gone and made treaties with them in which the government has undertaken to guarantee them certain rights, certain lands, and certain privileges in connection with these lands, and now to turn back on those guarantees is a most infamous act, because it is treachery on the part of power as against weakness.[350]

Poppleton then discussed the erroneous Dred Scott decision and expressed his gratitude that the Fourteenth Amendment had rectified it. He also pointed out that Lambertson erred when he told the Court that the government had "given" the Poncas tools, houses, and plows. This was not a gift, Poppleton reminded Lambertson, but "consideration" for the relinquishment of their rights to certain land they were ceding to the government. Poppleton argued that it was a contractual arrangement that did not authorize the government to unilaterally change the terms of the treaty when the Poncas had not broken its end of the bargain. During his two-hour argument, Poppleton displayed his reputation as a passionate trial lawyer who fought for justice for his clients, as his powerful words demonstrate:

> I tell your Honor it is an outrage – and the word outrage doesn't express it – it is an infamy difficult to grasp ... Is it possible that this great government, standing here dealing with this feeble remnant of a once powerful nation, claims the right to place them in a condition which is to them worse than slaves, without a syllable of law, without a syllable or contract or treaty? I don't believe, if your Honor please, that the courts will allow this; that they will agree to the proposition that these people are wild beasts; that they have no status in the courts. The argument of the gentleman representing the government comes to that - they are simply wild beasts.[351]

Poppleton said that the writ "has been the shield and protection of individual liberty until it has made every man a sovereign the world over."[352] In his argument, he asserted the right of the prisoners to petition the court for a writ of habeas corpus to protect themselves from lawless violence:

> Everything in this county not done by law is lawless violence. In looking over judicial decisions I found this language: 'No human being in this country can exercise any kind of public authority which is not conferred by law. In the United States it must be given by the express words of a written statute. Whatever is not given is withheld and the exercise of it is positively prohibited.' If there is any power in the military to hold these people, it must be under a positive statute. I protest against the power of the military to arrest them, and I think the military itself has a right to protest.[353]

Poppleton then shared a quote from the testimony given by Standing Bear on the witness stand the previous day, describing his "sacred desire" to bury his son:

> During the sixty days I was coming from the Indian Territory to the Omaha agency I carried the bones of my boy in a box, and I have got them now. It is my sacred desire, it is my absorbing purpose, it is my highest aspiration to carry the ashes of that boy and bury them where in his last hours he wished to be buried.[354]

Near the end of his closing argument, A.J. Poppleton paused for a moment, then turned and looked directly at Standing Bear, and asked this question:

That man not a human being? Who of us all would have done it? Look around this city and state and find, if you can, the man who has gathered up the ashes of his dead son, wandered for sixty days through a strange country without guide or compass, aided by the sun and stars only, that the bones of his son may be buried in the land of their birth. No! It is a libel upon religion; it is libel upon missionaries who sacrifice so much and risk their lives in order to take to these Indians that gospel which Christ proclaimed to all the wide earth, to say that these are not human beings. But if they are human beings, they cannot be barred from the right to this Writ.[355]

A.J. Poppleton sat down, exhausted. It was nearly 9:30 p.m. Court adjourned. Yet, Judge Dundy did not leave the courtroom, but remained seated on the bench. He signaled for Standing Bear to speak – this was an answer to Standing Bear's request made through Tibbles earlier that day that he would like to speak for himself.

Standing Bear Speaks

Another "first" was about to take place in this case. Late in the evening of Friday, May 2, 1879, a Native American was allowed to address the court, something that had never occurred before in any federal courtroom anywhere in the United States. Standing Bear, who did not speak or read English, spoke to the judge through an interpreter. He recounted the sufferings the Ponca Tribe had endured at the hands of the government without any justifiable reason. The Poncas were small, defenseless people. In less than two years, their population had been reduced by over twenty-five percent. If they were sent back to Indian Territory, Standing Bear told the court, his people would die.

Standing Bear spoke with passion and conviction for nearly 30 minutes. Near the end, he paused and raised his hand to the perpendicular for everyone in the courtroom to see. He held it there for a moment and then uttered these now famous words:

That hand is not the color of yours.
But if I pierce it, I shall feel pain.
If you pierce your hand, you also feel pain.
The blood that will flow from mine, will be
the same color as yours.
I AM A MAN.
The same God made us both.[356]

It was nearly 10:00 p.m. when Standing Bear finished. Thomas Tibbles wrote that his speech "was greeted with a round of applause."[357]

Judge Dundy's Decision

Judge Elmer S. Dundy rendered his landmark ruling on May 12, 1879, holding:

> That an *Indian* is a PERSON within the meaning of the laws of the United States, and has, therefore, the right to sue out a writ of *habeas corpus* in a federal court, or before a federal judge, in all cases where he may be confined or in custody under color of authority of the United States, or where he is restrained of liberty in violation of the constitution or laws of the United States ... Being restrained of liberty under color of authority of the United States, and in violation of the laws thereof, the relators must be discharged from custody, and it is so ordered.[358]

Standing Bears Thanks Tibbles, Webster, and Poppleton with Gifts

Before Standing Bear and his wife Suzette went home to an island on the Niobrara River to begin their life again and to bury their son Bear Shield, Standing Bear gave gifts from his few remaining earthly possessions to Tibbles, Webster, and Poppleton for their great assistance in the case.

To Thomas Tibbles, Standing Bear gave his beaded leggings calling him his "brother." To John Webster, he gave his tomahawk, saying he had no more need of it. Finally, to A.J. Poppleton, he gave his three-hundred-year-old war bonnet headdress saying it was his most valued possession.[359]

The War Bonnet

On January 5, 1915, Caroline Poppleton and her children loaned Standing Bear's war bonnet to the Nebraska State Historical Society for safekeeping and display to the public. Myron Learned, Caroline's son-in-law, formally presented the war bonnet to the Society in Lincoln, together with a letter Caroline wrote.[360] She shared the story of Standing Bear's visit to their home that Sunday afternoon, thirty-six years earlier, fondly recalling the scene:

> I remember in 1879, when Judge Dundy had rendered the decision in his favor, how Standing Bear with his interpreter called upon Mr. Poppleton at his rooms at Roswell Smith's, opposite the Withnell House, corner of Harney and Fifteenth, where we boarded after our house on Capitol Hill was burned, to personally thank him for his speech on his behalf and with the war bonnet in his hands, he offered it to Mr. Poppleton as his grateful act and his only pay for the words he had spoken for him and his tribe ... Out of the poverty of his worldly possessions, he gave such visible token of his appreciation as he could, while out of the wealth of his human soul, and out of the fullness of his manly heart, he uttered sentiments, and expressed purposes which distinguish him as chief among ten thousand, and as a character, dark though his skin may be, altogether lovely.[361]

Caroline Poppleton shared the memorable words Standing Bear spoke to Poppleton when he presented him with his war bonnet headdress:

> He informed Mr. Poppleton that he was about to leave for the North, and he thought he would call and bid him goodbye. He said: "I believe I told you in the court room, that God made me and that I was a man. For many years, we have been chased about, as a dog chases a wild beast. God sent you to help me. I thank you for what you have done. I want to get my land back. That is what I long for all the time. I wish to live there and be buried with my people. When you were speaking in the court room, of course I could not understand, but I could see that you were trying very hard to release me. I think you are doing for me and my people, something that never has been done before. If I had to pay you for it, I could never get enough to do it. I have here a relic which has come down to my people, through a great many generations. I do not know how old it is. It may be two or three hundred years old. I desire to present it to you, for what you have done for me.[362]

Caroline then shared her husband's response at the moment he received the war bonnet headdress from Standing Bear:

> Mr. Poppleton accepting the gift, said to Standing Bear, that he was more than repaid for what he may have done, in the satisfaction he felt in having rescued him and his people, and his satisfaction would be all the deeper, should they succeed in maintaining themselves in their new relations and achieving the arts and the freedom and peace of civilized life.[363]

A.J. and Caroline Poppleton treasured Standing Bear's gift and refused to sell it. After her husband died in 1896, Caroline and her children continued to treasure the war bonnet and its meaning for Standing Bear and A.J. But as Caroline neared the end of her life, she decided it could best be preserved for historical purposes in the hands of the Nebraska State Historical Society. In the final paragraph of her January 5, 1915, statement, Caroline wrote:

> The keepsake given by the Chief to the great attorney, is a rare gift, being esteemed the most sacred, as it is the most venerable object in the possession of the tribe. It resembles a wig and was worn by the head chief at their most weighty councils. Curiosity hunters have often sought to secure it at any price in money, but he has, to one and all, said that money could not buy it. Among occasions on which it has been worn was of the first treaty in 1858, we believe made between the Poncas and the government of the Unites States. Standing Bear informed us that when he was a little boy, his father told him that no one in the tribe knew how old it was, and that it had come into their possession in generations long past.[364]

Poppleton Remembers

A few years before he died, A.J. Poppleton reflected upon many of the people he had interacted with over his life, together with some of the more interesting and important cases he handled as general counsel for the Union Pacific Railroad Company, and in his private practice. Near the end of his memoirs, he recalled the moment he stood in the courtroom representing Standing Bear and the Poncas and the profound satisfaction it gave him, more than any other work:

> Without fee or reward or any hope or promise of compensation, Mr. Webster and myself entered upon this work and espoused the cause of the Indians. The hearing took place before District Court Judge Dundy at Omaha ... I delivered my argument upon that case in the evening in the large courtroom of the Federal Building on the corner of Dodge and Fifteenth Streets. There were present in addition to the court and its officers, an audience taxing the fine capacity of the room, including General Crook and other officers under his command, and many ladies. I have spoken to larger audiences, but I think never to one more intelligent and sympathetic, and in looking back I cannot now recall any two hours work of my life with which I feel better satisfied. Our movement was completely successful. The court sustained our claims to the fullest extent; Standing Bear was liberated.[365]

Standing Bear and his fellow Poncas had two of the best lawyers in the nation representing them—Andrew J. Poppleton and John L. Webster.[366] Without any financial compensation and at personal sacrifice, these two men researched the issues and, using creative language, drafted the pleadings to present to the court. Their closing arguments were extraordinary in attempting to achieve what no other lawyer in the nation had done before.

Judge Dundy's ruling that "an Indian is a person within the meaning of the laws of the United States and has therefore the right to sue out a writ of habeas corpus in a federal court," was unprecedented and became the first civil rights victory for Native Americans.

Together, they made history.

Fig. 36. Chief Standing Bear Washington D.C. November 1877

Courtesy of Nebraska State Historical Society

23

Poppleton and Webster Fight for Native Americans

A.J. Poppleton and John L. Webster continued fighting for Native Americans' civil rights after successfully defending Chief Standing Bear and the Poncas. Despite heavy workloads and civic commitments, they filed two more lawsuits in federal court in April 1880.

Ponca Tribe v. Red Cloud et.al. (1880)

On April 8, 1880, Poppleton and Webster filed a petition on behalf of the Ponca Tribe in the United States District Court for the District of Nebraska. They petitioned the Court to order the Sioux Nation to return the 96,000 acres of the Ponca's ancestral land, which the Sioux had wrongly been given by the government's "clerical error" in the Fort Laramie Treaty of 1868.[367]

The case was titled *Ponca Tribe of Indians (Plaintiff) v. Makh-pi-ah-lu-tah, or Red Cloud, in his own behalf and in behalf of the Sioux Tribe of Indians* (Defendant).[368] The petition pled that the Poncas had never voluntarily ceded their ancestral land to the government and had never received any compensation at the time of their forced removal to Indian Territory. Judge Elmer S. Dundy granted the plaintiff's petition on December 3, 1880 holding that: "The Ponca Tribe of Indians, Plaintiff, has a legal estate in and is entitled to the possession of the real estate described in the Petition, and that the Sioux Nation of Indians, unlawfully kept the Ponca Tribe of Indians out of the possession of the same."[369]

Three months later, in March 1881, Congress made an appropriation of $165,000 to indemnify the Ponca tribe for losses sustained in consequence of the removal and declared that the Poncas had the right to return to their old homeland.

Samuel J. Kirkwood, Secretary of the Interior, met a few months later in Washington D.C. with representatives of the Lakota Sioux and Ponca Tribes. The Lakota Sioux agreed to cede to the Poncas 26,000 acres of the original 96,000 acres of their ancestral land.[370]

Elk v. Wilkins (1880)

Poppleton and Webster filed another petition in April 1880 in the Circuit Court of the United States for the District of Nebraska on behalf of John Elk, a former member of the Winnebago Tribe of Northeast Nebraska. On April 5, 1880, Elk walked into the registrar's office for Omaha's Fifth Ward, and applied to vote in the city election. Charles Wilkins, registrar of the Fifth Ward, refused Elk's application on the grounds that he was ineligible to vote because Nebraska had not granted citizenship to Native Americans. Omaha's Fifth Ward included all land North of Davenport Street and East of 16th Street, extending to the Missouri River.

One day later, John Elk returned to the registrar's office and requested a ballot so he could vote. Again, Wilkins denied his request. Poppleton and Webster agreed to represent John Elk. Their petition asserted that under the 14th Amendment to the U.S. Constitution, John Elk, born within the United States and separated from his tribe, was a citizen and had the right to vote in the city elections:

> John Elk, plaintiff, complains of Charles Wilkins, defendant, and avers that the matter in dispute herein arises under the constitution and laws of the United States, and, for cause of action against the defendant, avers that he, the plaintiff, is an Indian, and was born within the United States; that more than one year prior to the grievances hereinafter complained of he had severed his tribal relation to the Indian tribes, and had fully and completely surrendered himself to the jurisdiction of the United States, and still so continues subject to the jurisdiction of the United States; and avers that, under and by virtue of the fourteenth amendment to the constitution of the United States, he is a citizen of the United States, and entitled to the right and privilege of citizens of the United States. That on the sixth day of April 1880, there was held in the city of Omaha a general election for the election of members of the city council and other officers for said city. That the defendant, Charles Wilkins, held the office of and acted as registrar in the Fifth Ward of said city, and that as such registrar it was the duty of such defendant to register the names of all persons entitled to exercise the elective franchise in said ward of said city at such general election.[371]

The case was heard before Judges Elmer S. Dundy and George Washington McCrary. Genio M. Lambertson, U.S. District Attorney for the District of Nebraska, represented the defendant Charles Wilkins. The same three lawyers who met in the Standing Bear case eleven months earlier, appeared in the same federal courtroom. Lambertson immediately filed a general demurrer in reply to the plaintiff's petition, citing the following causes: "That the petition did not state facts sufficient to constitute a cause of action; that the court had no jurisdiction of the person of the defendant; and that the court had no jurisdiction of the subject of the action."[372] Both sides proceeded to make their arguments regarding Lambertson's general demurrer. Judges Dundy and McCray sustained Lambertson's general demurrer and dismissed the petition, with costs assessed to the plaintiff.

Poppleton and Webster immediately filed a writ of error in the United States Supreme Court. Justice Horace Gray wrote the opinion for the high court, affirming the judgment of the Circuit Court in favor of Wilkins, in a 7-2 decision, issued November 3, 1884.[373]

The decision of the Supreme Court concluded its reasoning in the case, saying, "the plaintiff, not being a citizen of the United States under the fourteenth amendment of the constitution, has been deprived of no right secured by the fifteenth amendment, and cannot maintain this action."[374]

Poppleton & Webster Open Doors of Justice for Native Americans

Within one year of the Standing Bear decision, Poppleton and Webster had taken a Native American's case alleging a violation of his civil rights all the way to the highest court in the land.

The John Elk case proved the door would remain open, even if the decision reached at the end of the trial was not favorable to the cause of citizenship.

The Elk case was one of the first cases in which Supreme Court Justice John M. Harlan wrote a dissenting opinion in civil rights cases for minorities. In his dissent, Justice Harlan agreed with the argument made by Poppleton and Webster that the fourteenth amendment granted national citizenship to Native American John Elk:

> If he [John Elk] did not acquire national citizenship on abandoning his tribe and becoming, by residence in one of the states, subject to the complete jurisdiction of the United States, the fourteenth amendment has wholly failed to accomplish, in respect to the Indian race, what we think was intended by it; and there is still in this country a despised and rejected class of person with no nationality whatever, who, born in our territory, owing no allegiance to any foreign power, and subject as residents of the states, to all the burdens of government, are yet not members of any political community, nor entitled to any of the rights, privileges, or immunities of citizens of the United States.[375]

Although John Elk lost his case, Poppleton and Webster succeeded in bringing the issue of Native American citizenship to the forefront of national discussion. Congress finally passed a national citizenship act in 1924, *the Indian Freedom Citizenship Suffrage Act.*[376]

Fig. 37. John L. Webster
Courtesy Douglas County Historical Society

Profile: John L. Webster (1847-1929)

John Lee Webster was born in Harrison County, Ohio on March 18, 1847. After being wounded in the Civil War, he attended Mount Union College in Ohio and Washington College in Pennsylvania. With his wife Josephine Watson, he settled in Omaha in 1869 by accident. He was headed to Wyoming to open a law office, but due to a blizzard, his train was forced to stay in Omaha for a week. During that time, he decided Omaha would be a good place to live and work. He became a member of the state legislature in 1873, and served as president of the Nebraska Constitutional Convention in 1875. At the time of the Standing Bear Trial, Webster served with Poppleton on the board of directors for the Omaha Law Library Association. He later served as attorney for the Metropolitan Utilities District, local attorney for the Wabash Railroad Company, and argued rate cases before the Interstate Commerce Commission in Washington D.C. and before the U.S. Supreme Court. He was a speaker on opening day of the Omaha Trans-Mississippi Exposition in October 1898. Webster was elected President of the Nebraska Bar Association in 1903, and served for six years as President of the Nebraska State Historical Society from 1910 to 1916. He delivered annual addresses before the state bar associations of Iowa, Colorado, Minnesota and Nebraska; and lectured nationally on the U.S. Constitution. He was a founder of the Omaha Friends of Art Association. A street is named in Omaha in his honor. He died September 2, 1929, age 82. Funeral was at Trinity Cathedral with burial at Forest Lawn Cemetery.[377]

24

Promoter of Arts and Literature

In the fall of 1879, Poppleton and Webster loaned their precious gifts from Chief Standing Bear to be displayed at a special exhibition. The first Art Loan Exhibition in Omaha, organized by Meliora Clarkson, Caroline Poppleton, and other leading women of the city, displayed 1,500 artifacts from around the world for a fund-raising event.

Art Loan Exhibition

The Art Loan Exhibition opened from September 25th to October 9th, 1879, and occupied a building near 19th & Capitol Avenue. A reporter for The *Omaha Daily Herald* previewed this innovative event and wrote: "This exhibition will be the largest, most complete and varied, most entertaining, and most valuable ever seen in the west."[378]

The purpose of the art exhibition was to raise funds to complete construction of Trinity Episcopal Cathedral. At the same time, the event was intended to encourage public appreciation of the arts. The *Omaha Bee News*, September 11, 1879, described the exhibition that quickly found favor with the public:

> The plan of the art loan was proposed by a few citizens of Omaha belonging to different societies and denominations, and it found favor with the public at once. The interest increases to such an extent that the project promises to be a success. While the proceeds of the exhibition are to be devoted to the completion of Trinity Cathedral, an edifice which should be an object of interest to every citizen of Omaha, and while we are receiving cordial aid from the members of Trinity Guild, the Art Loan Exhibition it not under the especial direction of any sect or denomination.[379]

Meliora Clarkson, wife of Bishop Robert H. Clarkson of Trinity Cathedral, served as the President of the exhibition's steering committee, and Caroline Poppleton served as Secretary. The other officers were Mrs. James W. Savage, Mrs. John L. Redick, Mrs. George W. Doane, and Mrs. John L. Webster (Vice Presidents); Mrs. Lyman Richardson (Treasurer) and Mr. Henry W. Yates (Assistant Treasurer). Over one hundred and twenty men and women volunteered to serve on the twelve committees to help launch the project.[380]

Opening Night

On opening night, Thursday September 25, 1879, guests were greeted by the Ninth Regiment Band of Fort Omaha at 8 o'clock, who "filled the neighborhood with music from the large tent north of the church for a half hour, when they adjourned to the interior of the building and from the gallery played the remainder of the program."[381] Guests paid 25 cents to enter the building. For the next fourteen days, the exhibition was open from mid-morning to 10:00 p.m. Guests could enjoy refreshments of lemonade, chocolate, and tea, or purchase a light dinner which sometimes included oysters. For an additional 25 cents, they could attend a musical concert in the evening. Telephones were installed in the building by the Omaha Electric Company for the convenience of the guests.[382]

Meliora Clarkson and Caroline Poppleton stood outside the entrance to the building to personally greet the guests on opening night. They asked a reporter from the *Omaha Daily Herald* "to politely request gentlemen who can conveniently do so, to leave their canes and walking sticks at home. The use of these articles in pointing at pictures and various articles on exhibition was found to be in some instances a little threatening to the articles."[383]

A seventy-two page *"Art Loan Exhibition Catalogue"* guided the visitors through the twelve exhibition rooms with a detailed listing of the 1,500 individual items on display: Bric-a-brac and Household Art (273 items); Ceramics and Pottery (192 items); Jewelry (73 items); Rare Curiosities (58 items); Laces and Textile Fabrics (167 items); Art Gallery-Oil Paintings (122 items); Art Gallery-Water Colors (20 items); Art Gallery-Engravings and Etchings (32 items); Art Gallery-Bronzes and Statuary (25 items); Art Gallery-Miscellaneous (29 items); Books and Manuscripts (171 items); Mineral and Geological Specimens/Relics and Curiosities (338 items).[384]

In the *Rare Curiosities Room* both A.J. Poppleton and John L. Webster displayed their gifts from Chief Standing Bear. The Art Loan Catalog described this exhibit:

> Poppleton's Ponca War Bonnet said to have been worn in council by the head chiefs of the tribe for three hundred years. Presented by Standing Bear to A.J. Poppleton for services rendered in the Ponca Habeas Corpus case, in the United States court at Omaha, 1879.[385]
>
> Tomahawk carried for a great number of years by the Ponca Chief, Standing Bear, as emblematic of his rank among his people and by him, lately presented to John L. Webster for services rendered in the Ponca Habeas Corpus case, in the United States court at Omaha.[386]

The *Art Gallery Room* displayed three paintings loaned by the Poppleton family: a Bierstadt painting of the Rocky Mountains from Caroline;[387] a proof of Whistler's portrait of Thomas Carlyle, on whose life Elizabeth lectured across the nation;[388] and a painting of "Great Heart and the Pilgrims" from A.J.'s collection.[389]

In the *Books and Manuscripts Room*, the Poppleton family displayed additional items they felt would be of interest to the spectators. A.J. shared "two volumes of history and travel, by Jonas Handway published in London, 1753. Once a part of the library of Edmund Burke, whose autograph in pencil is still legible on the flyleaf."[390] Elizabeth loaned a volume of "The Old Bachelor," a series of letters written by William Wirt commencing 1810;"[391] and William loaned a pamphlet that contained an "authenticated copy of the Last Will and Testament of George Washington, with schedule of his real estate and notes thereto by the testator."[392]

The exhibition closed on Thursday evening October 9, 1879, with a musical presentation offered by the Ninth Infantry Band playing the works of Gilbert and Sullivan. Bishop Clarkson shared his pride in the collection, and thanked the audience for supporting the event:

> Omaha has reason to feel proud not only of the splendid collection itself, but of the gracefulness, the good feeling, the fidelity, and the enthusiasm that has characterized the whole enterprise from first to last. It is all this – with the good it has done, and the pleasure it has afforded, and not merely the money it has secured – which has made the art-loan exhibition a thing to be remembered with joy and thankfulness, as long as we live.[393]

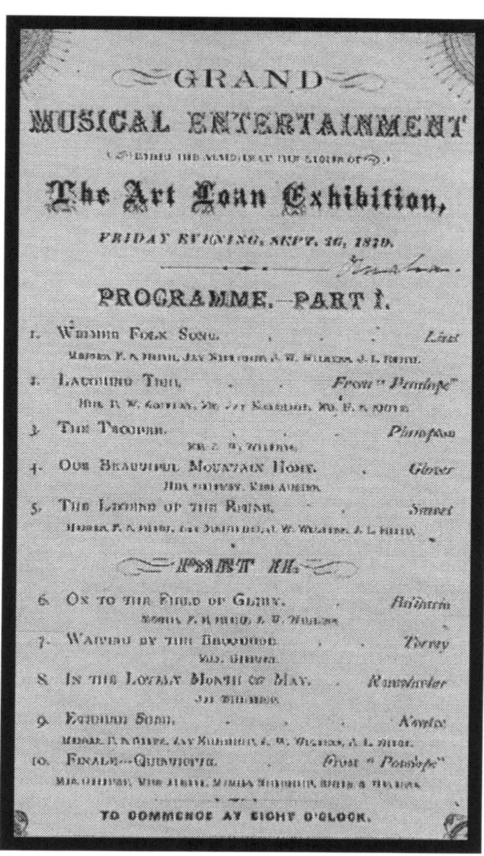

GRAND
MUSICAL ENTERTAINMENT
[illegible]
The Art Loan Exhibition,
FRIDAY EVENING, SEPT. 26, 1879.

PROGRAMME.—PART I.

1. [illegible] Folk Song. . . . [illegible]
2. Laughing Trio. . . From "Penelope"
3. The Trooper. . . . [illegible]
4. Our Beautiful Mountain Home. . Glover
5. The Legend of the Rhine. . . [illegible]

PART II.

6. On to the Field of Glory. . [illegible]
7. Waiting by the [illegible] . . [illegible]
8. In the Lovely Month of May. . [illegible]
9. [illegible] Song. . . . [illegible]
10. Finale—Quintette. . From "Penelope"

TO COMMENCE AT EIGHT O'CLOCK.

Fig. 38. Art Loan Exhibition Program September 26, 1879.
Courtesy of A.J. Poppleton III Personal Collection.

A New Exhibition Building and Dedication Speech by Poppleton

The great success of the two-week Art Loan Exhibition ignited a group of enterprising businessmen led by Max Meyer, William Wallace, Fred Gray, and Isaac Miner, to build a permanent structure where the people of Omaha could enjoy the fine arts, musical concerts, operas, lectures, and other cultural events on a permanent basis.

In 1886, the same four men, along with other investors, completed the "Exposition Building" at a cost of $50,000. This block-long edifice, located on Capitol Avenue, between Fourteenth and Fifteenth Streets, featured an auditorium with a seating capacity of 9,000. The building was formally dedicated on February 18, 1886. Mrs. Martin Cahn and the Norwegian Quartet sang, accompanied by the Musical Union orchestra. Six thousand people gathered in the hall to hear Max Meyer introduce A.J. Poppleton to deliver the dedication address. A.J. especially recognized Omaha's amazing growth since its founding 32 years earlier:

> Omaha should be proud of this grand structure, for in all the west, between Chicago and the coast, I do not believe its like can be found. Even San Francisco, I think, cannot produce its equal. It is an enterprise which will serve Omaha not only materially, but intellectually, morally, and spiritually. Here will the people gather to listen to grand music, brilliant oratory, and the utterances of the intellect of the country.[394]

Omaha Public Library

In 1857, three years after Omaha's founding, a group of early settlers organized the Omaha Public Library Association, with Dr. George Miller serving as its first president. The group opened a reading room on the second floor of the Western Exchange Bank Building on 12th & Farnam Street. In the beginning, the group held a series of lectures that proved successful in raising funds to operate the library. The first lecture was given by Judge Eleazer Wakeley entitled "Thoughts on American Government." Soon, it was evident that the library did not have adequate funding to continue. The difficult times brought on by the Panic of 1857 forced the association to dissolve after just three years.[395]

It would be another decade before A.J. Poppleton and another group of civic leaders decided Omaha was missing out on the benefits of a vibrant public library, so in December 1871, they incorporated a new association under the name of the Omaha Library Association. The board of directors elected the following officers:

President:	A.J. Poppleton
Vice-President:	Nathan Shelton
Recording Secretary:	Albert Swartzlander
Corresponding Secretary:	Albert H. Henry
Treasurer:	Lewis S. Reed

The public library occupied the same building as the law library on the second floor of the Simpson building on 14th Street between Dodge and Douglas. The post office occupied the first floor.[396] The 1872 Catalogue, published at the end of the library's first year of operation, listed 4,942 individual volumes in eight categories: Books of Reference, History, Biography, Voyages/Travels & Religious, Philosophical & Scientific, Essays/Speeches & Miscellaneous, Poetry, and Fiction.[397]

A.J. Poppleton was especially interested in reincorporating the public library because he was a voracious reader of histories and biographies of the ancient Greeks and Romans, as well as works of philosophy. Over the years, he had become a collector of first-edition books, especially those written by Charles Dickens, William Shakespeare, William Makepeace Thackeray, and other English novelists of the 19th century.

In December 1876, the Library Association sponsored a 'Home Lecture Course' to enhance the culture of the city. James M. Woolworth gave the first lecture entitled "An Afternoon in the Houses of Parliament."[398]

On the next weekend, A.J. Poppleton gave a lecture on Edmund Burke, a British statesman, parliamentarian, and orator.[399] A.J. admired Burke for his command of the English language. Even though he never heard Burke speak in person, A.J. believed he 'heard' Burke's voice clearly in his writings. He appreciated that an Englishman of Burke's stature empathized with the American point of view during our struggle for independence. Although Burke's opinions were in the minority in parliamentary debates, he continued to speak out.

Eighteen years after the public library association had been reorganized, its board of directors issued a report for the year ending May 31, 1890. The report noted there were 27,650 volumes in the library collection. The Reading Room held over 125 periodicals, including daily newspapers such as the Boston Advertiser, Chicago Tribune, Cincinnati Enquirer, Denver Republican, New York Tribune, New York World, Philadelphia Times, and the St. Louis Globe-Democrat. Also available for readers to peruse were monthly magazines such as Atlantic Monthly, Century, Harper's, Magazine of Art, Popular Science, Scribner's, Shakespearean, Edinburgh Review, and the Woman's Tribune.[400]

The 1890 Annual Report identified Elizabeth E. Poppleton as a member of the board of directors. As chair of the Library's Book Committee, Elizabeth submitted a report in which she responded to a concern of the board that students lacked interest in coming to the library: "Probably the library lacks appreciation from students because it is so poorly housed, and the public will not realize the value of this collection of books unit it is placed in a library building."[401]

Six months after Elizabeth's report addressed the poorly housed library and called for a new building, her father was elected by the Omaha City Council to serve as president of the library board due to the death of the board's president, Judge James W. Savage.[402] Within a month of beginning his term on the board, A.J. Poppleton introduced a resolution calling for the erection of "a suitable, indestructible, fire-proof library building" as soon as adequate funding could be obtained. The resolution was adopted by unanimous vote and sent to the City Council for discussion. Later in the year, a generous bequest from the Estate of

Byron Reed moved the project forward. Reed donated money, land on 19th & Harney Street, and his personal library and coin collection.[403]

The October 18, 1897, morning edition of the *Omaha World Herald* published a five-column article by Elizabeth Poppleton tracing the history of the Omaha Public Library. The paper carried an editorial complementing Elizabeth on the service she rendered to the historical record of the library:

> Miss Poppleton does a great service to the people of Omaha this morning in rescuing from threatened oblivion, and most certainly from long years of neglect, the history of the Omaha public library. To be sure, she tells us that "a soiled, brown and ragged pamphlet" containing the record of facts and names connected with the foundation of the library is in its archives, and also that she stumbled upon a duplicate of it in the hands of "an old settler of antiquarian tastes," [her father] but these two perishing pamphlets might soon have been lost in fact, and almost certainly to the sight of even the younger founders of the library, but for the timely vigilance in dealing with one of the most important histories of Omaha institutions, all things considered, that will ever be written by one so able and painstaking. On behalf of the living and the dead who shared in the work of establishing the Omaha public library ... we thank her for this gracious and important service to our people.[404]

Family Activities from Caroline's Diary

A.J. Poppleton and his family traveled frequently, but sometimes, his busy workload prevented him from joining them. Caroline's diary during the 1880s highlighted family activities and excursions:

Dec 1880 "Celebrated our Silver Anniversary."

July 1882 "Family had a 2-month trip to Montana & California, <u>except</u> Mr. Poppleton."

June 1886 "Mary and I attended cousin Jeannie Fisk's wedding in Ogdensburg, New York."

July 1886 "Mr. Poppleton and I took a month's trip to Portland on the Northern Pacific, through Puget Sound and then ocean voyage to San Francisco."

July 1887 "Will graduated from Harvard with his degree "cum laude, the family also present <u>except</u> Mr. Poppleton. Elizabeth elected alumnae trustee of Vassar College. Mother died February 1887."[405]

25

Silver Wedding Anniversary

A.J. and Caroline Poppleton's home on 19th & Capitol Avenue burned down in January 1879, a few months before the Standing Bear trial. They moved into rooms at Roswell Smith's across the street from the Withnell House Hotel on 15th & Harney Street and lived there for almost 22 months while their new home was being built. Finally, in October 1880, A.J. and Caroline moved into their new home, 2232 Sherman Avenue on 16th Street, just in time to celebrate their silver wedding anniversary. They called their new home "Elizabeth's Place" in honor of their daughter Libby.[406]

Caroline sent out 380 invitations to family and friends throughout the nation announcing their celebration to be held Thursday evening, December 2, 1880, at 8:00 p.m. Caroline and A.J. realized that most of their invitees who lived outside of Nebraska would likely be unable to travel such long distances in winter. Nevertheless, they wanted to share their joy with everyone, especially because the celebration would take place in their new home.

Congratulatory Letters

The Poppletons received scores of hand-written letters from out-of-towners who declined the invitation, but all expressed good wishes and thanked the couple for the impact on their lives, the community, and the nation. One example came from their long-time friends, Methodist minister Rev. Thomas B. Lemon and his wife Margaret, then living in North Platte, Nebraska:

My Dear Friends. North Platte, Neb. Dec 4th, 1880

Please accept the regrets of myself and wife at not being able to answer your invitation in person on the evening of the 2nd and our warm and sincere congratulations on the beautiful useful record you have made during the twenty-five past years of your married life. It is not every couple passes the wooded forest-village of life together – and they who do can say we have had changes – sorrows and disappointments but these things only render the union sanctified by God's smiles and blessings, stronger and holier. Within 25 years Omaha has grown into a mighty city, Nebraska has become a great state, the Union Pacific Railroad has brought the trade of the Pacific and China through Nebraska to Omaha. Youth has passed to mature age. Children have been born, educated and entered on life's course. At the close of 25 years, you enter a new home that rises above the ashes of a former one with the quiet of mind an upright life brings. Our prayer is that you may reach together the Golden period with the glory that grants us an evening of life found in the path of righteousness.

Ever your friends, Rev. & Mrs. T.B. Lemon[407]

Caroline received the following letter from her uncle William Foote living in Ogdensburg, New York, that included family wishes for the occasion:

My Dear Carrie: Ogdensburg, NY Nov 27, 1880

The lapse of time is in no way more emphatically illustrated than by the rapid return of those anniversaries of which I am reminded by the receipt this morning of an invitation to your silver wedding ... I am sure you will mark it, as you ought, with a very large white stone. Although separated from you by nearly half the continent, I shall be with you in spirit and enjoy your festivities with zest. We have held a family consultation, and vote: 1) we wish we could go; 2) we reluctantly concluded not to go; 3) we send our hearts full of love and wishes for many happy returns. Please also, assure your good mother of my love.

Your affectionate Uncle, William Foote[408]

A.J. received the following letter from his brother Orrin living in Birmingham, Michigan, who spoke of the difficulty of traveling in stormy winter months:

Dear Brother: Birmingham, Mich. Nov 30, 1880

I am in receipt of your kind invitation to be present at your silver wedding anniversary and regret to be compelled to say that it will not be prudent for me to undertake such a journey in extreme weather ... I am obliged to take precaution against taking cold on account of my hereditary difficulty. I hope you and your wife will enjoy this anniversary.

Your affectionate Brother, O. Poppleton[409]

Omaha Bee News Report

The fifteen-room residence with a detached carriage house was situated on five acres, perfect for hosting the 250 plus guests who attended the celebration. It was quite a change from a quarter of a century ago when A.J. and Caroline began their married life in a one-room apartment in a multi-use office building. In those early days, they hoped that one day they could afford to build their own home and raise a family in this new territory. The *Omaha Bee News* reported the exquisite celebration:

SILVER WEDDING DAY

On Thursday evening [December 2, 1880], Mr. and Mrs. A.J. Poppleton celebrated the twenty-fifth anniversary of their marriage, at their new and elegant residence in "Elizabeth Place." The occasion is reported to have been one of the most interesting and brilliant that has been enjoyed by the good people of this city for many years and was attended by a select number of friends of the fortunate couple. The floral decorations of the new mansion were profuse, fragrant and beautiful, and everything that could be done to give pleasure to the guests who were present, was anticipated. An orchestra furnished exquisite music for those who preferred to tread the mazy dance, while the more sedate could amuse themselves at cards in the music room. A common center of attraction was the supper room upstairs where a sumptuous repast was spread.[410]

There were no presents, that condition being inscribed upon the invitations sent out some days before the event took place. Mr. A.J. Poppleton, of Omaha, and Miss Carrie Sears of Council Bluffs, were married Dec. 2nd, 1855, by Rev. Mr. Rice, of the latter city, who with his wife were present at this anniversary jubilee. Mr. and Mrs. W.H. Robinson, of Council Bluffs, who acted as groomsman and bridesmaid a quarter of a century ago, were also present. The ceremony was again performed, and in the presence of the same minister and witnesses the vows were again spoken, after which Rev. Mr. Rice made some very beautiful and appropriate remarks. The guests included many prominent visitors from abroad and a very large number of citizens, both old and young, of Omaha.[411]

Omaha Daily Herald Report

The *Omaha Daily Herald,* December 3, 1880, described in detail the Poppleton's new elegant home as a residence ablaze with light and gaiety, and filled with congratulations from old settlers:[412]

A QUARTER-CENTURY

Mr. and Mrs. Poppleton Celebrate Their
Twenty-Fifth Wedding Anniversary

Throwing Open Their Elegant New
Residence to a Host of Friends

A Notable Day in the Annals of the
First Families of Omaha

Last evening in an elegant new residence on Sherman Avenue, in the city that twenty-five-years ago was a mere hamlet, and surrounded by numbers of friends, who with them had shared the life of the pioneer and lived to help build up a metropolis in the trans-Missouri empire, Mr. and Mrs. Poppleton celebrated their silver wedding. The place was ablaze with light and as carriage after carriage rolled up to the door, and guests alighted and entered, the groups increased to a throng and the gayety grew incrementally. The congratulations extended to the host and hostess were cordial and heartfelt and gained emphasis from the meeting of so many of the old settlers now living in different places, who had not been under the same roof for years. Notwithstanding its extent, every room in the new house was filled last evening. The dining room was converted into a ballroom for the dance, where the guests kept measure with the witching music of an orchestra.[413]

The Poppleton residence on Sherman Avenue, presents in the view of this visitor a spacious house built after the old English style with red and black brick laid in black mortar. Low, wide verandas run along the sides of the house and a carriage porch projects from the south front. To the west, and approached from either side, is situated the bar, erected after the same style of architecture that is exemplified in the house. The buildings are surrounded by level grounds, four or five acres in extent, the whole being a part of Elizabeth Place.[414]

Entering the door from the carriage porch, the first appurtenance on the right is the library, situated in the southeast corner of the house. It is eighteen feet square, finished in cherry, and lined with cases exquisitely adorned with hand carvings. The fireplace is high, formed of wood and inlaid with English tiles, those in front from Shakespeare, and those on the ends from Tennyson ... Across the east hall from the library, and in the northeast corner, the drawing room, eighteen by twenty-five feet, is located. Back of the drawing room and communicating with it by sliding doors, is the dining room, in which the woodwork and furniture are wholly of ash, and the walls are finished in rich reds and browns. The dimensions are eighteen by twenty-five feet.

The music room opens on the opposite side of the library. It is finished in butternut and has a high wood fireplace ... the upper hall is spacious and divided by open arches of solid oak. There are seven chambers on this floor, furnished in the Queen Anne style; a room twenty-four feet square is fitted up for Mr. Poppleton's study.[415]

The basement is divided into the laundry, men servant's rooms, servants' bathrooms, coal rooms and cellars. The kitchen, bathrooms and other departments for household and toilet use occupy the rear of the main floor. A system of electric bells communicates with the kitchen, speaking tubes lead from every floor, a special line runs to the barn, and the house is throughout heated by steam.[416]

The Architecture and Guests

The *Omaha Daily Herald* pointed out that the architect, interior furnishings, and decorations were all designed by Chicago companies. The Donaghue Co. of Omaha provided the floral arrangements. Of the 380 family and friends Caroline sent invitations to, the Herald named 253 guests in attendance for the evening, including Caroline's parents from Onawa, Iowa, and her sister Delia.

Dignitaries who attended the party included Judge Elmer S. Dundy and his wife Mary, John L. Webster and his wife Josephine, Byron Reed, J. Sterling Morton and Joseph W. Paddock. Many political figures came, past, present and future including U.S. Senator Manderson, Mayor B.E.B, Kennedy, Governor Saunders, Mayor Champion Chase, Mayor Lyman Richardson, and Marguerite Murphy Cuming, the widow of two-time Acting Governor, Thomas B. Cuming.

The Omaha legal community was well represented by James Woolworth, A.J. Hanscom, Judge George Lake, Judge Eleazer Wakeley, and Judge James Savage. Members of the Creighton and Clarkson families were also represented.[417]

Their Final Home Together

A.J. and Caroline Poppleton lived in their home on Sherman Avenue for the rest of their married life. A.J. died in the house in 1896. Caroline continued to live there until 1911, when she moved to live with her daughter Elizabeth.

The Poppleton's Silver Wedding Anniversary celebration was such a memorable social event in Omaha's first quarter of a century that thirty years later the December 2, 1919 edition of the *Omaha Bee News*, included a two-column story commemorating the event:

> **OMAHA SOCIETY 30 YEARS AGO:**
> **SILVER ANNIVERSARY RECEPTION OF**
> **MR. AND MRS. A.J. POPPLETON**
>
> Thirty years ago today, the silver wedding anniversary of Mr. and Mrs. A.J. Poppleton was celebrated at their residence on Sherman Avenue, which was new at that time. This was one of the largest and most brilliant social affairs of that period, and present were many of the pioneer residents of the city.[418]

Losing His Eyesight

Yet, the joy and happiness experienced by the Poppletons in celebrating their 25 years together and having a permanent place to call home after a fire destroyed their last home and most of their possessions was likely tempered by the realization that A.J. was gradually losing his eyesight.

In his memoirs A.J. wrote: "As early as 1880, the sight of my left eye had become impaired. Oculists have advised me that this had no necessary connection with and would probably have no effect upon the right.[419]

Sadly, the doctors were wrong.

Fig. 39. Poppleton Home 2232 Sherman Avenue
Courtesy of A.J. Poppleton III Personal Collection

26

Last Years of Practice

On April 3, 1882, A.J. Poppleton penned a letter to Caroline from the Riggs House Hotel in Washington D.C. where he was staying with his son William ("Will") who would turn 16 in a couple of days. Caroline was visiting her brother Stillman Foote Sears in Ogdensburg, New York. Will was ending his first year at Phillips Academy in Andover, Massachusetts and his father was giving him an early birthday present - a tour of the Capitol and other sights in Washington D.C. and Baltimore. They would also be privileged to attend the swearing-in ceremony of a family friend, Samuel Blatchford, as a newly appointed Justice to the United States Supreme Court:

> My Dear Carrie: Washington D.C. April 3, 1882
>
> It is now 3 bells. Will has tired me out, so while he is gone to the Capitol, and I am resting I will tell you what we have done today. We arrived at 6:20 and as soon as we were settled and breakfasted, we sallied out. First, we took cars for the Capitol and toured thoroughly over the building. This we finished at 10:30 and as we headed over there an hour and a half before the S.C. [Supreme Court] convened, we went to the Navy Yard. At 12 o'clock the S.C. room was full to see Judge Blatchford sworn in. The ceremony was very brief and simple ... Judge B. looks well and judicial. He will no doubt be a far better judge than [Roscoe] Conkling – he is not fit for it either in temperament or in legal attainment. Edmonds, though a good lawyer, is full of tricks and subtleties and lacking in the constitutional fairness necessary to make a great judge. Then we went first to the Senate – then to the House. Since lunch Will has gone back to the Capitol, but I concluded to rest the balance of the day. We have decided to give Wednesday to Baltimore and take our leave there for home.
>
> With a thousand kisses, love A.J. Poppleton[420]

Poppleton added a footnote to his letter naming five lawyers who "came and spoke to us at lunch" that day, including Genio Lambertson, the District Attorney for Nebraska, who fought against Poppleton and Webster in the Standing Bear Trial and also opposed them in the John Elk case. This showed the respect other lawyers in the country had for Poppleton.

UPRR Expands Poppleton's Jurisdiction

During the 1880's, A.J. Poppleton's workload for the Union Pacific Railroad Company ("UPRR") increased significantly. The UPRR acquired the Kansas Pacific and the Denver Pacific Railroads, leading the company to change its name to the Union Pacific Railway Company. Poppleton later wrote about the UPRR's consolidation and the impact it had on his growing workload and responsibilities:

> Following this consolidation my jurisdiction was greatly extended, and my power and labor greatly enlarged. In addition to the supervision of the strictly legal business of the consolidated company, I was vested with supervision of the Tax Department, of the Claim Department, and also of the preservation of the organization of about sixty auxiliary companies which had been created from time to time to carry out the plans of the Union Pacific Company ... From year to year the labor and responsibility of the General Attorney's office continued to increase, as well as general litigation, and more especially the litigation of titles to the granted lands as against homestead and pre-emption settlers, until the burden had become well-nigh intolerable. During the latter portion of the first presidency of Mr. Charles Francis Adams, the average current litigation as shown by the reports of the General Attorney at that time comprised over five hundred litigated cases each year, with a constant tendency to increase.[421]

On November 21, 1885, Charles Francis Adams, President of the UPRR, issued a Circular Letter on behalf of the Company in which he added Colorado to Poppleton's supervision and restated Poppleton's control over all legal matters for the Company, saying:

> The Circular of the Company, relating it to the Law Department, dated October 1, 1880, is modified as follows: All legal business in Colorado of the Union Pacific Railway Company and of other roads in that State operated by it or in its interest will be in the immediate charge of Messrs. Teller & Orahood of Denver, who will report in respect thereto to Mr. A. J. Poppleton, the Company's General Attorney at Omaha; Colorado being hereby added to Mr. Poppleton's supervisory jurisdiction. As the headquarters of the operation of the Company's railways are at Omaha, Mr. Poppleton is *ex officio* the adviser of the officers of the Departments located at that place, in respect of all questions arising upon any part of the Company's system of roads.[422]

On March 29, 1886, Poppleton received a letter from the Company's Executive Committee on behalf of the Board of Directors in Boston. The letter notified him that he had been appointed "appraiser of such lands situated within the limits of the land grant of the Union Pacific Railway Company as may from time to time become subject to sale."[423] As a result of this new role, Poppleton was now responsible for appraisals and the extra work associated with being the general attorney for all the railroad's business west of Chicago. His travel schedule became extremely demanding:

> My jurisdiction extended over every state or territory in which the Union Pacific Company owned or controlled railway and I was expected also to give attention to any suits commenced or pending west of Chicago. My special field covered California, Nevada, and after the acquisition of the Oregon Railway and Navigation Company, Oregon, as well as Idaho, Kansas, Missouri, Wyoming, Montana, Utah, Iowa and Nebraska.[424]

The Last Straw

On December 12, 1887, Poppleton received a letter from UPRR President Charles Francis Adams, requesting that he assume a rather challenging task - to control the workings of Paul Vandervoort, a man who likely was serving as a lobbyist for the UPPR, but doing so on his own terms and in his own indiscreet manner. Adams thought Vandervoort was doing more harm to the company than good. This 'request' was likely the last straw for Poppleton. He had decided he could do no more. Adams wrote:

> A.J. Poppleton, Esq.
> General Attorney, Omaha, Neb. Boston, December 12, 1887
>
> My Dear Sir:
>
> Referring to your favor to me covering a letter from Paul Vandervoort, I have communicated with our people at Washington. Our representative there sends me the following:
>
>> Referring to Mr. Paul Vanderwoort, I cannot see how he can render any direct service at this end of the line, yet his enmity might take a very mischievous direction. He is a man who talks rather loudly, and often indiscreetly. Nevertheless, he has fairly intimate relations with many prominent public men. In short, his power for evil exceeds his power for good. The premises considered, I think it would be well to have him employed through Mr. Poppleton, with the distinct understanding that he is not to assume to represent the company here or elsewhere, but upon all proper occasions to voice the friendly feelings of the people of his section toward the Union Pacific in connection with its enterprises in the West. This is as far as I think he ought to be allowed to go, requiring circumspection on his part.
>
> I do not want to deal directly with Mr. Vandervoort. Could not this thing be arranged, as suggested, through you? He wrote to you – could you not write back, making some financial arrangement with him, which you would report to me, and giving him instructions as if from yourself? He might write to you from time to time, such reports as he saw fit, and you could forward them to me. If he deemed it very essential, he might write directly to me, you explaining to him that you had advised me of the fact that you had employed him. I dislike having recourse to such very circuitous methods to accomplish results; but in Washington this seems to be necessary. I do not like to have anything which bears the appearance of an organized lobby there. I could not avoid having this appearance, were these parties to communicate directly with me and quote me.
>
> I remain, etc. Charles F. Adams, President[425]

Resignation From the Union Pacific

After 24 years as the UPRR's General Attorney, A.J. Poppleton decided the workload had become overwhelming and tedious. He realized that he had missed many family vacations, including his son William's college graduation. He felt it was time to retire from his work for the Company:

> From 1884 to 1888, when I resigned my connection with the Company, my duties were almost wholly advisory, aside from the supervision of pending litigation, and of the Departments heretofore mentioned. This advice extended to every department and to every phase of the Company's affairs, administrative, executive and otherwise. I soon came to feel that my burdens were increasing which my strength was failing and about the first of January 1888, I decided to resign as soon as the Company would accept my resignation, and accordingly it was tendered and accepted on the first day of February in that year.[426]

Poppleton was grateful for the people he worked with, and proud of the many accomplishments they achieved during his time with the railroad. However, he had genuine concern about the strategic direction the Company's leadership was taking for future growth and success:

> This ended my connection with the Union Pacific Railway Company and its affairs. I had been twenty-four years in its service and had participated in almost all of its trials, conflicts, failures and successes. I need not say that I had grown to feel a strong personal attachment to the corporation and an ardent desire to witness long-deferred success. Its affairs however do not seem to me to have improved, and I fear that the inherent infirmities entailed upon it by early mismanagement can never be healed or removed; and that litigation alone will clear it of the wreckage and make it useful to the people of the states and territories through which it runs and to the government of the United States. The enormous capitalization inflicted upon it through the agency of the so-called Credit Mobilier devices rendered it impossible that it should remain permanently a solvent corporation. It is impossible to predict the future of the Company. It can only be said with certainty that in the absence of a long extension upon very low interest by the United States, the Company and its affairs must inevitably come to bankruptcy.[427]

Poppleton was correct in his prediction. In 1893, less than five years after his resignation, the UPRR declared bankruptcy due in part to a national economic downturn known as the 'Panic of 1893.' Following the reorganization permitted by the bankruptcy court, the Company returned to its original name, which it held prior to its acquisition of the Kansas Pacific and Denver Pacific railroads in 1889 – The Union Pacific Railroad Company.

Omaha Bee News Interview - January 14, 1888

Hearing a rumor that A.J. Poppleton had resigned as general attorney for the UPRR, the *Omaha Bee News* sent a reporter to his office. The reporter asked if the report was true? Poppleton replied that it was true. Then the reporter asked when the resignation would take effect, and Poppleton replied, "At once, if possible, and not later than April 1st."[428] Finally, the reporter asked A.J. if he would share the reasons behind his resignation:

> Mr. Poppleton then stated that the principal reason for his resigning was that his health would not any longer permit him to continue the laborious duties of his office. The close confinement to business, he said, is becoming too great a tax upon his energies. Besides, he has reached that age when, if he ever intends to take a rest or have any recreation, he must at once cut loose from his present employment. He is not compelled to work any longer, and he desires to be in a position to do whatever he feels inclined, without any interference by routine duties. It is his intention to devote himself to his private interests, and to travel, not only in this country, but in Europe. He will have an office in the new First National Bank building.[429]

Accolades Pour In

The accolades came pouring into Poppleton from officials at the UPRR offices in New York and Boston, and from attorneys who worked with him across the nation:

> John F. Dillon, General Solicitor
> Union Pacific Railway Company New York City, January 6, 1888
>
> Dear Sir:
>
> I do not know when I was more surprised though I possibly ought not to have been than when I received yesterday your letter of the 4th enclosing resignation of your position as General Attorney of the Union Pacific Railway Company to take effect as soon as you can be relieved and not later than April 1st, 1888. Knowing as I do, that the fidelity and care with which you discharge your duties makes the place one of great labor and responsibility with corresponding anxiety, and appreciation how thoroughly these matters have absorbed your time and studies, and how natural it is to desire a little time for thought and reflection before the night cometh and all is dark and silent –I am not prepared to gainsay the wisdom of your step, deeply as I regret it. Mr. Adams happened to be here when your letter was received, and I laid it at once before him. He and I both indulged the hope that perhaps you might, on the expression of the company's regret, to accept it, be inclined to reconsider the matter.
>
> Very sincerely yours, John F. Dillon[430]

Charles Francis Adams, President
Union Pacific Railway Company Boston, January 9, 1888

My Dear Sir:

I have received the news of your resignation with very great regret. It is unnecessary for me to say that our official relations have on my part always been most agreeable, and I have been sincerely grateful to you for the kindly and energetic support you have always lent me.

I remain, etc. Charles F. Adams[431]

W. H. Savidy, Attorney
Union Pacific Railway Co. Pocatello, Idaho, January 23, 1888

Dear Sir:

I desire to thank you for the interest you have taken in me and for the opportunity you have given me, for had it not been for you, I should not be in the position I am today. It has been a pleasure to work under your instructions, and your integrity, energy and nobility, the success of your life has been an invaluable lesson to me; may I always have the honor to be.

Your friend & obedient servant, W.H. Savidy[432]

Vacation In Mexico

In March 1888, shortly after he resigned from the UPRR, A.J., and his family were finally able to travel outside the country. A.J., Caroline, and their daughter Libby, home from teaching at Vassar College, took an adventurous vacation to Mexico. Caroline wrote in her diary that it lasted about a month. They joined a tour group at El Paso, Texas that had originated in Buffalo, New York. During their stay in Mexico City, A.J. was granted the honor of meeting with the Justices of the Mexico Supreme Court in the capital city.[433]

William S. Poppleton

A few months after returning from his Mexico vacation, Poppleton opened a law office with his son William Sears Poppleton. Will was born on April 7, 1866, in Omaha. At the age of 13, after attending an Omaha public school, he enrolled in Phillips Academy in Massachusetts. He stayed in the East for college and graduated cum laude from Harvard in July 1887, with an A.B. degree and a double-honorable-mention in historical studies. Will returned to Omaha to "read the law" in the office of Judge Frank Irvine, who later was appointed Dean of Cornell Law School.

A. J. & W. S. Poppleton,
Attorneys and Counsellors

Rooms 314 - 316 First National Bank Building
Omaha, Nebraska

Two powerful families came together when Will married Charlotte H. Kennedy on October 17, 1888. Charlotte was the daughter of B.E.B. Kennedy, the former Mayor of Omaha. Rev. Charles Gardner, Dean of Trinity Cathedral, officiated the wedding which took place at the Kennedy home at 1919 St. Mary's Avenue. The *Omaha Excelsior* reported the social significance of the wedding:

> From a social point of view the marriage of Mr. Poppleton and Miss Kennedy is the leading event of the season as it takes from the circles of society two of its best-known devotees. It was a representative marriage, too, for it unites two houses that have been identified with Omaha's achievements for many years.[434]

Fig.40. William S. Poppleton
Courtesy A.J. Poppleton III Personal Collection

William proved to be a great help to his father in his last years of practice, taking over much of the day-to-day work under A.J.'s careful guidance. Will joined many civic and business organizations, including the Omaha Real Estate Owners Association, for which he was elected President in 1893. He also served on several committees of the Douglas County Democratic Party, which led to William's appointment in 1894 by the mayor, to a committee to review the City Charter. Two years later, the civic and business leaders of the city set up a committee system to organize the upcoming Trans-Mississippi Exposition. William served on a committee that met with the legislative bodies of Colorado and Wyoming. In 1900, he ran unsuccessfully as the Democratic party's candidate for Mayor.

Legal Counsel for First National Bank of Omaha

The Kountze brothers, Augustus and Herman, organized the First National Bank of Omaha in 1863 with a capital stock of $50,000. It was the first bank in Nebraska set up under the national banking law. Edward Creighton served as President until his death in 1874 when Herman Kountze took charge as president. Then Edward's brother, John Creighton was elected vice-president. A.J. Poppleton sat on the Board of Directors for a time, in addition to serving over the years as the bank's legal counsel. He also represented the Kountze and Creighton families in various legal matters, especially in the financial difficulties associated with the building of the Grand Central Hotel.[435], John Creighton, was elected vice president

City of Omaha Attorney (1890-1892)

In 1890, A.J. Poppleton was appointed to a two-year term as City Attorney for Omaha. He said that he performed "a vast amount of work, and dealt with an infinite variety of difficult, perplexing and important questions."[436] In addition, it was said that he "succeeded in bringing to a final disposition in the courts, 196 cases brought against the city, besides performing all the advisory duties of the office."[437] William assisted his father in many of these court cases.

Poppleton wrote that "my best legal work between 1888 and 1892, consisted in the preparation of the law authorizing the consolidation of the street railways of Omaha, and drafting, perfecting, defending and vindicating that consolidation in the courts."[438] [439] He also played a crucial role as City Attorney "in securing the city's acceptance of a bequest from the Estate of Byron Reed for public library purposes, and the voting of bonds to carry out its provisions."[440] During his forty-two years in Omaha, A.J. Poppleton never missed an opportunity to enrich the cultural life of the city he loved.

Then, in early 1892, the eyesight of his right eye started to deteriorate rapidly. The concern he expressed in 1880 regarding the deterioration of eyesight in his left eye that was then taking place and could eventually move to his right eye as well, had happened. A.J. Poppleton sadly realized that his legal career was coming to an end. He was going blind.

27

"My Life of Light Was Ended"

A.J. Poppleton struggled with his eyesight throughout his adult life. While attending Union College, his eye issues led to dizziness and headaches, which left him secluded in his dorm room. Being so far away from family and friends, worsened his situation.

In his memoirs, he wrote that over a twelve-year period his eyesight gradually left him. His left eye first, and finally his right eye. His life of light had come to an end – he was totally blind:

> As early as 1880, the sight of my left eye had become impaired. Oculists had advised me that this had no necessary connection with, and would probably have no effect upon, the right. Nevertheless, about the first of January 1892, the sight of my right eye began rapidly to fail. This continued until about the first of July of that year when I became totally blind. My life of light was ended, and my life of darkness began.[441]

Last Trip to Michigan

In March 1892, Caroline wrote in her Diary, "Mr. Poppleton and I took our last trip to Michigan to attend his brother's funeral."[442] Orrin Poppleton, A.J.'s oldest brother, died March 18th at the age of 75. In 1825, Orrin, age 8, and his sister Sally, age 5, journeyed with their parents from Richmond, New York to Troy, Michigan. Except for a few trips to visit cousins in New York, Orrin stayed for most of his life in Michigan, helping his parents on the farm. In his early twenties, he moved to nearby Birmingham to open a mercantile business, where he married Sarah Abbey and raised five children.

Like his father and brother, Orrin was active in party politics and served his community in many ways, including 10 years as president of the Oakland County Historical Society.[443] In 1856, his parents moved to a farm outside of Birmingham to be near him. Zada died in 1861, and William died in 1869.

After Orrin's funeral, A.J. and Caroline stayed in Michigan to visit family and friends and to consult with Dr. Knopp, whom Caroline called a "celebrated oculist," but with no positive results.[444] After their visit, the Poppletons returned to Omaha, whereupon Caroline began to write personal letters to family, friends, and many of A.J.'s colleagues in the legal fraternity throughout the nation to inform them of his tragic news. In June 1892, Caroline made the following entry in her diary, the last one she would write until her husband's death four years later:

> Mr. Poppleton suffered a complete loss of his sight – It was a dreadful calamity – and was for a time over-whelming - but his strong character prevailed and in November of his last year, he limited his visits to his office and took up the management of his own affairs as far as was possible, cheerfully, and uncomplainingly, with William's help.[445]

Last Case

Because of the loss of his eyesight, Poppleton was unable to make the final argument in a case filed in 1892 before the United States Court of Appeals for the Eighth Circuit. His co-counsel, James M. Woolworth, made the final argument to the court on his behalf. But before he did so, Woolworth asked the court leave to allow him to give the following heartfelt tribute to his colleague:

> May It Please the Court:
>
> We bring this cause to your Honors, oppressed by a great sorrow. We had the assistance of the luminous argument and wonderous gift of speech of Mr. Poppleton, upon the hearing of the case in the court below. His sight has since the last sittings of this Court, become dimmed, and it is probable the day is not far distant when the light and the joy of the sun will be to him extinguished. For more than thirty years, he and I have stood side by side, or face to face, in the most strenuous contentions of the bar; always, I believe, with mutual respect and regard. I am sure of the sympathy of the Court for him, and of its profound regret that the public will no longer be served by his great ability.
>
> James M. Woolworth[446]

Sympathy From Fellow Attorneys

A.J. Poppleton received numerous notes of sympathy from friends and colleagues across the nation, expressing their shock and sadness upon hearing of his blindness. One of the first letters came from John Thurston, who succeeded him as General Attorney for the UPRR. He was so sad at hearing the news, he felt unable to write for nearly a week. On May 13, 1892, Thurston finally expressed his feelings to his friend and mentor:

> Dear Mr. Poppleton: Omaha, May 13, 1892
>
> I have ever cherished for you a reverential admiration and affection which only this hour of trouble permits me to express. I cannot reconcile myself to this unjust situation. Your brave, honorable, useful life; your distinguished service to the community and the country; your invaluable example of robust integrity and manhood; deserve the choicest favor of a just providence. A multitude of friends hold you in tender sympathy and love. Of them, I am one,
>
> John M. Thurston.[447]

Stevenson Burke, president of two railroads, the Toledo & Ohio Central Railway and the Toledo, Columbus & Cincinnati Railway, penned Poppleton a three-page letter of encouragement:

My dear friend. Cleveland, July 28, 1892

I was greatly shocked and surprised a few days ago by a letter I received which stated that you had met with a great affliction in the loss of your eyesight ... I want to assure you of my most sincere and earnest sympathy with you in your great affliction. I am very glad to learn that you are cheerful and happy not withstanding this affliction. A philosophical mind like yours can adopt ties to all states and conditions. In this not distant future, we will all receive eyes that will never fail us. Life has many trials and many joys. You have suffered much, but you have had and still have much to enjoy and be thankful for, and most of all your loving and devoted wife and children. Besides, you have gained wealth and professional distinction such as has fallen to the lot of but few. Mrs. Burke desires me to express to you and your dear good wife her deep sympathy. With kindest regards to yourself and family, I am very sincerely grieving

Stevenson Burke.[448]

Poppleton received the following letter of condolence from his friend and fellow attorney, William V. Rooker of Indianapolis, Indiana:

Dear Sir: Indianapolis, Oct 14, 1892

I cannot tell you how much I regret that you have been thus afflicted, and perhaps, I should not try to do so, because to you all the words of friends, while they are duly appreciated, must be empty and fall short of the mark ... There is no man who more deserves the fullest measure of enjoyment in old age. You have worked hard, and you have worked well. You have long stood at the top of your profession. You have provided your family with all that it necessary. You have done your duty as a citizen. You have raised a family that is a worthy example to any parent under God's sun. There are only two members of your family with whom I am personally acquainted – your wife and your daughter Miss Elizabeth. But I must quit enumerating the good things you have to consider because, when I contemplate them, I persuade myself that you have attained all that any man ought to hope for and that even with your blindness, your situation excels that of most all your fellows.

Very Truly, Wm Rooker.[449]

Letter From J. Sterling Morton

J. Sterling Morton left Detroit on the day of his wedding to Caroline French, October 30, 1854, and headed to Nebraska at the recommendation of A.J. Poppleton.[450] He and A.J. met at the Michigan University and both were greatly upset when the University dropped literary/debating societies from campus life. The Mortons settled in Bellevue before later moving to Nebraska City.

J. Sterling became Clerk of the first Nebraska Territorial Supreme Court, and later served in the legislature. He became acting governor from December 5, 1858, to May 2, 1859. He later served in the cabinet of President Grover Cleveland as Secretary of Agriculture.

Morton wrote a letter to Poppleton from his office at Morton Salt Company in Chicago dated June 9, 1892. In his letter he refers to Carrie and Joy Morton. Carrie's mother was A.J.'s sister Zada Poppleton Lake, who was married to George B. Lake, A.J.'s former law partner. Joy Morton was the oldest son of J. Sterling Morton. Carrie and Joy Morton married on September 23, 1880, at Trinity Episcopal Cathedral in Omaha. The ceremony was presided over by Bishop Robert Clarkson.[451] Morton reminded Poppleton of their nearly four-decade friendship that saw growth and change in their lives and the state they loved:

> My Dear A.J. Chicago June 9, 1892
>
> I am really very sorry to hear from Carrie and Joy Morton of your profound affliction as to the sight of your eyes. And yet we have seen so much of change and growth, of joy and sadness, in the thirty-seven and a half years we have lived in Nebraska that one scarcely can wonder at tired eyes. And, more than that, your eyes have peered into law books and looked so intensely after the interest of your clients, that they far more than the optics of an indolent individual like myself – need rest. And perhaps with rest and tranquility, they may again become keen and strong. That they may be fully restored, and that your general health may be built up again, and "the glad light of day" be yours to enjoy fully in all its luxury for years to come, is my sincere hope, as it is also that of Carrie and Joy.
>
> Your friend, J. Sterling Morton[452]

Poppleton Elected Trustee of Union College

In 1890, Poppleton was elected Trustee of the governing board at his alma mater, Union College in Schenectady, New York. He cherished memories of the year he spent at the college, grateful for the guidance and mentorship of Dr. Nott, former president of the College, and Dr. Taylor Lewis, his highly respected professor of languages.

Poppleton received a letter dated May 9, 1895, from Andrew Raymond, then President of Union College, informing him of the college centennial celebration scheduled for the last week of June 1895. President Raymond asked Poppleton to help endow a professorship to honor Dr. Lewis, with a focus on Greek and Oriental languages. Raymond's letter mentioned the pleasant visit he had made to Poppleton's home the previous February and expressed regret that A.J. would be unable to attend the reunion.[453]

On May 15, 1895, Poppleton sent a response to Raymond's letter, pledging his support but at the same time expressing his inability to take on the project due to his current condition:

My Dear Sir: May 15, 1895

I have your note of the 9th of May. Since my disability I have dismissed connection with any movement or enterprise which would bring upon me public notice of any form ... I cannot do more than promise to make subscriptions in case such a movement is inaugurated. My sense of obligation to Dr. Lewis for whatever I have been able to accomplish is very great and I will be glad to become one of the rank and file in formalizing your proposed designs. I am under great obligations to you for your kind attention to me on your visit to Omaha and shall always hear of your personal and official success in your present position with the greatest pleasure. Very Respectfully, Your Obedient Servant,

Andrew J. Poppleton[454]

Michigan University Awards Poppleton Honorary Degree

A month later, A.J. Poppleton received the Honorary Degree of "Master of Arts" from Michigan University at its June 1895 commencement ceremonies in Ann Arbor. He was unable to attend in person. A friend at the University sent him a copy of the editorial from *The Ann Arbor Courier*, dated Saturday, June 29, 1895, which referred to the year the University cancelled the literary societies which had been so important to A.J.:

One of the interesting bits of history revived at commencement was of the old fraternity war, when the University authorities in 1850, told the students they must give up their connection with college or their secret societies. Among those who stood by their fraternity, the Beta Theta Pi, and left college, was A.J. Poppleton, who went to Union College. He afterwards became a man of great power in the Missouri valley, was the attorney of the Union Pacific railroad, and the leading corporation attorney at Omaha. But he always felt the University had done him a great injustice, especially after admitting its wrong position by allowing the societies to exist. Recently he has lost his eyesight and become entirely blind. In the light of these things, the regents did a significant act of justice Thursday by granting him a master's degree, which so far as possible, now rights the wrong of forty-five years ago.[455]

Marriages of Poppleton's Daughters

The Poppleton daughters, Elizabeth and Mary Delia, were married during the last years of A.J.'s life. Both ceremonies were held in their family home at 2232 Sherman Avenue, and both were officiated by Rev. Charles Gardner, Dean of Trinity Episcopal Cathedral. A.J. was able to walk Mary down the aisle in 1893 but was unable to escort Libby in 1895.

Mary Delia Poppleton

Mary Delia Poppleton, the youngest of the three surviving children, was born in Omaha on July 23, 1873. Like her sister Libby, Mary attended primary school at Brownell Hall. In September 1886, at age 13, Caroline enrolled Mary in the Catherine Aiken School for Girls in Stamford, Connecticut. Four years later, she attended the Anne Brown School in New York City. Caroline wrote in her diary, June 1891, that Mary graduated from Miss Brown's School, where she was the class poet and composed the class song with music, which Libby played at the ceremony.[456] Mary remained in New York City to train as a mezzo-soprano singer under the tutelage of famed composer and teacher Gottlieb Federleinin.

Fig. 41. Mary Delia Poppleton
Courtesy A.J. Poppleton III Personal Collection

The wedding of 20-year-old Mary to attorney Myron L. Learned, age 27, took place in the Poppleton home on Tuesday evening, April 18, 1893. Rev. Gardner was joined in officiating the ceremony by Rev. J.P. Llwyd of the Church of the Good Shepherd, an affiliate of Trinity Cathedral. The *Omaha Daily Bee* wrote that Mary was "one of Omaha's fairest flowers, a favorite in social and musical circles."[457] Mary became active in the Tuesday Musical Club, which was organized in 1892, and later served as its president. She also wrote essays and dramatic plays, some of which were performed in theaters throughout the Midwest. For four years, she was employed as the music critic for the *Omaha Daily Bee*. Mary and Libby organized programs held in their parents' home on Sherman Avenue and other venues for the Tuesday Musical Club or to support Trinity Church or some other Omaha charity for over 20 years. Mary would recite one of her own poems or sing one of her own ballads while Libby accompanied her on the piano.

Fig. 42. Mary Delia Poppleton Learned
Courtesy A.J. Poppleton III Personal Collection

Libby Gets Married

On May 8, 1895, Elizabeth, age 37, married Major Dr. William G. Shannon, age 44, a surgeon in the United States Army. Her brother William escorted Libby down the aisle because of her father's total loss of eyesight. The couple met while Major Shannon was stationed at Fort Omaha. After their honeymoon, they left for Major Shannon's next post, Fort Custer, Montana.[458]

A.J.'s Last Letter to Caroline

In early September 1895, Caroline and Mary went to visit Libby and Major Shannon in Montana. While they were absent from Omaha, A.J. moved out to the family farm in Elkhorn to be close to his quarter horses. The acreage reminded him of his boyhood farm in Michigan. He wrote his last letter to Caroline, dictating it to his son William. He signed his name with a scribble. Amidst a farm and weather report, A.J.'s gentle teasing of Carrie shines forth:

> My dear Carrie: Omaha, Neb. Sept. 11, 1895
>
> There is nothing new at home. I sent a basket of tomatoes up to Will yesterday. I received your letter written near Edgemont yesterday afternoon rather a long trip for a short letter. I think I told you Julian failed to find Grossman at the cottage but left directions with Alfred to explain to him about the pump. The weather has been rather warm since Sunday, in fact, I would call it hot, except that I might elicit an answer saying something about moving into the city before the summer was over. I hope the clear air of Custer has braced both you and Mary up and I presume the bottle of wine I sent has had a similar effect upon Elizabeth. There is such an absolute dearth of news that I shall not interrupt to write again. Hoping you may be greatly benefited by the journey, I am yours affectionately,
>
> A.J. Poppleton [459]

"His Strong Character Prevailed"

Caroline wrote in her diary that in the beginning of 1892, her husband's blindness was a "dreadful calamity – and was for a time over-whelming."[460] Many friends who saw him in those early days shared a similar reaction. A while later, they wrote that as Poppleton came to terms with the loss of his eyesight, to their amazement, he became resolved to make the best of this tragedy. In Caroline's words, "his strong character prevailed."[461] The weddings of his two daughters were a comfort to him, especially since he liked and respected both of his sons-in-law.

"Hold Up The Standard"

No couple in Omaha was closer friends to A.J. and Caroline than James and Elizabeth Woolworth. They socialized together, were active members and underwriters of many civic and cultural organizations in Omaha and were parishioners of Trinity Episcopal Cathedral.

A.J. Poppleton and James M. Woolworth were also dedicated members of the Omaha Bar Association, supporting and mentoring many attorneys, young and old. The Woolworths frequently visited the Poppleton home, encouraging and supporting A.J. and Caroline during the last difficult years. Woolworth wrote of one of his last visits to their home:

> Four years ago, last April, he called me to him to tell me of his impending calamity of blindness. No one of all his friends, except his wife and children, knew what was upon him. A long season of great distress followed; but when it was passed, he composed himself to his new condition with a calm and serene spirit. They were four years of happy life. He dwelt in the high places where the light first comes and shines the longest, not in the valleys. When he saw his end drawing near and he and I were about to separate never to meet again on this earth, prostrate as he was, his voice, strong as ever, gave me his high command, "hold up the standard." Mr. Poppleton's professional career was brought to a sudden and untimely end by the loss of his eyesight, while in the full enjoyment of his mental faculties, and before any serious impairment of his physical strength. Poppleton's life had been a successful one in all ways by which success is measured in human estimation. He had acquired reputation, wealth, the respect, and admiration of his brethren at the bar, the attachment of friends, commanding influence in the community, a position second to none at the bar of the state, as well as of the nation, and the love and affection of a true wife and devoted children, which are the best gifts of God to man. What was left for him to strive for? The battle of life had been fought; the victory had been won.[462]

28

"He Has Been Blind – He Can See Now"

The Evening Times of Washington D.C. featured a lengthy column in its September 30, 1896 edition: "Andrew J. Poppleton, who was general attorney of the Union Pacific Road from its organization until his voluntary retirement in 1888, to be succeeded by Senator Thurston, died this morning. For several years he has been blind. He Can See Now."[463]

Andrew Jackson Poppleton passed away at 4:30 p.m. in the afternoon of Thursday, September 24, 1896, at his home on Sherman Avenue. He was 66. The Certificate of Death listed his cause of death as Bright's disease.[464] Three months earlier, his doctors had diagnosed him with this disease. Three weeks before his death, he suffered a severe attack and thereafter was under continuous care of his medical team led by Dr. Bridges and Dr. J.E. Summers. Caroline never left his side.

A.J.'s daughters Elizabeth "Libby" Shannon and Mary Learned, who was visiting Libby, arrived from Fort Custer, Montana, ten days before his death, and were at his bedside with their brother William. A.J. was preceded in death by his three-year-old daughter Mary Zada Poppleton.[465]

The news of Poppleton's death quickly spread throughout the community. In response, lawyers from the Omaha Bar Association called a meeting to discuss the most appropriate way to honor the memory of their colleague. On Friday, September 25, 1896, at 4:00 p.m., the lawyers met at the Douglas County Courthouse, Courtroom No. 2, to appoint a committee to draft resolutions to honor Poppleton. Judge Frank Irvine, Commissioner of the Nebraska Supreme Court, presided over the meeting.

The resolutions would be discussed at a special meeting of the Bar the following Monday. The committee included Charles A. Baldwin, former Mayor Benedict Eli Kennedy, U.S. Senator Charles F. Manderson, Judge John C. Cowin, William D. Beckett, and Judge Eleazer Wakeley. James M. Woolworth, recently elected President of the American Bar Association, chaired the committee. The committee agreed to gather at the Poppleton home as a group for his funeral the next day.[466]

Funeral and Burial

The funeral service for A. J. Poppleton was held at his home on Saturday afternoon. The *Omaha Bee News* described the prominence of those in attendance:

> Among the throng that filled the spacious rooms was numbered nearly every man of prominence in the public and social circles of the city. With these were mingled others less prominently known, but equally sincere in their regret at the loss of a valued friend. The large rooms on the lower floor were all seated to their full capacity and the wide porch that traverses the entire front of the building was occupied by those who were unable to gain admittance to the interior.[467]

The *Omaha Bee News* also detailed the arrangement of the rooms with floral displays, as well as the placement of a magnificent casket adorned with roses and bearing his remains:

> A distinctive feature of the arrangements was the exceptional taste that marked the distribution of the floral offerings. There was none of the profuse and promiscuous heaping of heavy designs that so often is wearily monotonous on similar occasions. The atmosphere was fragrant, not heavy, with the perfume of clusters of rare blossoms, striking for their beauty rather than their elaborate design. The magnificent casket that occupied the center of the south parlor was simply adorned with two or three choice clusters of roses. The mantel bore simple bunches of roses, ferns and white carnations. Then every room in the house was similarly favored. There were flowers in profusion, but they were so distributed that the bloom of each cluster had a corner of its own.[468]

Rev. Alvin F. Sherill, a close friend and confidant of Poppleton from the time they worked together during and after the Standing Bear trial, earlier had been asked by A.J. to speak at his funeral. Then living in retirement, Rev. Sherill came from his home in Galesburg, Illinois to conduct the 3:00 p.m. service. The *Omaha Bee News* described the funeral as impressive:

> Before 2 o'clock the casket was uncovered and those who wished to see the face that would be, but a memory thereafter, passed through. Then the lid was closed and not opened again. Shortly after 3 o'clock the brief, but solemnly impressive services were held. Rev. A. F. Sherill, the former pastor of the First Congregational church, delivered a short discourse in which he spoke eloquently at the victory of death and earnestly of the sympathy that belonged to the sorrowing in their bereavement. The music was admirably rendered by the choir of Trinity Cathedral.[469]

At the close of the funeral services, a long line of carriages followed the remains of A. J. Poppleton to his final resting place in Prospect Hill Cemetery, 32nd & Parker Street. The men who were asked to carry his casket to the cemetery were Victor B. Caldwell, Gilbert M. Hitchcock, A. L. Reed, Curtiss C. Turner, L.M. Kuhns, William A. Redick, Charles T. Kountze and Randall K. Brown.

Another distinguished group of men were named honorary pallbearers: James M. Woolworth, Dr. George L. Miller, Joseph H. Millard, Lyman Richardson, William Pusey, J. Sterling Morton, George I. Gilbert, and Judge Eleazer Wakeley.[470]

Newspapers throughout the nation reported the death of A.J. Poppleton, including the *Detroit Free Press* which devoted a full column on the front page of its October 3, 1896 edition describing A.J.'s boyhood and education in Michigan, and highlighting his work on the Standing Bear case and for the Union Pacific Railroad. The newspaper praised his many qualities as a lawyer, orator, and leader with integrity: "Andrew J. Poppleton's clear and logical mind, his thorough knowledge of parliamentary rules, his sturdy honesty and integrity, combined with his rare powers as an orator, gave him great influence and strength in legislative bodies as well as in courts."[471]

Historical Note: Prospect Hill Cemetery

Between 1860 and 1875, real estate developer and civic patron, Byron Reed, purchased cemetery land near 32nd & Parker Street, originally developed by Moses Shinn and Jesse Lowe, to hold the remains of soldiers from Omaha Barracks (later known as Fort Omaha) who had died during the Civil War, as well as many of the early settlers of Omaha. Today, over 10,000 men, women and children are buried in this historic cemetery, a who's who of early Omaha: Poppleton, Hanscom, Reed, Woolworth, Paddock, Shinn, Enos Lowe, Metz, Snowden, Kountze, Lake, Krug, Millard, Sorenson, Hitchcock, Briggs, Dan Allen and Anna Wilson. "Omaha's developers, religious leaders, mayors, judges, those for whom Omaha streets, parks and schools have been named," are buried and honored here.[472]

Memorial Service of the Omaha Bar Association

On Monday, September 28, 1896, the Omaha Bar Association held a memorial service at the Douglas County Courthouse, Courtroom No.1. Nearly all of the members of the Bar were present, as well as other city residents. At 3:00 p.m., Judge Frank Irvine began the service, and James M. Woolworth, chair of the special committee, presented the resolutions honoring Poppleton:

> ANDREW J. POPPLETON, one of the foremost leaders of this bar ever since the first organization of the courts in Nebraska, and holding a high place among the great lawyers throughout the whole land, a citizen who had rendered to this community and state services of the highest value, and a man of singular purity of life and character, having departed this life at his residence in this city on the 24th day of September instant, we, his friends, associates and brethren assembled for the purpose of expressing our respect for his memory, have
>
> RESOLVED, that the great powers of our deceased brother in advocacy, his wide and varied learning, his lofty principles, and his pure and elevated character secured for him when he was among us our highest respect and admiration. And now, when by an inscrutable Providence he has been removed from our midst, and we are deprived of his good example and the inspiration of his impressive personality, with unfeigned sorrow we bear witness to his virtues and the fame which he achieved through all the borders of the nation.
>
> RESOLVED, that we tender to his widow and children our sincere sympathy, and direct that a copy of these resolutions be communicated to them.
>
> RESOLVED, that the chair appoint suitable committees to present this expression of our respect for the memory of Mr. Poppleton to all of the district courts of this country, the supreme court of this state, and the circuit courts of the United States for this district, and request that they be spread at large upon their records.[473]

After reading and adopting the resolutions, Woolworth delivered the first tribute to A.J. Poppleton. His speech and other eulogies were recorded in "*A Memorial Edition of The Omaha Mercury,*" the official paper of the Nebraska legal fraternity dated October 9, 1896.

MEMORIAL EDITION

THE OMAHA MERCURY

OFFICIAL PAPER NEBRASKA LEGAL FRATERNITY.

ESTABLISHED 1870. | OMAHA, NEBRASKA, OCTOBER 9, 1896. | VOL. XXVI. NO. 41

THE FINAL DECREE

Decision which Affects a Life. The Court of Last Resort, from whose Finding there is no Appeal, Enters Another Imperative Order.

AND THE MANDATE IS OBEYED

Andrew J. Poppleton, Lawyer, Citizen and Philosopher, is Called Above.—His Memory Honored by the Bar. Proceedings in Full.

Andrew J. Poppleton, one of the leading members of the Omaha bar, died at his residence in this city on Thursday, September 24, 1896. His last illness was of short duration and although Mr. Poppleton had been in ill-health for many months, his death was most unexpected when it occurred.

Mr. Poppleton was a lawyer of great ability and was beloved by all who knew him. By his death, the whole legal profession has lost a member who long

THE LATE ANDREW J. POPPLETON.

HIS WORK FOR NEBRASKA.

In 1855 he married Catherine L. Sears. Five children were born to them: two died in infancy; the others survive; the eldest, Elizabeth, wife of Maj. Shannon of the United States army; the next, William S., following his father's profession in this city, and Mary, wife of Myron L. Learned, also a member of the bar.

Mr. Poppleton was engaged in almost all the important controversies in the courts and his very remarkable gifts of public speech gave him power throughout the territory. He was a member of the territorial legislature in 1857, when the question of the relocation of the capitol was renewed and greatly agitated. He took a very active part in that contention. The following year he was elected mayor of the city, being the second person to hold that office. In the following spring he suffered a slight facial paralysis, which was followed by a protracted and dangerous illness. He was absent from the life of the city for about eighteen months, and returned to it with a vigor greatly impaired. Gradually he recovered his strength and afterward enjoyed for many years a large measure of health and vigor. He was obliged, however, to exercise great care and abstemiousness in his habits. When the state was admitted to the union in 1867, he received the entire vote of the democrats in the legislature for United States senator, and would

Fig 43. Memorial Edition of The Omaha Mercury, October 9, 1896
Courtesy of A.J. Poppleton III Personal Collection

James M. Woolworth Eulogy: Poppleton the Founder

James M. Woolworth described Poppleton's family background, education, and early career. He spoke about Poppleton's 24-year service to the Union Pacific Railroad, his venture into politics, his various battles with physical illnesses, and the complete loss of eyesight. Woolworth was present with his friend during many of the incidents he described, including court actions in which they collaborated as co-counsel, and even a few instances when they found themselves on opposing sides of a case. Woolworth's tribute before the Omaha Bar Association membership reflected the 40-year friendship they shared:

> To measure the usefulness of such a life as Mr. Poppleton's, we must consider the times and circumstances under which he lived. The greater part of his life was spent as a pioneer, in laying the foundation, and upon it erecting the superstructure of civilization in a new country. The structure of society and of

civil government was to be built from the foundation, and Mr. Poppleton was one of the chief architects. How well he and those associated with him planned, and how substantially they built, is attested by the marvelous growth of this commonwealth and the material wealth and prosperity we now enjoy.

To the young practitioner, just entering upon professional life, Mr. Poppleton was a helpful adviser and sympathetic brother. Through an extended practice of many years at the bar, side by side with Mr. Poppleton, and seeing him engaged in many bitterly contested trials, where the desire for success would naturally lead to personal controversy, I never saw him so far forget himself as to indulge in abusive or unkind remarks towards opposing counsel.[474]

Fig 44. James M. Woolworth
Courtesy Douglas County Historical Society

Profile: James Mills Woolworth (1829-1906)

No lawyer was closer to A.J. Poppleton than James M. Woolworth. Born in Onoddaga County, New York on June 28, 1829, Woolworth graduated from Hamilton College in 1849, and began practicing law in 1854 in Syracuse, New York. He moved to Omaha two years later. After serving one term in the Nebraska Territorial Legislature, he was appointed Omaha's first City Attorney, and later served as a member of the Nebraska Constitutional Convention in 1871. He remained active in the city, state and national bar associations for most of his career, being elected the second President of the Omaha Bar Association in 1891 following Poppleton; and then being elected President of the American Bar Association in 1896. Like Poppleton, he argued many cases before the U.S. Supreme Court and gave numerous addresses to civic groups and bar associations throughout the nation. In 1882, he was appointed attorney for the Chicago, Burlington and Quincy Railroad. He wrote the first history of Nebraska in 1857, and later served on the board of directors of the Nebraska Historical Society from 1880 to 1891. He died on June 16, 1906, age 77, from diabetes. His funeral was held at Trinity Episcopal Church conducted by Dean Beecher. Woolworth had been a member of Trinity's vestry, and was Chancellor of the Episcopal Diocese for over 20 years. He was buried in Prospect Hill cemetery and William S. Poppleton was a pallbearer. Woolworth was preceded in death by his first wife, Helen Beggs in 1867, and by his second wife Elizabeth Butterfield in 1897, and by five of his six children. An Omaha Avenue and Street are named in his honor.

Judge Eleazer Wakeley Eulogy: Poppleton the Professional

Immediately following Woolworth's eulogy, Judge Eleazer Wakeley spoke. He had known Poppleton since 1857 and had worked under him for seven years in the Law Department of the UPRR. He also served with Poppleton in founding the Omaha Law Library Association. Wakeley offered a unique perspective on Poppleton's uncanny ability to accomplish so much in a day, including time spent on legal matters and on behalf of the commercial and cultural life of Omaha:

> In his profession, as in all his pursuits, he was a severe economist of time. Industry, system, method, were among the chief aids to his success. I had means to know, as others here knew, that with a laborious practice constantly pressing upon him, he gave continual attention to important business matters with regular success so that much of his legal work was accomplished in the early hours of the day, before the time when many younger and more vigorous men had commenced their own. It was a maxim of his life that regulated labor was not only a duty, and for the profit and benefit of men, but for their fullest enjoyment and pleasure. The practice of law was his chosen vocation, the chief work of his life, but the qualities and the mental endowments which gave him success in that would have qualified him for the achievement of high success in any congenial field of intellectual effort.[475]

Judge William Kelly Eulogy: Poppleton the Mentor

A.J. Poppleton was committed to mentoring young men entering the legal profession because he had experienced the positive impact of mentoring in his own life. One of the attorneys who was grateful for Poppleton's mentorship was Judge William R. Kelly. He had "read the law" in Poppleton's office and later rose to head the office of general counsel for the Union Pacific. Judge Kelly spoke with gratitude of Poppleton's mentorship:

> I only became acquainted with Mr. Poppleton about ten years ago, perhaps twelve. I came into his office and under his direction and supervision. I found him generous. I found him earnest in advising me as his assistant, and yet he did not take away from me the responsibility that every man ought to exercise when he goes into a courthouse. I learned to love him as a man and to revere him as one of the leaders of the profession. Never in my knowledge of him was his standard of professional honor lowered, and every word of advice given by him was in the line of an elevated standard of professional honor and courtesy. Mr. Poppleton has been referred to as the builder of the policies of the Union Pacific Railway company through his work done in its law department. He has left behind him, in the archives of that office, the story of patient labor, careful thought, profound consideration for the people among whom he lived as well as for the corporation which he served. That record is a monument itself to the strength of this man's character as great as any that could be raised for him anywhere. Mr. Poppleton was strong. He fearlessly stated his views of the law. Through all of his policies, one thing was prominent, that is, the element of justice and fairness. This Andrew J. Poppleton has always insisted upon.[476]

George O. Calder Eulogy: Poppleton the Orator

Attorney George O. Calder shared a story of the first time he saw and heard Poppleton, not in a courtroom, but in a public forum arguing for prison reform and humane treatment of prisoners:

> I remember very well the first time I saw and heard Mr. Poppleton; it was in the old Boyd Opera House, at a meeting called in the interest of the prisoners and prison reform. I remember well the impassioned plea for the unfortunate and distressed, the direct recognition on his part of the fatherhood of Almighty God in comparison with whom we are all as nothing, and of the brotherhood of all mankind. Then, for the first time, Mr. Chairman, I both heard and saw eloquence. I heard eloquence from those lips silent now and silent forever; I saw eloquence beaming from the eye, informing his every feature, until to me the man approached sublimity. What he said at that time made a profound impression upon those who heard him, so much so as to myself, though years have since intervened, I have not and never will forget. Remember, he said, that any man, however debased, however low in the social scale, even though a convict, is still a man for all that. Then was revealed to me the mind, the heart, the soul of Andrew J. Poppleton. And the lesson imparted by him at that

meeting was this: that in whatever vocation of life we may be; however circumscribed or limited our sphere of action may be, yet live not for yourself alone, but for others.[477]

Dr. George L. Miller Eulogy: Poppleton the Friend

Other eulogies were given by distinguished members of the Bar and colleagues of Poppleton, including Judge John I. Redick, W.D. Beckett, and Judge Charles A. Baldwin. But there was another man in the audience who was not a lawyer, but who nonetheless was asked by Judge Wakeley to make a few remarks. He was Poppleton's close friend for over 40 years, Dr. George L. Miller:

> It was my fortune to know him on his first arrival in this region, and the first impressions that I got of him were more than realized in his stalwart and splendid life. I found him then as I have known him since, in the very prime and strength of his manhood as a dominant intellectual and moral force. From that hour to the day of his death, he remained an influential and powerful man in the community, and all, and always for the good of it. That he was one of the chief architects, sir, of this community, is a matter well known to the men who began their manhood lives with his own. Few men knew that man better than I did. In every act of his life, in his business and professional life, as I read him, sir, he had a method and object, and he elevated all of it into giving him the rank at this bar, not merely local, not merely state, but a reputation that reached the whole country. I have been with him for forty-two years, not always in harmony with Mr. Poppleton on some subjects, of local concern not always, but always ready to go to him for counsel, and in any of the relations I have held with him I have never found him withholding from me the candor of his judgment. The gratitude of Omaha will not be expressed in proper form until, accepting the suggestion of this distinguished gentleman to my left (Mr. Woolworth), a monument shall be erected in our public parks to the memory of Andrew J. Poppleton.[478]

Fig 45. Dr. George L. Miller.
Courtesy of Douglas County Historical Society

Profile: Dr. George L. Miller (1830-1920)

George LaForest Miller was born in Oneida County, New York on August 18, 1830. He graduated from the College of Physicians and Surgeons in New York City in 1852 and was appointed city physician in Syracuse. On October 19, 1854, he followed his parents to Omaha, six days after Poppleton arrived, becoming Omaha's first physician. His father Lorin Miller was Omaha's ninth mayor from 1865 to 1867. George Miller was elected to the Council in the first territorial legislature, and served for five years. In 1857, the Omaha City Council contracted with him and his associates to build the four-story Herndon House Hotel at 9th & Farnam Street, which he called home for many years. He left Omaha to be an editor of a newspaper in St. Joseph, Missouri, but returned in 1864 to run unsuccessfully for Congress. In 1865, he joined Daniel W. Carpenter, a reporter for the *Council Bluffs Bugle* newspaper, to found *The Omaha Daily News*. Dr. Miller used the newspaper as a platform to promote all things Omaha, as well as to make the nation aware of the injustice done to Standing Bear and the Ponca prisoners in 1879. He was elected President of the Western Associated Press (a regional predecessor of the Associated Press). He was always a strong supporter of animal care and joined others in founding the Nebraska Humane Society in 1875, leaving the Society a $100,000 bequest in his Will. In May 1869, he helped organize the parade and festivities in Omaha to commemorate completion of the Pacific Railroad. At the age of 77, he was elected President of the Nebraska State Historical Society and served from 1907 to 1909. His first wife, Harriette Dickinson, died in 1899, and his second wife Frances Briggs died in 1910. Dr. Miller was a member of the first vestry at Trinity Episcopal Cathedral along with Thomas Cuming and A.J. Hanscom. He had no children. Dr. Miller died on August 28, 1920, age 90, and was buried in Forest Lawn Cemetery. A park, street, and elementary school in Omaha are named in his honor.

Caroline's Diary Entry – September 1896

Caroline Poppleton wrote nothing in her diary during the four years of A.J.'s blindness, as she was consumed with caring for him. Now, after her husband's death and burial, she made the following entry at the end of September 1896:

> Mr. Poppleton's death came after an illness of three months. An attack of Brights disease. All his family were with him from the first to the end. He was buried in Prospect Hills where he wished to lie, and his funeral services were conducted by his friend Rev. A.F. Sherill at his request. Mary and Myron came to live with me immediately after Mr. Poppleton's death.[479]

Omaha City Council Tribute

On October 8, 1896, Daniel H. Wheeler, a member of the Omaha City Council, rose from his chair and paid the following tribute to A. J. Poppleton:

> Mr. President and Gentlemen of the Council: Our regular meeting this evening comes to us at a time of sorrow to a large circle of family and friends, and amid a general feeling of sadness in our community. Since our last regular meeting, our esteemed and worthy townsman, a former Mayor of this City, the Honorable Andrew J. Poppleton has joined the silent majority beyond the Unknown River. His body has been carried by loving hands and placed in the silent tomb in the city of the dead. There we left him, our friend with the peace of God in all his looks.[480]

The following resolution was adopted by unanimous vote of council members, and signed by Council President W.A. Saunders, and Mayor William J. Broatch:

> RESOLVED, Thinking of trials past, and knowing as we do, how well he had wrought for this life, trusting in the merits of an All Wise and loving God, we believe he would repeat the sweet lines of Bonari:
>
> " Beyond the smiling and the weeping, I shall be soon;
> Beyond the waking and the sleeping,
> Beyond the sowing and the reaping, I shall be soon.
> Love, rest and home. Sweet home.
> Lord, tarry not, but come."[481]

29

Caroline – The Pioneer Woman

Caroline Laura Poppleton was the light of Andrew Poppleton's life. In his *Reminiscences*, A.J. wrote of his heartfelt love for his wife of forty-one years:

> For me the most fortunate day of my life was that which brought the health and strength and sunshine of her nature into my own darker and more desponding life. Looking back nearly forty years, I can see very plainly that without her, my life might have become largely valueless and useless. She has been my stay and support and anchor in every worthy purpose and achievement, and in the darkness which now enshrouds me the light shines with undiminished radiance.[482]

Together, A. J. and Caroline helped Omaha grow from a small frontier village when they married in 1855 into a prosperous and vibrant community. Caroline raised their four children, served many organizations, and traveled with A.J. on numerous cross-country trips. Throughout her 21 years as a widow, she was surrounded by the love and support of her children, siblings, and countless friends. Caroline's leadership in various civic organizations such as the Bishop Clarkson Memorial Hospital and School of Nursing, and her loyal support of Trinity Episcopal Cathedral, are examples of her active and philanthropic life. Caroline's strong faith sustained her through the loss of her daughter Mary Zada in 1862, her husband A.J. in 1896, and her son William in 1913.

The 1913 Omaha Bee News Interview

On Sunday, June 8, 1913, The *Omaha Bee News* published an interview with Caroline under the front-page heading "The Pioneer Women of Omaha." The story began with these words: "One of the earliest of the pioneer women to come to Nebraska was Mrs. A.J. Poppleton, who came to Omaha in 1854, and she recalls in a most interesting way the early days of the city."[483]

> Mr. Poppleton was one of the first settlers of Omaha, coming here from his native state, Michigan, in 1854, and was a member of the first legislature. I came to Council Bluffs with my father's family from New York in the same year and Mr. Poppleton and I were married the second day of December 1855, and crossed the river to Omaha the next day, where we have always lived and where our children were born.[484]

The early part of the interview revealed the places where the young couple lived, because 'home' was always very important to Caroline:

> The first three months we boarded at the old Douglas House on Thirteenth Street. Then we began housekeeping in one room in the brick building built by Jesse Lowe, the site since occupied by the old United States National Bank building at Twelfth and Farnam streets. Mr. Poppleton's office was in the front, which was also partly occupied by J.W. Paddock, who was not married and often took breakfast with us. Across the hall was the bank of the Western Fire and Marine Insurance Company, organized in 1855. The building was filled with offices and the rest of the block was used by the Indians [Omaha Tribe] to receive their yearly annuities. The room which we used was the home of C.B. Smith, the private secretary of Governor T.B. Cuming, and his wife kindly offered it to us with its furniture while they were away on a visit to the east. There we cooked, ate, slept, and entertained our visitors for another three months.[485]

Caroline told the newspaper reporter how she and her husband met William Newton Byers, A.J.'s second law partner: "I well remember having Mr. and Mrs. W.N. Byers to dinner with us, who afterward became a partner with Mr. Poppleton in loans and real estate."[486] Byers served with Poppleton in the first territorial legislature and drafted the first plat map of the city. He left Omaha after only five years to search for gold in Colorado, where he later founded the *Rocky Mountain News.* He used his newspaper as a platform to promote Denver's growth as a booming mountain town and lived there until his death in 1903.

In 1856, Caroline and A.J. moved into the first home they owned. They no longer had to rent rooms in what otherwise were office buildings. She said it was a turning point in their marriage and an indication that her husband's law practice in the city was secure:

> In May, we moved into our own home, with orchard and garden, on the corner of Capitol Avenue and Fifteenth Street, where we lived for ten years. In 1866, we built on the forty acres fronting on which is now known as North Twenty-Fourth Street [Grand Avenue], opposite Brownell Hall, which was in the Saratoga Hotel near Fort Omaha. In 1868, the fever and ague [flu] drove us back to town, and we lived at Sixteenth and Cass streets in a large building which we owned and turned around, making two homes, one of which was occupied by J.M. Ham, of the Union Pacific. In 1870 we went into our new house on the corner of Dodge and Nineteenth streets, on Capitol Hill, where our youngest daughter [Elizabeth] was born. The house was burned to the ground on the second day of January 1879. That year we built our house on Sherman Avenue, where we celebrated our silver wedding and where I lived myself for thirty-one years.[487]

Caroline briefly described her travels with her husband and his last years: "Mr. Poppleton was general attorney for the Union Pacific Railway Company for nearly twenty-five years, and I think I traveled in every state in the union with him. He retired from the Union Pacific in 1888, and after four years of entire loss of sight, he died in Omaha in 1896."[488]

In the final paragraphs of the *Omaha Bee News* interview, Caroline spoke of her work and activities in church and community:

> I have been in Omaha almost fifty-eight years and have always been connected with Trinity church, since the days of the little Gothic church on the corner of Ninth and Farnam, where I was the soprano of the quartet choir. Since 1869, I have been closely associated with Bishop Clarkson Memorial Hospital. I have seen Omaha grow from infancy. We were then all strangers in a strange land, young and happy, and dependent upon each other for society. What strong and enduring friendships were formed in those days, whose companionships and loving kindness were to be life-long, and what pleasure we take in talking over the pleasantness of the old times![489]

Trinity Episcopal Cathedral

Trinity Episcopal Cathedral had an important role in the lives of the Poppleton family from the time of its founding in 1856, to the death of their daughter Mary Delia Learned in 1960. The church provided spiritual sustenance and fellowship for their family, as well as for many families who made a lasting mark on Omaha in its first fifty years. Andrew and Catherine Hanscom, James and Elizabeth Butterfield Woolworth, John and Josephine Webster, Joseph and Catherine Barker, Champion and Mary Butterfield Chase, Jesse and Sophie Lowe, Algernon and Emma Paddock, Joseph and Susie Paddock, Lieutenant John Bourke and Mary Horbach Bourke, Eleazer and Sabina Wakeley, Clinton and Emily Briggs, Dr. George and Harriette Miller, Thomas B. Cuming, Byron and Mary Reed were among its parishioners.[490]

Historic Note: Trinity Episcopal Cathedral

Charles W. Martin, in *A History of Trinity Episcopal Cathedral,* wrote that the first "lay services were held in the home of Acting Governor Cuming for both Episcopal services and Roman Catholic services. A small chair from the Cuming home used by the lay readers of both denominations is now owned by Joslyn Art Museum, Omaha."[491] On April 19, 1856, a meeting was held at the law office of Jonas Seely to organize a church. The first vestry was elected, consisting of Samuel Moffatt, Charles W. Hamilton, Thomas B. Cuming, A.J. Hanscom, Jonas Seely, A.F. Salisbury, and Dr. George L. Miller. In 1859, Mayor Jesse Lowe and his wife Sophie offered to lease, rent free for ten years, two lots on the Southwest corner of 9th and Farnam Streets for the church. Bishop Robert Harper Clarkson arrived in Omaha on December 3, 1865, as the newly elected leader of the jurisdiction of Nebraska and the Dakotas, and quickly led the effort to build a new church. After the new church burned down on November 10, 1869, a small wooden chapel was constructed in the middle of Capitol Ave until the present church could be completed in 1883. Bishop Clarkson died of pneumonia March 10, 1884. He and his wife Meliora McPherson Clarkson (1827-1902) were buried on the grounds of the Cathedral.[492]

Fig 46. Trinity Church in the Middle of the Street
Courtesy of Trinity Episcopal Cathedral.

On November 17, 1862, A.J. and Caroline's second daughter, Mary Zada Poppleton, died of typhoid fever at the age of three years and seven months. They turned to their church community for comfort and support during Mary Zada's suffering and death. In her memory, they donated funds to create the beautiful "Saint James the Minor" stained glass chancel window in the sanctuary of Trinity Cathedral, still visible today.[493]

On Easter Sunday, 1898, less than two years after her husband's death, Caroline donated the heavy brass cross with a pyramid eight-sided brass base to adorn the church's High Altar in his memory.

Caroline Poppleton was one of the founding members of the Trinity Parish Aid Society, which played a leading role in raising funds for various church expenses, including the music program, Sunday School operations, and church repairs. The Aid Society"also made dresses, nightgowns, baby clothes, sheets, towels, bedspreads, and face cloths which were given to Clarkson Hospital and to Dean Tancock to give to the poor," according to Martin's History of the Cathedral.[494] Caroline always loved music and was a soprano in the church choir.

All of Caroline and A.J.'s children were baptized at Trinity and became members of the congregation. Dean Charles Gardner organized the Woman's Auxiliary on December 13, 1886, and appointed Caroline as the first vice-president, and he was the first president.

Bishop Clarkson Memorial Hospital and School of Nursing

Caroline Poppleton was named to the first Board of Trustees of Bishop Clarkson Memorial Hospital and School of Nursing in 1892. She served in that role for 23 years. In addition, she served as the secretary-treasurer for the hospital for many years. When Meliora Clarkson died on May 13, 1902, Caroline was elected to take her place as manager of the hospital. At the Board of Trustees meeting held October 1, 1903, Caroline resigned as manager of the hospital. The minutes of the meeting recorded the Board's high esteem for her:

> Mrs. Poppleton has for many years taken a very deep interest in the Hospital, not only as a Director and Treasurer, but in its active management. She was the most confidential associate and advisor of Mrs. Clarkson during her life and rendered most efficient service. Since undertaking the duties of Manager, she has been wise and efficient in all respects. The Trustees regret exceedingly that she has felt compelled to withdraw from the position of Manager and they are gratified to know that she will continue to act as Treasurer and as a Trustee.[495]

Historic Note: Bishop Clarkson Memorial Hospital and School of Nursing. In 1869, Bishop Clarkson broke ground at 23rd & Webster Street for the first hospital in Omaha. It opened in 1870 as "Good Samaritan Hospital," but fire destroyed it in 1877. A small temporary hospital, "Ladies Hospital," was established next to Trinity Church by a group of women from Trinity in 1880. In three years, a new hospital was begun at 1716 Dodge Street, "Child's Hospital and Home." Caroline Poppleton spoke at the event. After Bishop Clarkson died in 1888, his wife Meliora was made lifetime manager of the hospital, and immediately worked to fulfill the bishop's dream and opened the "Bishop Clarkson Memorial School of Nursing," the first in Nebraska. The student nurses lived in a home at 628 S. 20th Street. In May 1892, the hospital was incorporated as "The Bishop Clarkson Memorial Hospital for Children." A new building at 21st & Howard Street was dedicated April 25, 1908, at which Caroline gave an address on the historical background and early work of the hospital.[496]

Death - November 22, 1917

On November 22, 1917, at age 82, Caroline Laura Sears Poppleton died within an hour of suffering a massive heart attack while residing at her daughter Elizabeth's home, 504 S. 26th Ave. in the Winona Apartments. Notice of her death was front-page news in *The Omaha Daily Bee*, morning edition, Friday, November 23, 1917. The article was one of very few stories on the front page not devoted to the pivotal battles taking place in Italy and Belgium in the last twelve months of World War I. The center of the front page carried the following headline and story:

Mrs. Poppleton,
Pioneer Woman of Omaha, Dead

Widow of A.J. Poppleton, and
Leader in Church and Society for Many Years
Taken by Death

The *Omaha Daily Bee* article spoke of her tireless work for over three decades on behalf of many charitable organizations, including Trinity Episcopal Cathedral and Bishop Clarkson Memorial Hospital and School of Nursing.[497]

Her funeral service was held at 3:00 p.m. on Sunday, November 24, 1917, at Trinity Episcopal Cathedral, conducted by Very Rev. James A. Tancock, Dean of the Cathedral.

Honorary pallbearers were J.H. Millard, C.E. Yost, M.T. Burlow, Fred H. Davis, Luther Drake, Judge Arthur C. Wakeley, Dr. J.E. Summers, and Dr. W.O. Bridges.

Active pallbearers were Henry F. Wyman, Frank Hamilton, Randall K. Brown, Charles L. Saunders, E.M. Fairfield, Samuel S. Caldwell, Thomas R. Kimball, Arthur C. Smith.

Caroline was buried next to her husband and daughter Mary Zada in Prospect Hill Cemetery, Omaha.[498] Caroline was survived by one sister, Delia Sears Ferguson of Omaha, and by one brother, Stillman Foote Sears of Long Pine, Nebraska; and by two children, Elizabeth Poppleton Shannon and Mary Poppleton Learned.

The *Omaha World Herald*, November 26, 1917, concluded its article on her funeral saying, "Acquaintances of the past half century gathered to pay their last respects to a lady who was respected and admired by all who knew her.[499]

Remembrance – February 4, 1936

Nineteen years after Caroline Poppleton's death, Rev. George Allen Beecher, former Bishop of Trinity Episcopal Cathedral (1905-10), wrote a letter to Caroline's daughter Elizabeth Poppleton Shannon, from his parish in Hastings, Nebraska, recalling his fond memories of Caroline and her support of his ministry:

> My dear Mrs. Shannon: February 4, 1936
>
> Those happy days we spent in the dear old Trinity Cathedral parish in Omaha, and the many visits in the Poppleton home on North 16th Street was a privilege we shall never forget. Mere things sometimes become so intricately associated with persons in our relationships with one another, that they are sacred. I often drove past the old home on our way to and from Fort Omaha while our daughter and her family were stationed there, just to have a look at the place. Even with all the changes, I could see the great lawn – trees- porch- and spacious living rooms – always so cheerful and bright with dear Mrs.

Poppleton's welcome smile and ever louder and cultured voice greeting all her friends who learned to appreciate that radiant landmark in Omaha's earliest social pilgrimage - in the days of the horse and carriage with their brilliant equipment and charming guests. I shall never forget the lawn party for the children when Charlie Martin took a moving picture of the "ring around the roses" and dear Mrs. Poppleton was the happiest and youngest playmate in the crowd- Oh! how I love to think of those wonderful days of my ministry! Then too – I cannot remember a Sunday morning when she was not in her usual place in the congregation at the Cathedral. It was as much a part of her life as the breath she breathed – and I recall that she always loved music – and served her day in the choir when – and before - a Cathedral was even dreamed of. How much Mrs. Beecher and I have enjoyed having this remembrance from you. Ever affectionately and gratefully yours,

Geo. A. Beecher[500]

Fig 47. Caroline Poppleton at Home
2232 Sherman Avenue (1911)
Courtesy of Douglas County Historical Society

Fig 48. Caroline Poppleton at Home
2232 Sherman Avenue (1911)
Courtesy of Douglas County Historical Society

30

Reminiscences

A.J. Poppleton, with fading eyesight, dictated his memoirs titled *"Reminiscences,"* a few years before his death. In the first sentence, he shared stories of his heritage, noting that his great-grandfather, Samuel Poppleton, with his wife and children, sailed across the Atlantic in 1751 from North Yorkshire, England, and became the first members of the Poppleton family to set foot on American soil.

Poppleton was grateful to his ancestors for instilling in him a fighting spirit, and exhibiting the virtues he would strive to emulate the rest of his life. As the first entry in his memoirs was a tribute to his great-grandparents, it seems appropriate that the last entry he made was a tribute to his parents:

> I recognize to its fullest extent the numerous obligations I have all of my life been under to my father and mother. They taught me industry, economy, and sobriety; to love knowledge; to shrink from no obstacles but to be patient and persistent in overcoming them; to scorn gratuities; to detest cards, tobacco and liquor; and that the only true order of nobility was that of labor, industry and virtue. They were plain and simple in their lives, but such success as I have attained, I attribute mainly to their teachings and examples.[501]

Go Forth with a Manly Heart

On February 16, 1851, A J. sat at his desk in his dorm room at Union College, pondering his future. He asked himself two questions: "What part of the Earth will I be in? " and "What will be my employment?"[502] His answer to both questions was, "It is all in the work of time. Go forth to meet the shadowy future without fear and with a manly heart."[503]

A.J. Poppleton went forth in his life with a manly heart, fighting for what he believed was right and just. He left his senior year at Michigan University when the school canceled the Literary Society, where he was a leader and friend to many. To stay would mean he supported what he felt was an unjust decision. He convinced his grieving parents to let him move 300 miles from home and enroll in Union College in Schenectady, New York, for his last year in college.

While at Union College, A.J. fought the loneliness of missing family and friends. But he met caring teachers who helped him overcome his loneliness and introduced him to noted historians and philosophers. He wrote, "After forty years of struggle with the world I look back upon the period I spent at Union College as the most profitable year in my whole life."[504]

At Union, he became exposed to "the law" as a possible career choice. He read legal commentaries by Kent and Blackstone, watched lawyers do battle in New York courtrooms, and was mesmerized by the eloquence of Daniel Webster.

At the same time, in the darkness of his dorm room, he began a lifelong struggle with his eyesight. In the beginning it came in the form of dizziness and headaches lasting for days, and resulting in a melancholy spirit that would grip his spirit. However, by the time he lost his eyesight 40 years later, living the last four years of his life in total darkness, he had learned how to fight that melancholy spirit and endure his burden with dignity and courage.

The Pioneer

A.J. Poppleton failed in his first attempt at practicing law with a few friends in Detroit, saying they had too many expenses and too few clients. He left Michigan a poor man and headed west in the hope of a better future. He arrived in Omaha City in October 1854, built a 10' x 14' log cabin with his own hands, and opened the city's first law office. This was intended to be a temporary solution to get him through the winter until spring came and he could leave for California. Clients were scarce in the young town when he arrived. There was no courthouse and no organized system of justice. There were no streets, only mud. Narrow pathways meandered through tall uncut prairie grass where a traveler may stumble upon the postmaster who carried the mail in his hat.

Life was a struggle in those early winter months, but A.J. found it exciting and challenging as a member of the first territorial legislature. It helped that he worked alongside Hanscom, Richardson, and Cuming, all from his home state of Michigan. Together, they led the fight to name Omaha City the capital of the new Nebraska Territory. These men understood this was the crucial first step in making the city attractive as a terminus for the discussed transcontinental railroad that would one day link the Atlantic to the Pacific coasts – hopefully through Omaha.

A.J.'s law practice grew as did his reputation for being an effective trial lawyer. In March 1858, he was elected Omaha's second Mayor. Five months after taking office, tragedy struck. He was forced to resign due to a stroke-like illness. This time, he would face a different fight – not in the courtroom or legislative chambers – but in training his body to rest, exercise, walk, and speak normally again. It would take 18 months to recover, but with fortitude, prayer, and the constant comfort and support of Caroline, he would begin again.

The Builder

When A.J. Poppleton resumed his law practice in the winter of 1860, he was determined to make the most of his second chance. The next three decades would prove to be the most productive in his life – for his practice, his profession, and his community.

In December 1863, he gave a speech on the banks of the Missouri River, celebrating with a thousand of his fellow citizens, the announcement that President Lincoln had selected Omaha as the Eastern terminus of the transcontinental railroad. Shortly thereafter, A.J. was appointed general attorney for the Union Pacific, a post he would hold for 24 years. He worked hard to create and build an efficient law department for the railroad, writing the first railway code, handling the administrative duties of a large corporation, and securing the contracts that made

Omaha the headquarters of operations for the Union Pacific. In addition, he personally argued cases in federal courtrooms throughout the nation, in the Nebraska Supreme Court, and before the U.S. Supreme Court.

A.J. and other like-minded citizens founded organizations that would benefit Omaha for generations to come. For example, they started a public library for the good of all residents, a law library and a bar association for the good of his profession, and a Trade and Commerce Association for the good of business. A.J. was often the man who provided the leadership and passion that inspired others to help establish these organizations.

The citizens of Omaha knew if A.J. Poppleton was behind a project, it would get done. He wrote the by-laws and constitutions and served as president of these organizations. He did everything in his power to ensure that a structure was in place to succeed. After only a year as president, he stepped aside and made room for others to lead but continued his support and encouragement. Thanks to his leadership skills, all four organizations are operating and benefiting Omaha citizens nearly 150 years later.

The Fighter

Despite his work schedule and responsibilities for the Union Pacific, plus his commitment to civic and professional organizations, A.J. Poppleton joined his colleague John L. Webster, to argue the unprecedented habeas corpus case in 1879 on behalf of Chief Standing Bear and the Ponca prisoners. These two outstanding lawyers worked tirelessly, pro-bono, to right a terrible wrong and bring justice to an unjust situation. Poppleton's two-hour closing argument validated his reputation as one of the great courtroom advocates in the nation. Judge Elmer Dundy's historic decision granted Standing Bear and these Poncas the status of 'persons' in the American legal system with standing to come into a federal court seeking a redress of their grievances. This was the first civil rights victory for Native Americans. For his great contribution to the cause, and in deeply felt gratitude, Chief Standing Bear gave A.J. his cherished headdress.

Poppleton and Webster teamed together in a second case in federal court to fight on behalf of the Ponca Tribe to recover their homeland. They also represented John Elk, a member of the Winnebago tribe, in his desire to vote in the city election as a citizen. Poppleton and Webster's efforts on behalf of Native Americans for the basic civil rights of personhood and citizenship was unprecedented in America at that time. The Standing Bear decision opened the door of the American judicial system for Native Americans; and the Elk decision and the arguments presented, garnered national attention on the issue of citizenship and moved that debate forward.

The Orator

A.J. Poppleton was a man of passion and piercing words. Throughout his life he expressed his thoughts and feelings in way that mesmerized audiences with his command of the English language. His brilliance and eloquence were evident when speaking at a college commencement, before fellow members of the Bar Association, at civic organizations, and in the courtroom. The ultimate source of Poppleton's oratorical skills was his desire to acquire knowledge. He never stopped learning.

Poppleton found inspiration at Michigan University and at Union College, where he studied Latin and Greek and delved into the great writings of Greek, Roman, and British historians and philosophers. Certain words and phrases stuck with him for life. Words like justice, fairness, integrity, industry, honesty, and most especially - honor. Poppleton was deeply passionate about these virtues. They became a part of his inner core.

Six months after his defense of Chief Standing Bear, Poppleton gave the keynote address before the Nebraska State Bar Association's annual meeting, January 7, 1880, at the Opera House in Lincoln, Nebraska. His address was so powerful and so well received that it was published by the Bar for public distribution. As with all published addresses Poppleton gave during his career, he referenced historical people and events from countries around the world, spanning a period from the Magna Carta to the Mayflower Compact to our Civil War. He spoke to the Bar Association with an unwavering belief in the importance to American society of an active, wise, honest, and impartial legal community:

> [A lawyer's] life is but another name for conflict; his footing is not in the clouds but upon the ignoble earth. The subject of his labor is the prosaic life of men ... Take from a free government the bar and the bench, and it would fall into chaos. No stable and just government can long exist without an able, upright, and impartial bench, and a wise and incorruptible judiciary is the outgrowth of a diligent, learned, and patriotic bar ...The bench and the bar are the custodians of the sacred vessels of liberty, the outposts and sentinels entrusted with the guardianship of the rights of property, the rights of person, the rights of belief, the rights of life.[505]

He closed his talk by inviting the attorneys and judges to assume their proper role in a nation that had recently endured five years of civil war, still in the throes of reconstruction, and wondering if a lasting reconciliation was truly possible. He challenged them to look to the future with hope:

> Let but the Bar, and its best flower and outgrowth, the Bench, wield their potential strength to develop, solidify, and establish a dominant national sentiment, holding allegiance rather to truth than to error, rather to people than to party, rather to nationality than confederacy, rather to progression than reaction, rather to the sacred preservation of every shred and syllable of the Magna Carta of personal liberty than to the abominable and bloody doctrine of

state necessity, and the sun of the next century will pour a flood of serene effulgence upon a people.[506]

A Courageous Heart and Vigorous Spirit

Of all the tributes given at the memorial gathering of the Omaha Bar Association on September 28, 1896, the only one found among Caroline Poppleton's papers at her death was given by Charles F. Manderson. He came to Omaha from Philadelphia in 1869 to open a law practice. At the time of Poppleton's death, he was serving his second term in the U.S. Senate. In 1899, he was elected President of the American Bar Association. He and Poppleton were of different political parties, but Manderson was a close friend and spoke of Poppleton's courageous heart and vigorous spirit:

> I feel that if there was any particular and distinctive feature in the make-up of Mr. Poppleton it was that he was possessed of those higher and more lovable attributes that come from the heart rather than the head. It is said that he was reserved and not communicative. In an acquaintance of thirty years with Mr. Poppleton I never found him so. True, he did not "wear his heart upon his sleeve for claws to peck at," but no man had more hearty generosity and feeling for his fellow men.
>
> Older than myself and having an experience that I may never hope to have, I never during my life in Omaha hesitated to go to him, advantaging myself of that ripe experience, as I would go to an older brother, for consolation and advice, and received from him always, not only words of wisdom, based upon his broad observation and splendid career, but words of encouragement; for one of the chief characteristics of Mr. Poppleton was that the element of envy was not in his make-up.
>
> He desired the advancement of all those with whom he came in contact, especially those of his own profession; his earnest wish seemed to be to help others in the particular achievement, wished for by them either in advancement in their calling or in any other which they might desire. We differed in politics, yet I recall with sad pleasure that during the years of my life when I was not in the practice of the profession, but in public life, that there came to me from him on several occasions letters that I cherish among my most precious belongings, words of commendation sometimes, and again, at times, those of criticism, that I know did me infinite good and were to my great advantage.
>
> There was another characteristic that I would speak of, also an attribute of the heart. That was this man's indomitable courage. He dared face some of the hardest ills of life and thus daring, overcame them. Mr. Woolworth has spoken of a period in his career when he was smitten with disease and when it looked as though his life must be a failure because of its physical effects. How bravely he battled. Then came the great affliction of the loss of sight.

I returned to Omaha from a brief absence a few years ago and felt as though it would be a painful duty, and yet a duty that I must perform, to call upon this afflicted brother, stricken as he was with total blindness. It was but a few months after this dreadful misfortune came to him. I cannot find words to express, Mr. Chairman, the pain of that interview. A strong man had been stricken with the most dreaded of all infirmities and he seemed to me to be utterly crushed beneath the dire calamity. I left his presence sad and disheartened, feeling that the end of all had come to him.

I did not see him again until nearly a year had elapsed when I again called upon him and saw the splendid evidence of his unfailing courage, manly determination and how he had overcome all fear and fought against disaster. He cheerfully talked upon the subjects of the day with an interest and appreciation that charmed me. I left his presence cheered again, realizing that his was the same vigorous spirit that I had found it, one to suffer and be strong, to endure and finally to win, to suffer temporary defeat and achieve final victory. He was not only a prime factor in the past of this community, but an example to those who in the future shall compose its citizenship.[507]

A .J. Poppleton met the future without fear, and with a manly heart; full of love for his family, his profession, his city, and his country. He lived his life fearlessly fighting for justice with integrity, honesty, courage and honor.

Fig 49. A.J. Poppleton 1890
Courtesy A.J. Poppleton III Personal Collection

EPILOGUE

The Legacy of A.J. Poppleton and the Early Settlers

Twelve years after the founding of Omaha in January 1866, Dr. George Miller invited a group of men to his residence at the Herndon House Hotel, 9th & Harney Street, to discuss how to preserve the history of the early settlers. Among the men attending were A.J. Poppleton, William D. Brown, William Snowden, James Megeath, Joseph W. Paddock, and John Withnell. The goal of the gathering was to organize *The Old Settlers Association* with membership limited to those living in the city prior to 1858. The officers elected were Dr. Enos Lowe, president; Dr. George Miller, vice-president; and A.D. Jones, secretary/treasurer.[508] The group disbanded after only two years, most likely because they were not yet ready to focus on the past; their thinking was future-oriented.

Twenty-one years later, on January 12, 1889, Dr. George Miller held an elaborate dinner event at the Omaha Club located at the U.S. National Bank building, 4th floor. He proposed to the sons of the early settlers that they should organize and re-name a successor to the Old Settlers Association, which they did - *The Sons of Omaha.* The preamble to its constitution listed a three-fold purpose: "(1) to perpetuate the history, memories and associations of early days in Omaha, (2) to promote good fellowship and common effort, and (3) to advance the best interests of the city."

No one was eligible for membership "unless the family of such applicant shall have resided in Omaha prior to the year 1870." Appropriately, William S. Poppleton, A.J.'s son, was the toastmaster at many subsequent dinners, and served as president in 1892.[509]

If we look back to the men and women who founded Omaha and saw it grow from a muddy pathway meandering through uncut grassland when Poppleton arrived in 1854 finding less than 20 people present, to the metropolis it became by Poppleton's death in 1896, when the city's population reached nearly 100,000, one might ask: How did they do it? What did they have in common?

- They valued education, many had a college or professional degree.
- They were religious, belonged to churches, yet were ecumenical.
- They promoted the arts, libraries, concerts, lectures, and cultural events.
- They built schools to provide their children with a good education.
- They fought to make Omaha the capital of the territory and develop a strong business environment attractive to national investment.
- They were generous with their time, talent and resources to support others.
- They enjoyed being together and celebrating their friendships with dances, festivals, open houses, receptions, and more.

Caroline Poppleton summarized the feelings the early settlers had for each other that lasted until the time of their deaths:

> I have seen Omaha grow from infancy. We were then all strangers in a strange land, young and happy, and dependent upon each other for society. What strong and enduring friendships were formed in those days, whose companionships and loving kindness were to be life-long, and what pleasure we take in talking over the pleasantness of the old times![510]

In his closing remarks to the faculty and students at the commencement ceremony for the University of Nebraska in Lincoln, June 1877, A.J. Poppleton shared the desire of the early settlers to leave a legacy for future generations based on peace, virtue and happiness:

> We, at least of the citizens of the State early cast our lot within its borders, and have long looked forward to the everlasting repose beneath its surface, may descend to our final rest assured that, however feebly and imperfectly, our hands have helped, in some measure, to rear a commonwealth under whose safe shelter, ages hence, shall rest in peace and virtue, a prosperous and happy people.[511]

Poppleton concluded his address with a poem expressing his love for his city and state with words like "goodly shore" and "earth's loveliest paradise." These words contrasted sharply with the words used in 1820 by Major Stephen A. Long, who led an expedition on behalf of the U.S. Corps of Topographical Engineers across the Great Plains to determine its suitability for settlement and growth. Major Long reported to the federal government that the area, which included Nebraska, was a "great desert ... and it is almost wholly unfit for cultivation and of course uninhabitable by a people depending upon agriculture for their subsistence."[512]

A. J. Poppleton countered Major Long's negative report, with a positive and uplifting poem:

> Great God! We thank Thee for this goodly shore;
> This bounteous birth land of the free;
> Where wanderers from afar may come
> And breathe the air of liberty.
> Still may her flowers untrampled spring;
> Her harvests wave and cities rise;
> And long till time shall fold his wing,
> Remain earth's loveliest paradise.[513]

ACKNOWLEDGEMENTS

I am grateful for the kindness shown to me by so many people who have generously shared their time and knowledge as I researched and wrote this book.

Thank you, Jill Jackson, historian and archivist at Trinity Episcopal Cathedral, for your hours of research, which provided me with photos and information about the lives of many of Omaha's early settlers who were also members of Trinity. It was touching to gaze at the window of Saint James the Minor, which has a memorial to Poppleton's three-year-old daughter, who died of typhoid fever.

Thank you to the staff at the Douglas County Historical Society, for your tireless work in locating photos, drawings and files on the early settlers: Whitney West, Executive Director; Elise O'Neil, Archivist; and Cynthia Hadsell, volunteer extraordinaire who were always ready and able to help me even when I dropped into the Crook House unannounced. I was honored to serve as a member of the Society's Board of Directors for six years and was privileged to be asked to create its Foundation and serve as its first president.

Thank you Haiden Nelson, Collection Technican, and Katie Dykstra, Photo Archivist at the Durham Museum for photos from the incomparable Bostwick/Frohardt collection.

Thank you, Tom Mooney, Curator of Manuscripts at the Nebraska State Historical Society, for a copy of Poppleton's Union Pacific file, as well as the early history of the Nebraska State Bar Association. Thank you Mary Jo Miller, Photo Archivist at the History Society, especially for the unique photo of the Rock Bluffs Precinct house where the "ballot box went to lunch", costing Poppleton election to the U.S. Senate.

Thank you, Charles Jan Headley, my former law partner, for reading portions of my early manuscript and raising pertinent questions that led me to further research.

Special thanks to John Mullen, a Fellow of the American College of Trial Lawyers and my friend for over 45 years, who read portions of the manuscript with his "fine-tooth pen." As former legal counsel to a number of railway companies, John's knowledge of railroad history in Nebraska was extremely beneficial, as was his analysis of some cases Poppleton handled for the UPRR.

Thanks to my brother Thomas Dwyer for discovering in the basement of our family home, a pristine edition of *Wolfe's City Directory* for the years 1878-79, as well as a first edition of many of the early histories of Omaha and Nebraska, especially Savage and Bell's *History of Omaha.*

Thank you, Kelly Golden, for locating the probate file of A.J. Poppleton's estate in the basement vault of the Douglas County Courthouse.

Thank you Wade Popp, Archive Specialist at the National Archives at Kansas City for the Federal Court of Nebraska; and Jessica May, Special Collections Archivist at the State Historical Society of Iowa; and Laura Steinman, Coordinator at Arbor Day Farm in Nebraska City; and Patricia LaBounty, Curator of the Union Pacific Railroad Museum in Council Bluffs, for answering questions and research topics on my behalf.

Thanks to Mike Nolan and the Board of Directors of Prospect Hill Cemetery organization who invited me to give the May 2024 Memorial Day address on the grounds of the cemetery. Standing among the graves of A.J. and Caroline

Poppleton, Hanscom, Woolworth, Reed, Lowe, Paddock, Lake, and hundreds more whom I respectfully referred to as "the living stones of Omaha history." Thank you Shannon Justice for the tour you gave me of the cemetery and monuments with your amazing recall of information.

Thank you Michelle Gullett, News Archives and Licensing Manager at Lee Enterprises, for the drawing of the Cyrus Tator hanging.

Thanks to Phil and Beth Black, of *The Bookworm,* an independently owned bookstore in Omaha, for your encouragement and support in writing and promoting my books.

Thanks to William R. Scanlin, J.D., for your research efforts at the United States Supreme Court for Poppleton's case filings.

No one who writes a story about a person or event in Omaha's early history can do so without a deep sense of gratitude to the scores of local historians who meet to discuss and preserve our history: Mike Nolan, Paul Hedren, Paul Berg, Michael Wagner of The Westerners International-Omaha Corral; Mitch McConnell and Kira Gale of The Trans-Mississippi Exposition Society; Betty Davis, Kathy Aultz, Pat Pixley of the Douglas County Historical Society; Harold Becker of the Omaha Dundee Sun; Dave Harding, Bob Marks and Stu Pospisil of the Omaha World Herald; Linda Meigs of The Florence Mill; my history professors at the University of Nebraska at Omaha, Dr. Harl Dalstrom and his wife Kay, Dr, Fred Adrian, Dr. Roy Robbins, Dr. Orville Menard and Dr. Bill Pratt; and Ron Hunter, Jeffrey Spencer, Joni Fogarty, Don Snoddy, Charles Martin, Barry Combes, Jim Fogarty, Eileen Wirth, and so many others.

Special thanks to Dr. Troy Johnson J.D., Director of Law Library, and Hans Herzl-Betz J.D., Reference and Instructional Service Librarian at the Creighton University School of Law Library, who were a tremendous help in locating information regarding the federal and state court cases in which Poppleton was involved. Thanks to Troy for inviting me to speak at the Midwest Law Librarians convention in November 2024, sharing that Poppleton was a founder of the first Law Library Association in Omaha. Special thanks to Hans for his extraordinary detective work regarding the Kidnapping and Snowplow cases.

Finally, I have been blessed with 40 years of marriage this year to my beautiful wife, Karen Kangas Dwyer, Ph.D., Professor Emeritus of the School of Communications, University of Nebraska-Omaha. In the midst of writing her own books, Karen listened to my story of A.J. Poppleton, read several drafts, offered many suggestions, and was my chief editor of the book. We enjoyed pouring over the many letters written between A.J. and Caroline and admiring their love and their joy of living in such an exciting era. I am grateful, Karen, that you have helped me tell the story of this great couple and their friends. There would be no book without you. All my love!

APPENDIX

Illustrations (By Fig. Number)

45. George L. Miller (ch. 28)
46. Trinity Church in Middle of Street (ch.29)
47. Caroline Poppleton at Home 1911 (ch. 29)
48. Caroline Poppleton at Home 1911 (ch. 29)
49. A.J. Poppleton 1892 (ch. 30)

Note: Illustrations #5, #12, #19, were drawn by Charles S. Huntington for Alfred Sorenson's History of Omaha (1889). Courtesy of Douglas County Historical Society.

Profiles (in alphabetical order)

- Baldwin, Charles A. (ch. 28 endnote)
- Barker Family (ch. 29 endnote)
- Beecher, Bishop George (ch. 29 endnote)
- Blatchford, Samuel (ch. 26 endnote)
- Briggs, Clinton (ch.17 endnote)
- Chase, Champion S. (ch. 29 endnote)
- Cowin, John C. (ch. 28 endnote)
- Creighton, Edward (ch. 12 endnote)
- Cuming, Thomas B. (ch. 5 & 11)
- Davis, Herbert (ch. 17 endnote)
- Dodge, Grenville (ch. 12)
- Estabrook, Experience (ch. 17 endnote)
- Hanscom, A.J. (ch. 3)
- Irvine, Frank (ch. 17 endnote)
- Jones, Alfred D. (ch .9)
- Kennedy, B.E. B. (ch.17 endnote)
- Learned, Myron (ch. 27 endnote)
- Lowe, Jesse (ch. 9)
- Manderson, Charles (ch. 17 endnote)
- Miller, Dr. George (ch. 28)
- Nott, Eliphalet (ch. 2)
- Paddock,. Algernon S. (ch. 29 endnote)
- Paddock, Joseph W. (ch. 8)
- Poppleton, Charlotte Kennedy (ch. 26 endnote)
- Poppleton, Helen Clarke Smith (ch. 26 endnote)
- Richardson, O.D. (ch. 4)
- Savage, James W. (ch. 17 endnote)
- Shannon, Major William (ch 27. endnote)
- Sherill, Rev. Alvin (ch. 28 endnote)
- Swartzlander, Albert (ch. 17 endnote)
- Train, George (ch.12 endnote)
- Wakeley, Eleazer (ch. 17)
- Webster, John L. (ch. 23)
- Woolworth, James M. (ch. 28)
- Yates, Henry W. (ch. 24 endnote)

Historical Notes (by chapter)

- A.J. Poppleton's Siblings (ch.1 endnote)
- Council Bluffs & Nebraska Ferry Co. (ch.3)
- Omaha's First Survey (ch.3 endnote)
- Omaha Tribe Cedes Land (ch. 4)
- First Settlers of Omaha (ch.4)
- Omaha's Earliest Homes (ch.4 endnote)
- Kansas-Nebraska Act 1854 (ch. 4 endnote)
- Nebraska Territory(ch.5)
- Francis Burt's Arduous Journey to Nebraska (ch.5)
- Results of First Census (ch.5)
- Organic Law of the Nebraska Territory (ch.5)
- Nebraska Territory Governors (ch. 5 endnote)
- Nebraska Territory Counties (ch.5 endnote)
- Initial Officers of Nebraska Territory (ch 5. endnote)
- Nebraska Territory First Code of Laws (ch. 7 endnote)
- Caroline Poppleton's Siblings (ch. 8 endnote)
- A.J. & Caroline Poppleton's Children (ch. 8 endnote)
- Enforcement of Claim Club Rules (ch.9)
- First Officers of City of Omaha (ch. 9 endnote)
- Preemption Act 1841 (ch.9 endnote)
- Thomas & Marguerite Cuming (ch.11)
- Stroke or Guillain-Barre Syndrome (ch.11)
- The Ballot Box That Went to Lunch
- Cozzens Hotel (ch.14 endnote)
- Brigham Young (ch 14 endnote)
- Pacific Railroad Act 1862 (ch. 15 endnote)
- Original Members of Omaha Bar Association (ch. 17 endnote)
- Omaha in 1868 (ch. 19)
- Brownell Hall (ch. 21 endnote)
- Standing Bear's War Bonnett (ch. 22 endnote)
- Poppleton homes (ch.25 endnote)
- Bright's Disease (ch. 29 endnote)
- Prospect Hill Cemetery (ch. 28)
- Trinity Episcopal Cathedral (ch. 29
- Bishop Clarkson Memorial Hospital & School of Nursing (ch. 29)

BIBLIOGRAPHY

Published Works

Aldrich, Robert S. *Omaha World Herald Centennial Edition.* May 9, 1954.

Ambrose, Stephen E. *Nothing Like It in the World. The Men Who Built the Transcontinental Railroad* 1863-1869. New York: Simon & Schuster, 2000.

Andreas, Alfred T. *History of the State of Nebraska.* Chicago: The Western Historical Company, 1882.

Antieau, Chester J. *Modern Constitutional Law. vol. 1.* Rochester, NY: The Lawyers Co-operative Publishing Company, 1969

Baker v. Morton, 79 U.S.150, (1870).

Baker, Ray P. Ed. *The Collected Works of Abraham Lincoln.* New Brunswick: Rutgers University Press, vol I. 1953.

Bain, David Howard. *Empire Express: Building The First Transcontinental Railroad.* New York: Penguin Books, 1999.

Baldwin, Sara Mullin, ed. *Who's Who In Omaha 1928.* Omaha: Robert M. Baldwin Publishers, 1928.

Ballowe, James. *The Life of Joy Morton. A Man of Salt and Trees.* DeKalb: Northern Illinois University Press, 2009.

Barrett, Jay Amos. *The History and Government of Nebraska.* Lincoln: J.H. Miller Publishers, 1892.

Barrett, Jay Amos. *Legislators of 1855: Biographical Fragments. Proceedings and Collection of the Nebraska State Historical Society, Second Series Vol II.* Lincoln: State Journal Printing Company (1898), 124-134.

Baydo, Gerald. *"Overland from Missouri to Washington Territory in 1854."* Nebraska History 52, no.1 (Spring 1971): 65-87.

Beadle, Erastus F. *To Nebraska in 1857.* N.Y. Public Library Bulletin, February-March 1923, reprinted by Omaha Public Library, 1923.

Black's Law Dictionary. 6th ed. St. Paul: West, 1990.

Blackstone, William. *Commentaries on the Laws of England.* Edited by W.M. Hardcastle Browne. St. Paul: West, 1897 [1750].

Bodayla, Stephen D. *"Can an Indian Vote?: Elk V. Wilkins: A setback for Indian Citizenship."* Nebraska History 67, no.4 (Winter 1986): 372-80.

Boughter, Judith A. *Betraying The Omaha Nation 1790-1916.* Norman: University of Oklahoma Press, 1998.

Bristow, David. *A Dirty Wicked Town: Tales of 19th Century Omaha.* Caldwell ID: Caxton Press, 2009.

Broadfield, Wm.E. *Stories of Omaha. Historical Sketches of the Midland City.* Omaha: Nichols & Broadfield, 1898.

Brown v. Pierce 74 U.S. 205. (1868).

Brown, Dee. *Bury My Heart At Wounded Knee.* New York: Holt, Rinehart and Winston, 1970.

Brown, Dee. *Hear That Lonesome Whistle Blow.* New York: Holt, Rinehart and Winston, 1977.

Brown, Wallace. *"George L. Miller and the Boosting of Omaha."* Nebraska History 50, no.3 (Fall 1969): 277-91.

Burkley, Frank. *The Faded Frontier.* Omaha: Burkley Envelope and Printing Company, 1935.

Byers, William N. History Nebraska. https://history.nebraska.gov/publications_section/william-n-byers/

Cameron, J. S. *Bright's Disease Today: The Pathogenesis and Treatment of Glomerulonephritis.* British Medical Journal, 1972, 4:87-90.

Canellos, Peter S. *The Great Dissenter, The Story of John Marshall Harlan, America's Judicial Hero.* New York: Simon & Schuster, 2021.

Cases Determined in the United States, Circuit Courts for the Eighth Circuit. 5. Reported by John F. Dillon, the Circuit Judge. Davenport IA: Egbert, Fidlar & Chambers, 1880.

Casper, Henry W. S.J. *History of The Catholic Church In Nebraska. Vol 1.* Milwaukee: Bruce Press, 1960.

Chudacoff, Howard P. *"Where Rolls the Dark Missouri Down."* Nebraska History 52, no.1 (Spring 1971): 1-30.

Combes, Barry. *"The Union Pacific Railroad and the Early Settlement of Nebraska 1868-1880."* Nebraska History 50, no.1 (Spring 1969): 1-26.

Combes, Barry. *Westward to Promontory.* Palo Alto CA: American West Publishing Co. (1969)

Constitution & By-Laws of the Nebraska State Bar Association. Lincoln: Beach's State Capitol Book and Job Printing House. 1876. Nebraska State Historical Society.

Council Bluffs Remembered, Council Bluffs: Nonpareil Publishing, 2004.

Curley, Edwin A. *Nebraska 1875.* Lincoln: University of Nebraska Press, 2006.

Davis, Betty J. *Above All Others on a Stream.* Omaha: Douglas County Historical Society, 2009.

Deloria, Vine Jr. and Clifford M. Lytle. *American Indians, American Justice.* Austin: University of Texas Press, 1983.

Diffendal, Anne Polk. *A Centennial History of the Nebraska State Historical Society. 1878-1978.* Lincoln: Nebraska State Historical Society, 1978.

Dodge, Grenville M. *How We Built the Union Pacific Railway and Other Railway Papers and Addresses.* Council Bluffs: The Monarch Printing Co., 1914.

Dodge, Grenville M. *Personal Recollections of Lincoln.* Council Bluffs: The Monarch Printing Co., 1911.

Dorsey, James Owen. *"Migrations of Siouan Tribes."* American Naturalist 20, no.30 (March 1886):211-22.

Douglas County Historical Society. *The Banner* (Omaha, NE). December 2008.

Douglas County Historical Society. *The Connection* (Omaha, NE). Issue 2, 2019.

Durant, Samuel W. *History of Oakland County.* 1877.

Dustin, Dorothy Devereux. *Omaha & Douglas County. A Panoramic History.* Woodland Hills, CA: Windsor Pub., 1980.

Dwyer, Lawrence A. *Standing Bear's Quest For Freedom: The First Civil Rights Victory for Native Americans.* Lincoln: University of Nebraska Press, 2022.

Dwyer, Lawrence A. *Before We Came - They Were Here: The Meaning of the Law.* Douglas County Historical Society. The Banner (Omaha, NE) , Summer 2010.

Edmunds, A.C. *Pen Sketches of Nebraskans.* Omaha: R & J. Wilbur Stationers, 1871.
Farnham, Wallace D. "The Pacific Railroad Act of 1862." Nebraska History 43, (September 1962): 141-168.

Fletcher, Alice C. and Francis LaFlesche. *The Omaha Tribe, vol. I.* Lincoln: University of Nebraska Press, 1992. (Originally published by Smithsonian Institution Bureau of American Ethnology [Washington DC: Government Printing Office, 1911).]

Fletcher, Alice C. and Francis LaFlesche. *The Omaha Tribe, vol. II.* Lincoln: University of Nebraska Press, 1992. (Originally published by Smithsonian Institution Bureau of American Ethnology [Washington DC: Government Printing Office, 1911).]

Fox, Dixon Ryan. *Dr. Eliphalet Nott (1773-1866) – and the American Spirit.* Princeton: N.J. 1944.

Frisbie v. Whitney, 76 U.S. 187, 194 (1869).

Gaylord, Mrs. Mary M. *Life & Labors of Rev. Reuben Gaylord.* Omaha: Rees Printing Company 1889.

Gendler, Carol. *"Territorial Omaha as a Staging and Freighting Center."* Nebraska History 49, no.2 (Summer 1968): 103-120.

Gless, Alan G., ed. *The History of Nebraska Law.* Athens: Ohio University Press, 2008.

Goss, J.Q. *Bellevue: It Past and Present.* Proceedings and Collection of the Nebraska State Historical Society, Second Series Vol II. Lincoln: State Journal Printing Company (1898), 36-47.

Guentzel, Richard. *"The Department of the Platte and Western Settlement."* Nebraska History 56, no.3 (Fall 1975): 389-417.

Hall, A.J. *History of Omaha 1857-1870.* Omaha: Daily Republican Steam Printing House, 1870.

Harding, David. *Wildly Colorful George Francis Train.* Omaha World Herald, November 9, 2008.

Harding, David. *Herald Publisher George L. Miller Sought To Astonish The World.* Omaha World Herald, Nov 15, 2015.

Harkins, Michael J. *"George Washington Lininger: Pioneer Merchant and Art Patron."* Nebraska History 52, no.4 (Winter 1971): 347-357.

Hirshson, Stanley P. *Grenville M. Dodge.* Bloomington: Indiana University Press, 1967.

History Nebraska. *Charles Frederick Manderson 1837-1911.* https://history.nebraska.gov/collection_section/charles- frederick-manderson-1837-1911-rg1211-am/

History Nebraska. *Thomas B. Cuming 1827-1858.* https://history.nebraska.gov/collection_section/thomas-b-cuming-rg3654-am/

Historic Prospect Hill Cemetery Walking or Driving Tour Guide. Omaha, 2007.

Homer, Michael W. *"The Territorial Judiciary: An Overview of the Nebraska Experience, 1854-1867.* Nebraska History 63, no.3 (Fall 1982): 349-380.

Howard, James H. *The Ponca Tribe.* Lincoln: University of Nebraska Press, 1995. Originally published by the Smithsonian Institution Bureau of American Ethnology, Bulletin no. 195 (Washington: U.S. GPO, 1965).

In The Matter of the Estate of Andrew J. Poppleton with Last Will & Testament, First Codicil, Second Codicil. File of County Court of Douglas County, Nebraska.

In Memoriam. Andrew J. Poppleton. Report of Cases In The Supreme Court of Nebraska January Term 1896. vol xlviii. Lincoln: State Journal Company, Law Publishers (1896).

Isaacs, Garvin A. *"With Liberty and Justice for All."* The Oklahoma Bar Journal 87, no.21 (2016): 1508, 1547.

Jefferson, Thomas. *A Manual of Parliamentary Practice for the Use of the Senate of the United States, 1801.*https://digitalarchive.wm.edu/hndle/10288/13433

Jensen, Oliver. *The American Heritage History of Railroads in America.* New York: American Heritage Publishing Co. a subsidiary of McGraw-Hill Inc., 1975.

Jensen, Richard E. *"Bellevue: The First Twenty Years, 1822-1842."* Nebraska History 56, no.3 (Fall 1975): 339-374.

Johnson, Harrison. *History of Nebraska.* Omaha: Herald Printing House, 1880.

Johnson and Graham's Lessee v. William M'Intosh, 21 U.S. 543 (1823).

Kalisch, Philip A. *"High Culture on the Frontier: The Omaha Library Association."* Nebraska History 52, no.4 (Winter 1971): 411-417.

Kammer, Sean. *Public Opinion is More than Law: Popular Sovereignty and Vigilantism in the Nebraska Territory.* University of South Dakota Law School. 2011.

Katz, Wendy Jean, ed. *The Trans-Mississippi and International Expositions of 1898-1899.* Lincoln: University of Nebraska Press, 2018.

Kelly, Alfred H. and Winfred A. Harbison. *The American Constitution: It Origins and Development.* New York: W.W. Norton & Company, 1948.

Kent, James. *Commentaries On American Law. Edi*ted by John M. Gould. Boston: Little, Brown, Co.1896 [1826].

Klein, Maury. *Union Pacific: Vol I, The Birth of a Railroad 1862-1893.* Garden City, NY: Doubleday (1987).

Kratville, William. *Images of Rail: Railroads of Omaha and Council Bluffs.* Charleston: Arcadia Publishing, 2002.

Lake, Carlos W. *The Kidnapping of Judge A.W. Stone.* Denver: The Colorado Magazine, vol. xvii, no 1 (January 1940) 19-26.

Lambertson, Genio M. *"Indian Citizenship."* American Law Review 20 (March-April 1886): 183-85.

Larsen, Lawrence H., and Barbara J. Cottrell. *The Gate City: A History of Omaha.* Lincoln: University of Nebraska Press, 1997.

Larsen, Lawrence H., and Barbara J. Cottrell and Harl A. Dalstrom and Kay Calame Dalstrom. *Upstream Metropolis. An Urban Biography of Omaha & Council Bluffs.* Lincoln: University of Nebraska Press, 2007.

MacMurphy, Harriet S. *Nebraska Women in 1855.* Proceedings and Collection of the Nebraska State Historical Society, Second Series Vol II. Lincoln: State Journal Printing Company (1898), 162-178.

Magid, Paul. *An Honest Enemy. George Crook and the Struggles for Indian Rights.* Norman: University of Oklahoma Press, 2020.

Marks, Bob. *Omaha History Detective. Mysteries, Myths & Memories For Our Last 220 Years.* Wadsworth Publishing, 2022.

Marquett, T.M.. *"The Effect of Early Legislation Upon the Courts of Nebraska."* Proceedings and Collection of the Nebraska State Historical Society vol 1, no 2. (1894), 103-106.

Martin, Albro. *Railroads Triumphant.* New York: Oxford University Press, 1992.
Martin, Charles W. "Herndon House Register, 1865-1866." Nebraska History 48, no.1 (Spring 1967): 27-43.

Martin, Charles W. *"Joseph Barker and the 1868 Union Pacific Railroad Excursion From Omaha."* Nebraska History 58, no.2 (Summer 1977): 123-148.

Martin, Charles W. *"Omaha in 1868-1869: Selections From the Letters of Joseph Barker."* Nebraska History 59, no.4 (Winter 1978): 501-525.

Martin, Charles W. *The Church In the Middle of The Street: A History of Trinity Episcopal Cathedral Omaha, Nebraska.* The Bishop and Vestry of Trinity Cathedral Dilley Manufacturing Co. 1983.

Mayo Clinic https://www.mayoclinic.org/diseases-conditions/guillain-barre-syndrome/diagnosis-treatment/drc-20363006

Territorial Legislature Meeting. Winter Session 1865-57. https://www.historicflorence.org/HistoricEvents/TerritorailLegislatureX.php

Morton, Julius Sterling, George Miller, Albert Watkins. *Illustrated History of Nebraska. Vol 1.* Lincoln: Western Publisher and Engraving Company. 1911.

Morton, J. Sterling. *Tribute to A.J. Poppleton.* Proceedings and Collection of the Nebraska State Historical Society, Second Series Vol II. Lincoln: State Journal Printing Company (1898), 108-110.

Morton, J. Sterling. *J.W. Paddock.* Proceedings and Collection of the Nebraska State Historical Society, Second Series Vol II. Lincoln: State Journal Printing Company (1898), 110-115.

McKay v. Campbell, 2 Sawy.118,134, 5 Am. Law T. Rep. U.S. Cts 407 (Dist. Oregon) 1871.

Moriarty, Ed. F. *Omaha Memories 1880-1916.* Omaha: Swartz Printing Co. 1917.

National Kidney Foundation. *What is Glomerulonephritis?* 2024.

National Register of Historic Places Inventory – Nomination Form. 1982.

Nebraska Authors. *James Mills Woolworth.* https://nebraskaauthors.org/authors/james-m-woolworth.

Nichols, Roger L. *"Stephen Long And Scientific Exploration On The Plains."* Nebraska History 52, no.1 (Spring 1971): 51-63.

Nichols, Roger L. And Patrick L. Halley. *Stephen Long And American Frontier Exploration.* Norman: University of Oklahoma Press , 1995.

Nicholas, Roy F. *"The Kansas-Nebraska Act: A Century of Historiography:* Mississippi Valley Historical Review 43 (September 1956), 187-212.

NIH https://www.ninds.nih.gov/health-information/disorders/guillain-barre-syndrome

Olson, James C. *History of Nebraska.* Lincoln: University of Nebraska Press, 1974.

Olson, James C. J. *Sterling Morton.* Lincoln: University of Nebraska Press, 1942.

Otis, Harry B. and Donald H. Erickson. *E Pluribus Omaha. Immigrants All.* Omaha: Lamplighter Press, Douglas County Historical Society, 2000.

Paz, D.G. *"A study in Adaptability: The Episcopal Church in Omaha, 1856-1919."* Nebraska History 62, no.1 (Spring 1981): 107-130.

Pattison, Robert E.; et al. *Report of the United States Pacific Railway Commission* [and testimony taken by the Commission]. Washington, U.S. G.P.O. (1887).

Price, David H. *"Sectionalism In Nebraska: When Kansas Considered Annexing Southern Nebraska, 1856-1860."* Nebraska History 53, no.4 (Winter 1972): 411-417.

Poppleton, Andrew J. *Reminiscences.* Lincoln: Nebraska Historical Society, 1915.

Poppleton, Andrew J. *An Address. The Lawyer In Politics.* Nebraska State Bar Association. Lincoln: Journal Company, State Printing, 1880.

Poppleton, Andrew J. *An Address. Character. Its Development and Exaltation The True End of Education.* University of Nebraska Fifth Annual Commencement. Lincoln: University Publishing Co. 1877.

Proceedings and Collection of the Nebraska State Historical Society, Second Series Vol II. Lincoln: State Journal Printing Company, 1898.

Reeves, Thomas C. *Gentleman Boss: The Life and Times of Chester Alan Arthur.* Newtown, Connecticut: American Political Biography Press, 1975.

Reilly, Bob and Hugh Reilly and Pegeen Reilly. *Historic Omaha. An Illustrated History of Omaha and Douglas County.* Omaha: Douglas County Historical Society. 2003.

Rogers, S.E. *Sketches of Members of the Legislature of 1855.* Proceedings and Collection of the Nebraska State Historical Society, Second Series Vol II. Lincoln: State Journal Printing Company (1898), 115-120.

Rollings, Willard Hughes. *"Citizenship and Suffrage: The Native American Struggles For Civil Rights In the American West, 1830-1965.* 5 Nev. Law Journal 126 (2004).

Runnymede and Magna Carta. Rotherham, England: The National Trust, 2019.

Savage, James W. and John T. Bell. *History of the City of Omaha, Nebraska and South Omaha.* New York: Munsell and Company 1894.

Schleicher, John. *First Omaha Doctor Served Nebraska Territory and State.* McGoogan Library of Medicine, University of Nebraska Medical Center. March 1, 2017. https://www.unmc.edu/newsroom/2017/03/01/first-omaha-doctor-served-nebraska-territory-and-state/

Seymour, Silas. *"The Great Union Pacific Excursion, 1866."* Nebraska History 50, no.1 (Spring 1969): 27-53.

Sheldon, Addison E. *History and Stories of Nebraska.* Lincoln: University Publishing Company. 1913.

Sheldon, Addison E. *Nebraska-The Land and the People, Vol 1.* New York: The Lewis Publishing Company, 1931.

Sheldon, Addison E. *Nebraska Old and New: History, Stories, Folklore.* Lincoln: University Publishing Company. 1937.

Snoddy, Don, Barry Combes, Bob Marks, and Del Webber, eds. *Their Man in Omaha. The Barker Letters: I, 1860-1868.* Omaha: Douglas County Historical Society, 2004.

Snoddy, Don, Barry Combes, Bob Marks, and Del Webber, eds. *Their Man in Omaha. The Barker Letters: II, 1860-1868.* Omaha: Douglas County Historical Society, 2004.

Sorensen, Alfred. *The Story of Omaha From The Pioneer Days to the Present Time.* Omaha: Gibson, Miller & Richardson Printers, 1889.

Spencer, Jeffrey. *Historic Photos of Omaha.* Nashville, TN: Turner Publishing Company, 2007.

Stahr, Walter. *Seward: Lincoln's Indispensable Man.* New York: Simon & Schuster, 2012.

Stevens, Thomas M. *The Union Pacific Railroad and the Mormon Church, 1868-1871.* Brigham Young University. 1972. https://scholarsarchive.byu.edu/etd

Stowell, C.R. ed. *The Pioneer Record.* Stowell & Kent Publishers, Auburn, NE: May 1896.

Sun, J., Gao, Y., Chi, L., Cao, Q., Ning, Z., & Nan, G. (2021). *Case Report: Early-Onset Guillain–Barre Syndrome Mimicking Stroke.* Frontiers in \urology, 12, 525699. https://doi.org/10.3389/fneur.2021.525699

Thavenet, Dennis. *"The Territorial Governorship: Nebraska Territory As Example."* Nebraska History 51, no.4 (Winter 1970): 387-409.

Thavenet, Dennis. *"Governor William A. Richardson: Champion of Popular Sovereignty in Territorial Nebraska."* Nebraska History 53, no.4 (Winter 1972): 463-476.

The Constitution of the United States. Washington DC: Smithsonian Institution, 2022.

"The Life of Governor Burt." Proceedings and Collection of the Nebraska State Historical Society vol 1, no 1. (1894), 25-38.

The Omaha Bee. *Nebraskans 1854-1904.* The Bee Publishing Co. Omaha: 1904.

The Cherokee Nation v. The State of Georgia, 30 U.S. 1 (1831).

The Omaha Mercury. Official Paper Nebraska Legal Fraternity. Omaha, Vol. XXVI. no 11.

Tibbles, Thomas H. *Buckskin and Blanket Days.* Lincoln: University of Nebraska Press, 1969.

Tibbles, Thomas H. *The Ponca Chiefs: An Account of the Trial of Standing Bear.* Edited by Kay Graber. Lincoln: University of Nebraska Press, 1972 [1880].

Tocqueville, Alexis de. *Democracy in America. 1835.* Edited by Richard D. Heffner. New York: New American Library 1956.

Train, George Francis. *My Life In Many States and in Foreign Lands, Dictated in My Seventy-Fourth Year.* New York: D. Appleton and Company, 1902.

"Typhoid." World Health Organization, March 30, 2003. https://www.who.int/news-room/fact sheets/detail/typhoid#:~:text=Persons%20with%20 typhoid%20fever%20carry,serious%20 Implications%20or%20even%20death.

U.S. Congress. *Habeas Corpus Act of 1867.*14 Stat.385.

U.S. Congress. *Homestead Act of 1862.* Pub L. 37-64.

U.S. Congress. *Kansas-Nebraska Act of 1854.* 10 Stat.277.33rd Cong.

U.S. Congress. *Indian Freedom Citizenship Suffrage Act. of 1924* (Snyder Act). 8 U.S.C. ch.12, subch.111, 1041b. 68th Cong. 1st Sess. hhtps://legislink.org/us/stat

U.S. Congress. *Message of the President of the United States.* 38th Cong. 1st Sess. Senate Ex. Doc. No. 27.

U.S. Congress. *Pacific Railroad Act. 1862.*

U.S. Congress Senate. *Report of the Secretary of the Interior.* H.R. Ex. Doc. No.1, 47th Cong 1st Sess 1881.

U.S. Congress. *The Preemption Act* (27th Congress, Ch 16, 5 Stat.453 (1841). Repealed 1891.

United States and Johnson, 1865-1869, '*Treaty between the United States of America and the Omaha Tribe of Indians. Concluded Mary 6, 1865. Ratification advised February 13, 1866. Proclaimed February 15, 1866.*' (1866) https://digitalcommons.unomaha.edu/ascdigitizedbooks/19S.- Omaha Tribe Treaty of 1854.

United States Department of Justice. Justice Manual 215. *Mandamus.*

U.S. Dept of the Interior, *National Register of Historical Places Inventory – Nomination Form 1982.*

United States v. Omaha Tribe of Indians, 253 U.S. 275 (1920.)

Union Pacific Rail Road 1864-1880 Timeline. UtahRails.Net. https://utahrails.net/up/up-timeline-1864-1880.php

Wakeley, Arthur C. Omaha: The Gate City and Douglas County, Nebraska. Vol 1. Chicago: The S.J. Clarke Publishing Company 1917.

Wakeley, Eleazer. *"Reminiscences of the Third Judicial District, 1857-1861."* Proceedings and Collection of the Nebraska State Historical Society vol 1, no 1. (1895), 150-163.

Warner, Dr. Richard and Ryan Rosenfeld. *Images of America: Council Bluffs Broadway.* Chicago: Arcadia Publishing, 2007.

Welsch, Roger L. *"The Myth of the Great American Desert."* Nebraska History 52, no.3 (Fall 1971): 255-265.

Williams, John Hoyt. *A Great and Shining Road. The Epic Story of The Transcontinental Railroad.* New York: Random House, Times Books. (1989).

Wirth, Eileen. *The Women Who Built Omaha.* Lincoln: University of Nebraska Press, 2022.

Wirth, Eileen. *We Belong Here: The Story of St. John's Church and Its People.* Omaha: St. John's Parish, 2023.

Wolfe J.M. *Omaha City Directory 1878-79.* Omaha: Herald Publishing.

Woolworth, James M. and William S. Poppleton. *Biography of Andrew Jackson Poppleton.* Proceedings and Collection of the Nebraska State Historical Society, Second Series Vol II. Lincoln: State Journal Printing Company (1898), 94-108.

Woolworth, James M. *Nebraska in 1857.* New York: C.C. Woolworth A.S. Barnes & Co. 1857.

Woolworth, James M. *John Marshall: An Address Delivered before the Omaha Bar Association on John Marshall day, February 4, 1901.* Omaha: The Association (1901).

Woolworth, James M. *The Dignity, Service & Prospects of the Profession of Law: An Address delivered before the Nebraska Bar Association January 1877.* Omaha: G.W. Gray Law Brief and Job Printer (1901)

Woolworth, James M. *Reports of Cases in the Supreme Court of Nebraska.* Chicago: Callaghan & Cockcroft, 1871.

Wright, Charles E. *Law At Little Big Horn. Due Process Denied.* Lubbock: Texas Tech University Press, 2016.

Wunder, John R. *Retained by The People. A History of American Indians and the Bill of Rights.* New York: Oxford University Press, 1994.

Wunder, John R. and Mark R. Scherer. *Echo of It Time: The History of the Federal District Court of Nebraska, 1867-1933*. Lincoln: University of Nebraska Press, 2019.

Wyman, Walker D. *"Omaha: Frontier Depot and Prodigy of Council Bluffs."* Nebraska History 27, (July-September 1936): 143-155.

Catalogues, Diaries, Journals, Letters

(Courtesy of the A. J. Poppleton III Personal Collection except as noted)

Adams, Charles F. *Charles F. Adams to A.J. Poppleton*. Boston: January 9, 1888.

Adams, Charles F. *Charles F. Adams Circular Letter*. Boston: November 21, 1885.

Adams, Charles F. *Charles F. Adams to A.J. Poppleton*. Boston: December 12, 1887.

Ames, Fred L. *Fred L. Ames to A.J. Poppleton*. Boston: January 18, 1888.

Art Loan Catalogue, 1879.

Burke, Stevenson. *Burke Stevenson to Hon. A.J. Poppleton,* Cleveland: July 28, 1892.

Catalogue of Books. The Omaha Public Library Association. 1877.

Circular of Brownell Hall, Omaha, Nebraska, September 17, 1867.

City of Omaha, Council Chamber. October 6, 1896.

Cuming, Thomas B. *Thomas B. Cuming to Marguerite Murphy*. Keokuk, IA: December 12, 1852. Douglas County Historical Society.

Cuming, Thomas B. *Thomas B. Cuming to Marguerite Murphy*. Keokuk, IA: January 9, 1853. Douglas County Historical Society.

Cumming, G.M. *G.M. Cumming to A.J. Poppleton*. Boston: December 16, 1886.

Dillion, John F. *John F. Dillon to Andrew J. Poppleton*, New York: January 6, 1888.

Dillion, John F. *John F. Dillon to Andrew J. Poppleton*, New York: January 13, 1888.

Dillion, John F. *John F. Dillon to Andrew J. Poppleton*. New York: February 14, 1888.

Douglas County Bar Association. *Constitution and By-Laws*. 1875.

First Annual Report of the Trade and Commerce of Omaha Nebraska for the Board of Trade for the Year Ending December 31, 1877.

Foote, William. *William Foote to Caroline Poppleton.* Ogdensburg, NY: November 27, 1889.

Groves, John. *John Groves to A.J. Poppleton.* Omaha: December 16, 1890.

Hooker, William V. *William V. Hooker to A.J. Poppleton.* Indianapolis: October 14, 1892.

Kelly, William R. *William R. Kelly to A.J. Poppleton.* Lincoln: January 21, 1888.

Laws, Resolutions and Memorials Passed at The Regular Session of the First General Assembly of the Territory of Nebraska Convened at Omaha City, on the 16th Day of January, Anno Domini, 1855.

Learned, Myron L. Myron L. Learned to Clarence S. Paine Secretary of the Nebraska State Historical Society. Omaha: January 26, 1915.

Lemon, Thomas B. *Thomas B. Lemon to A.J. and Caroline Poppleton.* North Platte, NE: December 4, 1880.

Lemon, Margaret. Margaret Lemon to Caroline Poppleton. December 30, 1908.

Manderson, Charles W. *Eulogy* September 28, 1896.

Maxwell, Samuel. *Judge Samuel Maxwell to A.J. Poppleton.* Lincoln: July 3, 1877.

Morton, J. Sterling. *J. Sterling Morton to Andrew J. Poppleton.* Chicago: June 9, 1892.

Morton, J. Sterling. *J. Sterling Morton to Andrew J. Poppleto.* Washington D.C. November 6, 1893.

Omaha Bar Association. *Constitution and By-Laws.* 1889.

Omaha Library Association Annual Report 1890.

Poppleton, Andrew J. Journal of the Thoughts, Feelings and Lurubrations, of Andrew J. Poppleton While A Student In Union College. Schenectady, NY: 1850-1851.

Poppleton, Andrew J. Address Delivered Before The Agricultural Society of the County of Oakland. September 30, 1852.

Poppleton, Andrew J. *A. J. Poppleton to Andrew Raymond.* Omaha: May 15, 1895.

Poppleton, Andrew J. *A.J. Poppleton to Caroline Poppleton.* Washington D.C.: January 25, 1878.

Poppleton, Andrew J. *A.J. Poppleton to Libby Poppleton.* Washington D.C.: February 9, 1878.

Poppleton, Andrew J. *A.J. Poppleton to Caroline Poppleton.* Washington D.C.: April 3, 1882.

Poppleton, Andrew J. *A. J. Poppleton to C.W. Hatch.* Omaha: August 8, 1889.

Poppleton, Andrew J. *A. J. Poppleton to John F. Dillon.* Omaha: January 4, 1888.

Poppleton, Andrew J. *A. J. Poppleton to John F. Dillon.* Omaha: January 10, 1888.

Poppleton, Andrew J. *A. J. Poppleton to John F. Dillon.* Omaha: May 15, 1895.

Poppleton, Andrew J. *A. J. Poppleton to M.F. Sears.* Omaha: February 28, 1887.

Poppleton, Andrew J. *A.J. Poppleton to Sidney Dillon.* Omaha: December 10, 1875. Nebraska State Historical Society.

Poppleton, Andrew J. *A. J. Poppleton to Thomas C. Durant.* Omaha: July 4, 1870.

Poppleton, Andrew J. *The Pacific Railroads: Suggestions submitted to the Hon. Charles Devens, attorney general of the United States,* on the resolutions of the Senate and House of Representatives in respect to the operation of the Union Pacific Railroad and branches: on behalf of said railroad company. Washington DC: Gibson Brothers Printers. (1877)

Poppleton, Caroline. *Caroline Poppleton to A.J. Poppleton.* Omaha: September 27, 1860.

Poppleton, Caroline. *Diary of Events.* Omaha: May 2, 1854 -August 18, 1905.

Poppleton, Caroline. *Caroline Poppleton to Mary Rockwood Powers.* Omaha: December 8, 1854. Douglas County Historical Society.

Poppleton, Caroline. *The War Bonnet.* Lincoln: Nebraska Historical Society, 1915.

Poppleton, Elizabeth. *Elizabeth "Libby" Poppleton to A.J. and Caroline Poppleton.* Poughkeepsie, NY: November 12, 1877.

Poppleton, Elizabeth, *Thomas Carlyle: A Study of His Life and Work.* Omaha: F.C. Festner & Son Printing House, 1877.

Poppleton, Elizabeth, *Saint Paul.* (unpublished manuscript).

Poppleton, Orrin. *Orrin Poppleton to A.J. Poppleton.* Birmingham, MI: November 30, 1880.

Poppleton, Orrin. *Sketch of William Poppleton.* Michigan Pioneer Collections, vol 297, 1886.

Potter, T.J. *T.J. Potter to A.J. Poppleton.* Burlington, IA. January 19, 1888.

Raymond, Andrew. *Andrew Raymond to A.J. Poppleton.* Schenectady, NY: May 9, 1895.

Rockwood, Mary Powers. *Overland Journal April to October 1856.* Douglas County Historical Society.

Rooker, William. *William Rooker to A.J. Poppleton.* Indianapolis, October 14, 1892.

Savidy, W.H. *W.H. Savidy to A.J. Poppleton.* Pocatello, ID: January 23, 1888.

Sickels, Frederick E. *Frederick E. Sickels to A.J. Poppleton.* Philadelphia: March 20, 1878. Nebraska State Historical Society.

Thurston, John M. *John M. Thurston to A. J. Poppleton.* Omaha: May 13, 1892.

Twenty-Fifth Annual Catalogue of Vassar College, 1889-1890. Poughkeepsie: A.V. Haight, Printer, 1890. Union Pacific Railroad Co. Corporate Resolution. Boston: March 29, 1886.

Union College. *Invitation to Centennial Celebration, 1895.*

Weidensall, Robert. *Robert Weidensall to A. J. Poppleton.* Chicago: January 16, 1888.

Williams, P.J. *P.J. Williams to A.J. Poppleton.* Salt Lake City: January 25, 1888.

Word, Samuel. *Samuel Word to A.J. Poppleton.* Butte City, MT: July 1, 1888.

Newspapers

Ann Arbor Courier
Deseret News of Salt Lake City, Utah
Detroit Free Press
New York Tribune
Omaha Arrow
Omaha Bee News
Omaha Daily Herald
Omaha Excelsion
Omaha Times
Omaha World Herald
Poughkeepsie Eagle-News
The Nebraska Palladium
Wheeling Intelligencer
Lincoln Journal

U.S. Supreme Court: Cases Filed by Poppleton

(incomplete list)

Elk v. Wilkins, 112 U.S. 94 (1884)

Kansas Pacific Railway Company and The Denver Pacific Railway and Telegraph Company v. The Union Pacific Railroad Company, Filed in the Circuit Court of the United States District of Nebraska (1868) Appealed to the United States Supreme Court 95 U. S. 279 (1877).

Ponca Tribe of Indians v. Makh-pi-ah-lu-tah, or Red Cloud, in his own behalf and in behalf of the Sioux Tribe of Indians, Fed. Dist. Ct. (D. Nebraska 1880).
Railroad Company v. Durant, 95 U.S. 576, (1877)

United States ex.rel Standing Bear v. Crook, 5 Dill.453, 25 F.Cas.695 (D. Nebraska 1879).

Union Pacific Railway Co. v. Cheyenne, 113 U.S. 516 (1885)

Union Pacific Railway Company, et.al. v. The Chicago, Rock Island & Pacific, and The Chicago, Milwaukee & St. Paul Railway Companies. An Argument Made In The United States Court of Appeals For the Eighth Circuit. Omaha: Rees Printing Company (1892).

United States ex.rel Hall et all. v. Union Pacific Railroad Co. (4 Dill.479. Circuit Court, D. Iowa. May Term 1875. Affirmed by United States Supreme Court at the October Term 1875, 91 U.S. 343.

Wardell v. Railroad Company, 103 U.S. 651, 26 L.Ed.509 (1880)

Nebraska Supreme Court: Cases Filed by Poppleton

(incomplete list)

Aumock v. Jamison. 1 Neb. 432 ; 1871 Neb. LEXIS 54
Ballou v. Sherwood. 32 Neb. 666 ; 49 N.W. 790 ; 1891 Neb. LEXIS 340
Burlington & M.R.R. Co. v. Kearney Co.17 Neb. 511 ; 23 N.W. 559 ; 1885 Neb. LEXIS 202
Damon v. Omaha. 38 Neb. 583 ; 1894 Neb. LEXIS 551 ; 57 N.W. 287
Franklin v. Kelley. 2 Neb. 79 ; 1873 Neb. LEXIS 11
Gerrard v. Omaha, N.& B. H. R. Co. 14 Neb. 270 ; 1883 Neb. LEXIS 35 ; 15 N.W. 231
Homan v. Laboo. 2 Neb. 291 ; 1873 Neb. LEXIS 29
In re Senate File 31. 25 Neb. 864 ; 41 N.W. 981 ; 1889 Neb. LEXIS 92
Jameson v. Butler. 1 Neb. 115 ; 1871 Neb. LEXIS 12
Kirkendall v. Omaha. 39 Neb. 1 ; 57 N.W. 752 ; 1894 Neb. LEXIS 4
Kyger v. Ryley. 2 Neb. 20 ; 1873 Neb. LEXIS 7
Lowe v. Omaha. 33 Neb. 587 ; 50 N.W. 760 ; 1891 Neb. LEXIS 211
Mattis v. Robinson. 1 Neb. 3 ; 1871 Neb. LEXIS 1
McCann v. Aetna Ins. Co. 3 Neb. 198 ; 1874 Neb. LEXIS 5
McCormick v. Omaha. 37 Neb. 829 ; 56 N.W. 626 ; 1893 Neb. LEXIS 283
McGavock v. Omaha. 40 Neb. 64 ; 58 N.W. 543 ; 1894 Neb. LEXIS 247
Merrill v. Omaha. 39 Neb. 304 ; 58 N.W. 121 ; 1894 Neb. LEXIS 45
Mills v. Murry. 1 Neb. 327 ; 1871 Neb. LEXIS 33
Monroe v. Elburt. 1 Neb. 174 ; 1871 Neb. LEXIS 21
Murphy v. Omaha. 33 Neb. 402 ; 50 N.W. 265 ; 1891 Neb. LEXIS 185
North v. Platte County.29 Neb. 447 ; 45 N.W. 692 ; 1890 Neb. LEXIS 260
Oberfelder v. Doran. 26 Neb. 118 ; 41 N.W. 1094 ; 1889 Neb. LEXIS 114
Omaha & R. v. R. Co. v. Brown. 14 Neb. 170 ; 15 N.W. 321 ; 1883 Neb. LEXIS 43
Omaha & R. v. R. Co. v. Brown. 16 Neb. 161 ; 20 N.W. 202 ; 1884 Neb. LEXIS 145
Omaha & Republican Valley R.R. Co, v. Rogers. 16 Neb. 117 ; 19 N.W. 603 ; 1884 Neb. LEXIS 102

Omaha & Republican Valley R.R. Co. v. Martin. 14 Neb. 295 ; 15 N.W. 696 ; 1883 Neb. LEXIS 80
Omaha v. Ayer. 32 Neb. 375 ; 49 N.W. 445 ; 1891 Neb. LEXIS 301
Omaha v. Cochran. 30 Neb. 637 ; 46 N.W. 920 ; 1890 Neb. LEXIS 148
Omaha v. Hansen. 36 Neb. 135 ; 54 N.W. 83 ; 1893 Neb. LEXIS 18
Omaha v. Howell Lumber Co. 30 Neb. 633 ; 46 N.W. 919 ; 1890 Neb. LEXIS 145
Omaha v. Jensen. 35 Neb. 68 ; 52 N.W. 833 ; 1892 Neb. LEXIS 251
Omaha v. Randolph. 30 Neb. 699 ; 46 N.W. 1013 ; 1890 Neb. LEXIS 151
Omaha v. South Omaha. 31 Neb. 378 ; 47 N.W. 1113 ; 1891 Neb. LEXIS 57
Omaha, N. & B. H. R. Co. v. Gerrard. 17 Neb. 587 ; 24 N.W. 279 ; 1885 Neb. LEXIS 219
Omaha, N. & B. H. R. Co. v. O'Donnell. 22 Neb. 475 ; 35 N.W. 235 ; 1887 Neb. LEXIS 173
Omaha, N. & B. H. R. Co. v. Umstead.17 Neb. 459 ; 23 N.W. 350 ; 1885 Neb. LEXIS 181
Orr v. Orr. 2 Neb. 170 ; 1873 Neb. LEXIS 18
Orr v. Orr.1 Neb. 359 ; 1871 Neb. LEXIS 39
Pennock v. Douglas County 39 Neb. 293 ; 58 N.W. 117 ; 1894 Neb. LEXIS 44
Poland v. O'Connor. 1 Neb. 50 ; 1871 Neb. LEXIS 6
Pomeroy v. Bridge. 1 Neb. 462 ; 1871 Neb. LEXIS 66 .
Redick v. Omaha. 35 Neb. 125 ; 52 N.W. 847 ; 1892 Neb. LEXIS 261
Robinson v. Jones. 31 Neb. 20 ; 47 N.W. 480 ; 1890 Neb. LEXIS 188
Rogers v. Ware. 2 Neb. 29 ; 1873 Neb. LEXIS 8
Savage v. Aiken. 14 Neb. 315 ; 15 N.W. 693 ; 1883 Neb. LEXIS 78
Savage v. Hazard. 11 Neb. 323 ; 9 N.W. 83 ; 1881 Neb. LEXIS 61
Second Congregational Church Soc. v. Omaha. 35 Neb. 103 ; 52 N.W. 829 ; 1892 Neb. LEXIS 248
Smiley v. Sampson. 1 Neb. 56 ; 1871 Neb. LEXIS 7
State ex. rel. Leese v. Wilkinson. 20 Neb. 610 ; 31 N.W. 376 ; 1886 Neb. LEXIS 106
State ex. rel. Townsend v. Hill. 10 Neb. 58 ; 4 N.W. 514 ; 1880 Neb. LEXIS 22
Streitz v. Hartman. 35 Neb. 406 ; 53 N.W. 215 ; 1892 Neb. LEXIS 31
Townsend v. Lamb. 14 Neb. 324 ; 15 N.W. 727 ; 1883 Neb. LEXIS 96
Traver v. Merrick County. 14 Neb. 327 ; 15 N.W. 690 ; 1883 Neb. LEXIS 77
Union P.R. Co, v. Schwenck. 13 Neb. 478 ; 14 N.W. 376 ; 1882 Neb. LEXIS 193
Union P.R. Co. v. Blum. 23 Neb. 404 ; 36 N.W. 589 ; 1888 Neb. LEXIS 154
Union P.R. Co. v. Burlington & M.R.R. Co. 19 Neb. 386 ; 27 N.W. 238 ; 1886 Neb. LEXIS 174
Union P.R. Co. v. Commissioners of Buffalo County. 9 Neb. 449; 4 N.W. 53; 1880 Neb. LEXIS 143
Union P.R. Co. v. Commissioners of Colfax County. 4 Neb. 450 ; 1876 Neb. LEXIS 42
Union P.R. Co. v. Commissioners of Saunders County. 7 Neb. 228 ; 1878 Neb. LEXIS 47
Union P.R. Co. v. County of Dawson. 12 Neb. 254 ; 11 N.W. 307 ; 1882 Neb. LEXIS 8
Union P.R. Co. v. County of York County.10 Neb. 612 ; 7 N.W. 270 ; 1880 Neb. LEXIS 116
Union P.R. Co. v. High. 14 Neb. 14 ; 14 N.W. 547 ; 1883 Neb. LEXIS 5
Union P.R. Co. v. Mertes. 35 Neb. 204 ; 52 N.W. 1099 ; 1892 Neb. LEXIS 270
Union P.R. Co. v. Ogilvy. 18 Neb. 638 ; 26 N.W. 464 ; 1886 Neb. LEXIS 264
Union P.R. Co. v. Smersh. 22 Neb. 751 ; 36 N.W. 139 ; 1888 Neb. LEXIS 79
Van Sickel v. Buffalo County. 13 Neb. 103 ; 13 N.W. 19 ; 1882 Neb. LEXIS 124
Whitlock v. State. 30 Neb. 815 ; 47 N.W. 284 ; 1890 Neb. LEXIS 175
Williams v. Lowe. 4 Neb. 382 ; 1876 Neb. LEXIS 29

ENDNOTES

1 Heritage

[1] King William the Conqueror's survey was known as *The Domesday Book*. The king used it to determine who owned land, how it was being used, and its value. The information was then used to levy taxes and outline the duties owed to the King by the landowners.

[2] A. Poppleton, *Reminiscences,* 3

[3] A. Poppleton, *Reminiscences,* 3

[4] A. Poppleton, *Reminiscences,* 3

[5] Orrin Poppleton, Sketch of William Poppleton.

[6] A. Poppleton, *Reminiscences,* 3. **William & Zada Poppleton's Children:** Zada gave birth to seven children: an unnamed baby who died in infancy, Orrin Poppleton (1817-1892), Sally Poppleton Hoxsey (1820-1895), Hannah E. Poppleton Bateman (1828-1854), Andrew Jackson Poppleton (1830-1896), Carrie Poppleton (1820-1854), and Zada Jane Poppleton Lake (1835-1860).

[7] A. Poppleton, *Reminiscences,* 3.

[8] Orrin Poppleton, Sketch of William Poppleton..

[9] A. Poppleton, *Reminiscences,* 3.

[10] A. Poppleton, *Reminiscences,* 4.

[11] A. Poppleton, *Reminiscences,* 4.

[12] A. Poppleton, *Reminiscences,* 4.

[13] A. Poppleton, *Reminiscences,* 4-5.

[14] A. Poppleton, *Reminiscences,* 5.

[15] A. Poppleton, *Reminiscences,* 5.

2 Union College: "The Most Profitable Year in My Whole Life"

[16] A. Poppleton, *Reminiscences,* 5.

[17] Distinguished men who graduated from Union College prior to Poppleton, were Chester A. Arthur (American President who graduated in 1848), and William H. Seward (Secretary of State under Lincoln who graduated in 1820). Seward's biographer Walter Stahr quoted Seward as saying Dr. Nott was a "very able smart good old man great orator but strict; I suppose that never was a President of a college more loved and respected than Dr. Nott." Walter Stahr. *Seward: Lincoln's Indispensable Man.*

[18] A. Poppleton, *Journal,* 144.

[19] Webster's Dictionary.

[20] A. Poppleton, *Journal,* November 1, 1850, 3.

[21] A. Poppleton, *Journal,* November 1, 1850, 3.

[22] https://www.presbyteriansofthepast.com/2020/03/20/eliphalet-nott-1773-1866 https://www.union.edu/about/history-and-traditions/presidents/eliphalet-nott

[23] A. Poppleton, *Journal,* November 3, 1850, 6.

[24] A. Poppleton, *Journal,* November 6, 1850, 7.

[25] A. Poppleton, *Journal,* November 7, 1850, 7.

[26] A. Poppleton, *Journal,* November 10, 1850, 8.

[27] A. Poppleton, *Journal,* November 11, 1850, 8.

[28] A. Poppleton, *Journal,* November 11, 1850, 8.

[29] A. Poppleton, *Journal,* November 16, 1850, 10.

[30] A. Poppleton, *Journal,* November 16, 1850, 10.

[31] A. Poppleton, *Journal,* November 19, 1850, 12.

[32] A. Poppleton, *Journal,* November 21, 1850, 13.

[33] A. Poppleton, *Journal,* December 17, 1850, 29.

[34] A. Poppleton, *Reminiscences,* 5. **Blackstone's Commentaries on the Laws of England** was written by Sir William Blackstone, a Justice in His Majesty's Court of Common Pleas, in four volumes, 1765-1769. They were required reading in most law schools in the 19th Century in England and America. Many young men living in obscure rural areas who had no opportunity to attend law school or to sit in a law office and learn from an attorney taught themselves the basic principles of the law by reading Blackstone's Commentaries. Abraham Lincoln took this same path while working at Denton Offutt's store in New Salem, Illinois. **Kent's Commentaries on American Law** were published in four volumes in 1826, based on the lectures of James Kent, the first Professor of law at the Columbia School of Law, beginning in 1794. Kent served in the New York legislature and as Chief Justice of the New York Supreme Court from 1804-1814.

[35] A. Poppleton, *Reminiscences,* 5-6.

[36] A. Poppleton, *Journal,* February 16, 1851, 52.

[37] A. Poppleton, *Reminiscences,* 6-7.

[38] A. Poppleton, *Journal,* April 24, 1851, 79-80.

[39] A. Poppleton, *Journal,* August 1851, 137.

[40] A. Poppleton, *Reminiscences,* 7.

3 A Ferry Boat to Omaha City

[41] A. Poppleton, *Reminiscences,* 7

[42] A. Poppleton, *Journal,* January 18, 1852, 133.

[43] A. Poppleton, *Reminiscences,* 8.

[44] A. Poppleton, *Reminiscences,* 8.

[45] A. Poppleton, *Journal,* June 26, 1851, 111

[46] A. Poppleton, *Journal,* June 26, 1851, 111.

[47] A. Poppleton, *Journal,* June 26, 1851, 113.

[48] A. Poppleton, *Reminiscences,* 8.

[49] Woolworth, *Biography,* 97.

[50] *A. Poppleton, Reminiscences, 8.*

[51] A. Poppleton, *Reminiscences,* 9.

[52] A. Poppleton, Reminiscences, 8.

[53] Brown, Dee. Hear That Lonesome Whistle Blow: The Epic Story of the Transcontinental Railroad, 5-6. See also A. Poppleton, Reminiscences, 8.

[54] A. Poppleton, *Reminiscences,* 9. See also Sorenson, 231.

[55] Sorenson, 231.

[56] A. Poppleton, *Reminiscences,* 9.

[57] A. Poppleton, *Reminiscences,* 9.

[58] A. Poppleton, *Reminiscences,* 9.

[59] *The Pioneer Record,* May 1896. **First Omaha Survey**. The survey completed by A.D. Jones and C.H. Downs in June-July 1854 by chain and stakes was as follows: "The city was laid out in 320 blocks, each being 264 feet square; the streets 100 feet wide, except Capitol Avenue which was made 120 feet wide, but which was given no alley in the blocks on each side of it. The lots were staked out 66 by 132 feet. Two squares were reserved – Jefferson square, 264 by 280 feet, and Capitol square,, 600 feet square." Sorenson 51.

[60] A. Poppleton, *Reminiscences,* 9.

[61] A. Poppleton, *Reminiscences,* 9. The area had already proven its practical use and importance as a jumping-off site for various groups heading west searching for a better life, such as the Mormons (1846), and gold seekers (1850).

[62] A. Poppleton, *Reminiscences,* 9.

[63] A. Poppleton, *Reminiscences,* 10.

[64]A. Poppleton, *Reminiscences,* 10.

4 Omaha City 1854

65 **Kansas-Nebraska Act.** Congress passed the Kansas-Nebraska Act signed by President Franklin Pierce on May 30, 1854. It was introduced into the Senate on December 14, 1853 by Iowa Senator Augustus C. Dodge. Senator Stephen A. Douglas of Illinois supported it as a way to promote the construction of a transcontinental railroad to link the eastern coast of the United States with the western coast to create one united route of transportation for goods, services, and people. But to get the Act passed through the southern-controlled Senate, Douglas had to agree to effectively repeal the 1820 Missouri Compromise and give settlers in the new Kansas-Nebraska Territory the right to vote on whether or not they wanted to permit slavery. This policy became known as "popular sovereignty." It led to the eruption of violence in Kansas known as "Bleeding Kansas" and an influx of settlers on both sides of the issue into the new territory. Dodge Street in Omaha was named in honor of Augustus C. Dodge.

66 A. Poppleton, *Reminiscences,* 10.

67 A. Poppleton, *Reminiscences,* 10.

68 *Treaty with the Omaha, 1854*. 10 Stats., 1043. See also Boughter; and Dorsey,, 235; and Fletcher & LaFlesche, 36;. and J. Howard, 15.

69 Broadfield, 34.

70 A. Poppleton, *Reminiscences,* 10-11. To identify **Omaha's Earliest Homes** see Arthur C. Wakeley, 78; and Johnson, 279-281. The first was built by Thomas Allen in February 1854 for the Ferry Company on 12th Jackson Street. It was known as "St. Nichols" and was used as a store and hotel. Its first residents were William and Rachel Snowden. The Snowdens later built their own home on 10th and Jackson Street. M.C. Gaylord built his home on 22nd Burt Street. William Clancy built a home and business known as "Big Six" on 13th and Chicago Street. Sheriff Peterson's home/saloon/early jail was on 10th between Farnam and Harney Streets. And historian Johnson built his own residence on the South side of St. Mary's Ave between 21st and 22nd Street where he lived 1854 to 1869.

71 Savage, 575.

72 A.D. Andreas, History of the State of Nebraska: Douglas County 2.

73 A.D. Andreas, History of the State of Nebraska: Douglas County 2, 6-7. See also Hall, 33.

74 Savage, 105.

75 Johnson, 41.

76 Wakeley,60.

[77] Morton, 1: 160-63. The resolution supported by then assemblyman Burt was intended to nullify the protective tariff acts of 1828 and 1832. "The resolutions which the convention adopted declared that the objectionable tariff laws "are unauthorized by the Constitution of the United States, and violate the true meaning and intent thereof, are null, void and no law, not binding upon the state, its officers or citizens."(Morton, 1:160)

5 The First Territorial Legislature

[78] **The Initial Officers of The Nebraska Territory:** Francis Burt of South Carolina (Governor), Thomas B. Cuming of Michigan (Secretary), Experience Estabrook of Wisconsin (Attorney General), Mark W. Izard of Arkansas (Marshall), Fenner Ferguson of Michigan (Chief Justice), and Edward R. Hardin of Georgia and James Bradley of Indiana (Associate Justices).

[79] Johnson 41. See Olson, *History of Nebraska,* 354 for the following names and terms of the **Territorial Governors** before Nebraska statehood: Francis Burt of South Carolina, Democrat (October 16-18, 1854 died); vacancy filled by acting governor Thomas B. Cuming of Michigan, Democrat (October 18, 1854, to February 20, 1855); Mark W. Izard of Arkansas, Democrat (February 20, 1855 – October 25, 1857 resigned); vacancy filled by acting governor Thomas B. Cuming, Democrat (October 25, 1857 to January 12, 1858); William A. Richardson of Illinois, Democrat (January 12, 1858 – December 5, 1858 resigned); vacancy filled by acting governor J. Sterling Morton of Michigan, Democrat (December 5, 1858 to May 2, 1859); Samuel W. Black of Pennsylvania, Democrat (May 2, 1859 – February 24, 1861, resigned); vacancy filled by acting governor J. Sterling Morton of Michigan, Democrat (February 24, 1861 – May 15, 1861); Alvin Saunders of Iowa, Republican (May 15, 1861 – March 27, 1867). See also Thavenet, *The Territorial Governorship.* The Mission House was overseen by Rev. William J. Hamilton, a Presbyterian minister to the Omaha Tribe. A county north of Omaha was named in honor of Francis Burt, as was a street (this author grew up on Burt Street).

[80] Morton, 1:163.

[81] Johnson, 41-42

[82] Morton, 1:164. Cuming appointed Barton Green, Colonel Ward B. Howard, James Doyle and W.R. Jones as the official escort. He also ordered that they be reimbursed for actual traveling expenses.

83 Woolworth, *Nebraska in 1857,* 36-37. Addison Sheldon summarized the conflicting opinions held by the opposing sides of the census and capital location issues of the first legislative session concerning Thomas Cuming. Writing in 1931, Sheldon said that Cuming "In his character were combined some of the most essential elements of success in the political arena. In native sagacity, force of will and executive ability, he was scarcely equaled by any other among the territorial governors ... He had courage equal to any emergency. Quick and resolute in decision and prompt in action, he was usually able to forestall his political adversaries and win the victory before they had fully decided what to do. If his enemies may be believed, he was not inclined to be overscrupulous, and his conscience allowed him to make use of methods that would hardly have been adopted by a man of fine moral standards." Sheldon, *History of Nebraska*, 244.

84 Kansas-Nebraska Act 1854. Addison Sheldon said that the eligible voters were "free, white, male inhabitants above the age of 21 years, actual residents in the territory and citizens of the United States. No officer, soldier, or other member of the United States army or navy was allowed to vote or hold office." (Sheldon, *Nebraska -The Land and the People*, I:241).

85 **First Counties in Nebraska Territory** were named for the following individuals: **Douglas** (Stephen A. Douglas, Illinois senator who championed the Kansas-Nebraska Act of 1854 in the U.S. Senate); **Dodge** (Augustus C. Dodge, Iowa senator who introduced the Kansas-Nebraska Act in the U.S. Senate); **Burt** (Francis Burt, first governor of Nebraska Territory); **Washington** (George Washington, first president); **Cass** (General Lewis Cass of Michigan, secretary of state in cabinet of President James Buchanan and mentor of Governor Cuming); **Pierce** (President Franklin Pierce who appointed the initial territorial officers); **Richardson** (William A. Richardson, Illinois congressman who sponsored the Kansas-Nebraska Act in the U.S. House of Representatives and later served as third governor of Nebraska Territory); **Forney** (John W. Forney, clerk of U.S. House of Representatives, 1851-56, during debate on Kansas-Nebraska Act and also ran Buchanan's campaign for presidency). See Johnson 42-45 for a description of the boundaries of each county.

86 An analysis of the results of the census can be found in Olsen, *History of Nebraska*, 83; and in Morton, 1:180-81. Addison Sheldon, Secretary of the Nebraska State Historical Society wrote in 1931: "This census was taken before the boundary line between Kansas and Nebraska had been surveyed; hence it very naturally happened that some inhabitants in the former territory were counted as residents of Nebraska." (*Nebraska The Land and the People*, 1:249). This may provide some explanation why the vote total in the most southern county of Richardson boarding Kansas was so high.

87 Savage, 51; and Morton 1:180-81. Cuming was sharply criticized by the South Platte faction who believed the results of the census showed a greater number of voting residents lived South of the Platte so they should have received a larger number of members than those counties North of the Platte River.

[88] Woolworth, *Biography*, 99

[89] Olson, History of Nebraska, 85.

[90] Morton, 1:199.

[91] Morton, 1:202. The *Nebraska Palladium* was the first newspaper published in the Nebraska Territory and lasted from July 1, 1854, to April 11, 1855.

[92] Morton, 1:198, 202.

[93]House Journal, 1855, 144.

[94] Kansas-Nebraska Act of 1854.

[95] Savage, 51.

[96] Cuming's first term as acting governor was from October 18, 1854, to February 20, 1855. His second term was from October 25, 1857, to January 12, 1858. Cuming Street is one block from this author's childhood home on Burt Street.

6 Bludgeons, Brickbats, Pistols and the Grand Ball

[97] *Morton, 1:163 footnote.*

[98] Savage, 52; and Sorenson 73.

[99] A. Poppleton, *Reminiscences,* 11

[100] *Omaha Daily Herald*, January 14, 1867.

[101] Savage 53; and Sheldon, Nebraska the Land and the People, 260.

[102] Morton, 1:297. While serving as Vice-President of the United States and President of the Senate from 1797-1801, Thomas Jefferson wrote *"A Manual of Parliamentary Practice for the Use of the Senate of the United States."* It was published in 1801 and was the first such manual published for use in America.

[103] Woolworth, *History of Nebraska*, 18-19.

[104] Morton, I: 206-07

[105] Johnson, 46. **The First Capitol Building** was erected in the fall of 1854 on 9th & Harney Street as the first brick building in Omaha City. It served as the legislative chambers for the first and second sessions. Later, it housed various businesses before it became the headquarters for the UPRR (until it moved across the street to the Herndon House Hotel in the fall of 1869). See Morton 1:267 for details of the construction of the second capitol building on 20th Street.

106 Hall 34-35

107 Sorensen 83. Jim Orton was the courageous fiddler.

7 First Trials and a July Fourth Celebration

108 Kansas-Nebraska Act of 1854, **Section 9.**

109 Kansas-Nebraska Act of 1854, **Section 17**. Morton, 1:251 identifies the districts and justices. **Section 27** of the Act stated that "each of the said district courts shall have and exercise the same jurisdiction in all cases arising under the Constitution and laws of the United States as is vested in the Circuit and District Courts of the United States; and the said supreme and district courts of the said Territory, and the respective judges thereof, shall and may grant writs of habeas corpus in all cases in which the same are granted by the judges of the United States in the District of Columbia." See also Homer, 356.

110 Morton, I:253. See the footnote in Morton 1:252-55 for the speeches made at the swearing in by members of the Bar, by the attorney general, and by the other justices. J. Sterling Morton was appointed first clerk of the Territorial Supreme Court.

111 A. Poppleton, *Reminiscences,* 11-12.

112 The murder victim, **George W. Hollister**, is the same man who was named in the first territorial legislature as "Clerk of the Belleview Precinct of Douglas County" for purposes of voting for members of the legislature. He graduated from Gale College, Illinois and studied law. His funeral service was conducted by Rev. G. Rice in Council Bluffs, and his body was returned to Illinois for burial. Morton 1.185 footnote.

113 Sorensen, 85.

114 Sorensen, 85.

115 Sorenson, 85. See also Andres, *History of the State of Nebraska: Douglas County* History Section 3: 23; and Morton 1:191-93. During the Civil War, Dr. Henry served with distinction as an army surgeon, and even handled some secret spy operations by sneaking through southern lines. He was commissioned as a lieutenant-colonel for his services. He died in 1880, age 49.

116 Sorenson, 86-87.

117 C. Poppleton Interview, *Omaha Bee News*, July 9, 1905.

118 C. Poppleton Interview, *Omaha Bee News*, July 9, 1905.

119 C. Poppleton Interview, *Omaha Bee News*, July 9, 1905.

120 C. Poppleton Interview, *Omaha Bee News*, July 9, 1905.

121 C. Poppleton Interview, *Omaha Bee News*, July 9, 1905.

122 C. Poppleton Interview, *Omaha Bee News*, July 9, 1905.

123 Rev. George G. Rice, *a* resident of Council Bluffs, wrote in the July 1855 edition of the eastern magazine *Home Missionary* entitled "Appeal for Nebraska" that gave an encouraging outlook for the future of Omaha City: "Yesterday, I spent in Omaha City and preached in the hall of the House of Representatives, having arranged to exchange with the chaplain. Omaha City has been made the capitol of Nebraska by the legislature. It is growing very rapidly and seems destined to be a place of much importance. There are in the town about forty houses, and probably from 150 to 200 inhabitants."

124 The 517-page **Code of Laws** was titled: "Laws, Resolutions and Memorials Passed at The Regular Session of the First General Assembly of the Territory of Nebraska Convened at Omaha City, on the 16th Day of January, Anno Domini, 1855." It was published by Sherman & Strickland, Territorial Printers, Omaha City, N.T. 1855. The Code consisted of 8 parts: **Part First:** To adopt certain parts of the Code of Iowa. **Part Second:** General laws. **Part Third:** Criminal Code (being Part Fourth of the Code of Iowa). **Part Fourth:** Territorial Roads. **Part Fifth:** County Seats and County Boundaries. **Part Sixth:** Incorporations, Insurance, Railroad, Land, Manufacturing and Milling Companies, Towns and Cities. **Part Seventh**: Ferries and Bridges. **Part Eighth:** Joint Resolutions and Memorials. The incorporation of the University of Nebraska (page 375) and the incorporation of the Nebraska Medical Society (page 396) are found in Part Sixth. Regulations concerning Habeas Corpus are found in Part First (pages 130-34)

8 "The Most Fortunate Day of My Life"

125 A. Poppleton, *Reminiscences,* 12

126 **Children born to Leonard and Delia Sears**: Elizabeth Sears (1830-1830), Mary Pember Sears (1833-1835), Caroline Laura Sears (1835-1917), Charles West Sears (1837-1870), Stillman Foote Sears (1839-1840), Stillman Foote Sears (1842-1921), Mary Rust Sears (1844-1911), Joseph Leonard Sears (1846-1883), Millard Fillmore Sears (1848-1914), Delia Louise Sears (1851-1924), Elizbeth W. Sears (1853-1854). Their first two children died before they left New York; their eleventh and youngest child died two months after the family arrived in Council Bluffs.

127 C. Poppleton, *Diary,* May 2, 1854

128 *Omaha Excelsior,* April 21, 1917.

129 C. Poppleton to her cousin "Lib" December 8, 1854.

[130] C. Poppleton, *Diary,* June 10, 1855.

[131] C. Poppleton, *Diary,* December 2, 1855.

[132] A. Poppleton, *Reminiscences*, 12. **Children born to A.J. and Caroline Poppleton:** Ellen Elizabeth Poppleton (Sept 10, 1856 – May 2, 1936, age 79), Mary Zada Poppleton (April 4, 1859 – Nov 17, 1862, age 3), William Sears Poppleton (April 7, 1866 - Nov 15, 1913, age 47), Mary Delia Poppleton Learned (July 23, 1873- January 15, 1960, age 87)

[133] *Omaha Bee News,* June 8, 1913. William Byers and his wife stayed only 5 years in Omaha before moving to Denver, where he later founded *The Rocky Mountain News* and became active in Colorado politics.

[134] Savage, 115.

[135] C. Poppleton, *Diary*, September 10, 1856.

[136] Overland Journal of Mary Rockwood Powers, April to October 1856, Douglas County Historical Society,

[137] Overland Journal of Mary Rockwood Powers, April to October 1856, Douglas County Historical Society.

9 The Gathering Under the Lone Tree

[138] A. Poppleton, *Reminiscences,* 12.

[139] Woolworth, *Biography,* 100. Poppleton and Woolworth sometimes found themselves on opposing sides of land dispute cases, such as *Mattis v. Robinson* 1 Neb 3, 1871 Neb .LEXIS 1. But, most often they worked together as co-counsel such as in the case of *Smiley v. Sampson* 1 Neb 56, 1871 Neb. LEXIS 7.

[140] **The Preemption Act** *(27th Congress, Ch 16, 5 Stat.453 (1841)* was repealed by Congress in 1891. Thirteen years before Congress created the Nebraska Territory and Omaha was founded, Henry Clay spearheaded *The Preemption Act* through Congress to create a system in which the newly established territories and the individuals desiring to settle there could acquire legal title to land by filing a claim with the federal land office for "any number of acres not exceeding one hundred and sixty, or a quarter section of land, to include the residence of such claimant, upon paying to the United States $1.25 per acre." For a review of a federal case pertaining to the Preemptive Act of 1841 see *Frisbie v. Whitney* 76 U.S. 187, 194 (1869).

[141] Johnson, 287.

[142] Savage, 98.

143 Morton, 1:231.

144 Gaylord was a carpenter by trade who built his own home on 22nd & Jackson Street. When he died, it was reported that "he was buried on the present site of Creighton College, his remains being taken up and reburied when the college building was erected in 1877." Morton, 1: 231.

145 Poppleton land claim recorded in the Office of the Recorder, Douglas County, at Book No. 2, Page 18.

146 Morton, 1:234

147 Sorensen, 107-108.

148 Savage, 98.

149 Sorenson, 113-114.

150 Wakeley, Arthur C. 108-09.

151 Sorenson, 151; Johnson, 285-286. **Omaha's First City Officers***:* Jesse Lowe (Mayor), L.R. Tuttle (Recorder), J.A. Miller (Marshall), Charles Grant (Solicitor), Lyman Richardson (Assessor), A.S. Morgan (Engineer), A. Chappel (Health Officer), John H. Kellom (Treasurer). The men elected to Omaha's First City Council: A.D. Jones, T. G. Goodwill, George C. Bovey, H.H. Visscher, Thomas Davis, William N. Byers, W.W. Wyman, Thomas O'Connor, C.H. Downs, and James Creighton. The city council sat for the first time on March 5, 1857.

10 Brawl in the House

152 A. Poppleton, *Reminiscences,* 13

153 A. Poppleton, *Reminiscences,* 13.

154 Morton, 1:315. The following reason is suggested for Morton's change of mind on the capital issue: "Mr. Morton's attitude toward the capital question had been completely reversed and at a public meeting held at Nebraska City after the adjournment of the legislature, where the members from Otoe County were called upon to explain their action in the Florence affair, Morton boldly stated that two years before in the capital contest he had struggled to the end for removal; a year later when he became a candidate for re-election he was defeated on this record (by 20 votes), and he came to the conclusion that his constituents cared but little about the removal, and he himself believed that it was impolitic and inexpedient to raise the question at the late session."

155 Sorenson 97.

156 Savage, 66

157 Jefferson's Manual of Parliamentary Practice.

158 Savage, 66.

159 Savage, 66.

160 Sorenson, 96-97.

161 Savage, 69

162 Savage, 69-70. **William A. Richardson** had been chairman of the House Committee on Territories and introduced a bill in the House of Representatives on February 1853, to organize the Nebraska Territory. It passed the House by a 2 to 1 margin and headed to the Senate for debate and eventual passage in March 1854.

163 Savage, 71

164 Savage, 71

165 *Omaha Times* vol 2 no 7, 91.

11 Mayor of Omaha

166 Morton, 1:337-340.

167 There is little historical record positively identifying Thomas Cuming's disease that caused his death. A medical research pathologist consulted by the author suggested Cuming may have suffered and died from Tuberculosis. It was a leading cause of death in the United States at that time and was called "Consumption" because the disease would consume the person through weight loss and a progressive wasting away of vitality and energy.

168 **Thomas and Marguerite Cumming** lived in a small house on the southwest corner of 18th & Dodge Street. At night, they always kept a lighted lantern in the window. The lantern, a chair and briefcase from their home were kept by Joslyn Art Museum Omaha. *(Omaha World Herald* October 25, 1959). When Thomas Cuming fell in love with Marguerite Murphy, he was concerned that because she was a Roman Catholic, his father, an Episcopalian minister living in Grand Rapids, Michigan, may not give his blessing to their marriage. On December 12, 1852, Thomas Cuming wrote a letter to Marguerite saying: "I wrote a very long letter this morning to my father telling him, very frankly, and for the first time, that I am engaged, and that you are a confirmed Romanist [Catholic]. I told him that the conflict between my own most sacred feelings and filial love was indeed severe, but that I was prepared for it, and indulged the hope, too (a faint one, I confess) that upon deliberate reflection he would not oppose me. I told him that I felt that you were essential to my happiness and welfare here and hereafter. I told him of your virtue, sincerity, discretion, etc. As well as I could, and entreated him, by his love for his only son, not to interpose even his disapproval." On January 9, 1853, Thomas Cuming wrote a second letter to Marguerite sharing his father's reply: "My father (noble old man that he is) writes to me, by the very same mail, that he will not oppose us – that your religion is between you and your God – and that no Catholic can regard this betrothal more sacred than he. He is a man of honor – my father. You must love him and he you." (correspondence courtesy of *Douglas County Historical Society*).

Thomas and Marguerite Cuming were very ecumenical during their lifetime in Omaha. Thomas remained an active member, contributor and a vestryman at Trinity Episcopal Cathedral, and Marguerite remained an active member of the Catholic Church. Historian of the Catholic Church in Nebraska, Fr. Henry Casper S.J. wrote that one of the earliest Masses in Omaha was presided over by Fr. Thomas Scanlon of St. Joseph, Missouri in the parlor of the Cuming home in early 1856. Fr. Casper further wrote that Thomas Cuming gave $125.00 for the building of St. Mary's, the first Catholic Church in Omaha located on the east side of 8th Street between Harney and Howard Streets, dedicated in August 1856 by Fr. Scanlon. According to Fr. Casper, Thomas and Marguerite were close friends of Bishop John Baptist Miege S.J. who helped raise the funds necessary to build the church. (Casper, 48-51). The *Nebraskian,* July 16, 1856 printed in Omaha commented: "It is somewhat significant that the first public house of worship now in progress in Omaha City and perhaps in the Territory, is a Catholic Church, a nice fine brick building on Park Place. Whoever may be the first promotors and supporters of this enterprise, and to whatever denomination they may belong, it gives them much credit and shows that there exists a true Christian spirit of religious toleration among the population of the Territory." (Casper, 51).

[169] **St. John's Church at Creighton College** after it was dedicated May 6, 1888 it became the home parish for Marguerite Cuming, even though when she died on February 12, 1915, at 82, she was buried from St. Cecilia's Cathedral with services conducted by Fr. Daniel P. Harrington. (*Omaha World Herald* February 13, 1915). She left a $40,000 bequest to St. John's in her Last Will and Testament that was used to enlarge the church's sanctuary and nave in 1923: "Enlarging the sanctuary required dismantling and reassembling the original three altars. Four more altars were added for Jesuit daily Masses. Enlarging the nave doubled seating capacity to accommodate more than a thousand worshippers." Eileen Wirth, *We Belong Here: The Story of St. John's Church and Its People.* 24.

[170] The *Omaha Daily Bee*, February 12, 1915.

[171] The *Omaha Daily Bee*, February 12, 1915. Harriet S. MacMurphy wrote an article for the Nebraska State Historical Society in 1898 confirming Caroline's description of that New Year's Day reception in the Cuming home in 1856: "In 1855 Governor Cuming built the house on Dodge Street near Nineteenth, which with some additions, remained the house of Mrs. Cuming until about ten years ago (1888). The Governor and Mrs. Cuming set out trees and shrubbery and made a garden so the grounds also were soon conspicuous for their beauty. The gradual slope, with the outlook upon the river and hills in the distance made it a lovely location, made many a pleasant occasion, upon which the settlers of those times look back with affections ... "I well remember, said one gentleman, New Year's day, 1856. Several of us called upon Mrs. Cuming and her mother and sister Fanny, afterwards Mrs. C. W. Hamilton, who were keeping open house. Mrs. Murphy had made a delicious egg-nog, the first tasted since we came to the territory, and we had a merry time." There were many social functions in those days; receptions, balls, dances, given at the Douglas House, or the state house, which was down on Ninth street between Farnam and Douglas, or upon the steamboats, which always made the occasion of their landing the opportunity for a ball in their spacious saloons ... with it all was that hearty comradeship which is one of the delights of a new country, and which once participated in is never forgotten. The universal statement to the writer was, "there has never been such hearty sociability since in Nebraska as in those early days."

[172] C. Poppleton, Diary, April 1857.

[173] A. Poppleton, *Reminiscences,* 13.

[174] C. Poppleton, *Diary*, March 1858,

[175] Woolworth, *Biography,* 100-01.

[176] Sun, J., Gao, Y., Chi, L., Cao, Q., Ning, Z., & Nan, G. (2021). Case Report: Early-Onset Guillain–Barre Syndrome Mimicking Stroke. *Frontiers in Neurology*, *12*, 525699. https://doi.org/10.3389/fneur.2021.525699

[177] NIH https://www.ninds.nih.gov/health-information/disorders/guillain-barre-syndrome

[178] Mayo Clinic https://www.mayoclinic.org/diseases-conditions/guillain-barre-syndrome/diagnosis-treatment/drc-20363006

[179] C. Poppleton, *Diary*, June 1859.

12 Abraham Lincoln Impacts Poppleton's Life

[180] C. Poppleton, *Diary,* April 4, 1859, and June 1859.

[181] W.H. Pusey to A. Poppleton January 17, 1878. This letter shows Pusey's ownership of the banking house since 1857 and his working relationship with Poppleton. Pusey was an honorary pallbearer at Poppleton's funeral in 1896. After Lincoln's speech at the Concert Hall in Council Bluffs, a reception was held in his honor at the home of William and Eleanor Pusey. The site later served as the Carnegie Library. Today it is the home of the **Union Pacific Railroad Museum,** 200 Pearl Street, Council Bluffs, Iowa 51502 . (712-329-8307).

[182] Hirshson, *30-31.*

[183] The Collected Works of Abraham Lincoln, Ray P. Basler, Editor. 1953. 1:5.

[184] Dodge, How We Built the Union Pacific Railway, 5-6.

[185] Dodge Personal Recollections.

[186] Dodge, *How We Built the Union Pacific Railway*, 9-11; Ambrose, 31; Williams, 24-25.

[187] **Edward Creighton** (1820-1874) was born in Ohio on August 31, 1820 and came to Omaha in 1856. He parlayed the investment he made in stock he owned in the Pacific Telegraph Company into a variety of business opportunities in Omaha, including a successful freighting operation across the plains to the Pacific. Later he invested in the cattle business and joined the Kountze brothers in forming the First National Bank of Omaha. He died November 5, 1874, age 54, from the effects of a stroke. His wife, Mary Lucretia Wareham, died two years later leaving a sizable bequest to build a Catholic college in Omaha called Creighton College (now Creighton University), opened 1878. Edward and Mary Creighton were an influential couple in the growth and development of Omaha. For more information on the transcontinental telegraph line see *The Pacific Telegraph Act of 1860*, 137 U.S. Statutes 36th Congress, 1st Session; and Sorenson, 215-221.

[188] C. Poppleton, *Diary*, November 1859.

[189] C. Poppleton to A. Poppleton, September 27, 1860.

[190] C. Poppleton, Diary, November 15, 1862. Earlier that year, Willie Lincoln, the 11-year-old son of the President, died of typhoid fever in his bed in the White House, February 20, 1862. For a review of the various health issues in Omaha at the time, see Michael J. Harkins, "Public Health Nuisances in Omaha, 1870-1900." 471-492. The World Health Organization reports that typhoid fever "is a threatening infection caused by the bacterium Salmonella Typhis. It is usually spread through contaminated food or water. Once Salmonella Typhi bacteria are ingested, they multiply and spread into the bloodstream. Symptoms include prolonged high fever, nausea, abdominal pain, constipation or diarrhea." Today, it can be treated with antibiotics. "Typhoid," World Health Organization, March 30, 2023, *https://www.who.int/news-room/fact-heets/detail/typhoid#:~:text=Persons%20with%20typhoid%20fever%20carry,serious%20 complications%20or%20even%20death.*

[191] Savage, 136.

[192] Sorensen, 126.

[193] Poppleton filed an appeal of the decision to the Nebraska Supreme Court, but it was denied. (Savage, 137). The first edition of the Nebraska Reports of 1871 includes a few earlier cases but not the Tator appeal and Poppleton does not discuss the case in his memoirs. Sorenson did added a sentence to his discussion of the case: "The argument of Mr. Poppleton was a most brilliant, eloquent and logical effort- in fact, it is said by those who have known Mr. Poppleton for thirty years to have been the best speech to a jury that he ever made." (Sorenson, 126).

[194] Savage, 137; Sorensen, 126-127.

[195] Pacific Railroad Act 1962; Dodge, *How We Built the Union Pacific Railway*, 11.

[196] President Executive Order 1863.

[197] Sorensen, 224.

[198] The exact spot of the groundbreaking is not absolutely certain because of the "shifting channel, at that time, near the foot of Capitol Avenue, a spot long since washed away." (*Omaha World Herald* 1954). However, the consensus of commentators over the years points to "Seventh and Davenport"(Klein 1:25). *The Omaha Daily Bee, December 1, 1883,* looking back 20 years wrote "The spot was near the ferry landing and the old telegraph poles and not far from the point where the water works are now located." (also, Johnson 1880, 116). Most likely the ground-breaking ceremony took place near the area of 7th Street between Davenport Street and Capitol Avenue.

[199] The *Omaha Daily Bee* December 4, 1863, described Methodist minister Thomas B. Lemon as "tall, gaunt and gawky as Abraham Lincoln himself who delivered himself of prayers and blessings." Lemon and his wife remained close friends of the Poppleton family for the next 40 years.

[200] Sorensen, 230.

[201] *Omaha Daily Bee*, June 19, 1904. *George Francis Train* (1829-1904)was one of the most colorful characters to ever live in Omaha. Born in Boston, March 24, 1829, his father sent him to live in New Orleans with his mother and three sisters. At age four, his mother and sisters died of typhoid fever, so George returned to Boston to be raised by his grandparents. All of this traveling as a youth, put the wanderlust in George and as an adult he traveled the world. While in Europe, he helped build a street-railway system in London, Geneva, Copenhagen and elsewhere and then was hired by Thomas C. Durant to raise funds to build the UPRR, lobby Congress for legislation supporting the work of the Union Pacific, and handle various marketing and public relation activities. He came to Omaha on UPRR business and began to invest heavily in real estate. He purchased 500 acres in the region of the city later called "Little Italy." In his autobiography he wrote that "the development of Omaha owes its prosperity directly to the Union Pacific Railway." (Train, *My Life*, 171). British authorities arrested him for his outspoken support of Irish independence. Over his lifetime, he said he spent time in 15 jails. George Pickering Bemis, Omaha's 26th Mayor (1892-1896), for a time acted as Train's personal secretary and tried to handle his business affairs in Omaha while Train was away, however eventually he had to sue Train for back wages as Train squandered most of his money and as a result, his land holdings in Omaha were foreclosed. A primary school near his home on 8th & Worthington Street in Omaha was later constructed and named in his honor. In 1870, he embarked on a voyage around the world, which he said inspired Jules Verne's *Around the World in Eighty Days*, published two years later. He said he later did the same trip in only 60 days. Train died alone and destitute in a New York City hotel room, January 18, 1904. His wife preceded him in death. He had four children.

[202] Sorenson, 231-233.

[203] Sorenson, 238.

[204] Omaha World Herald May 9, 1954.

[205] A. Poppleton, *Reminiscences* 12-13.

[206] Kratville, 9.

13 "The Legal Career Which I Cherish"

[207] A. Poppleton. *Reminiscences*, 13-14.

[208] Wakeley, Arthur C. 249; Sorenson, 239.

[209] Klein, 70.

[210] C. Poppleton, *Diary* entries for April 7, 1866, and December 1866.

[211] A. Poppleton, *Reminiscences,* 14.

[212] A. Poppleton, *Reminiscences,* 24.

[213] Wakeley, Arthur C. 71. Senator J.N. Patrick of Omaha is said to have made the actual motion to adopt the name "Lincoln" in the legislative session (Olson, *History of Nebraska*, 146).

[214] C. Poppleton, *Diary*, May 1870.

[215] U.S. Constitution 17th Amendment.

[216] A. Poppleton, *Reminiscences,* 17.

[217] Sheldon, History and Stories of Nebraska, 168.

[218] Sheldon, History and Stories of Nebraska, 169-170; also, Sheldon, Nebraska the Land and People, 348-49.

[219] A. Poppleton, *Reminiscences* 18.

14 "Safe in Mr. Poppleton's Hands"

[220] A. Poppleton, *Reminiscences* 16.

[221] A. Poppleton, *Reminiscences* 15.

[222] A. Poppleton, *Reminiscences* 15.

[223] A. Poppleton, *Reminiscences* 16-17.

224 A. Poppleton, *Reminiscences,* 17. **Brigham Young** was one of the 30 men named to the initial Board of Directors of the Union Pacific in 1862 (Williams, 71). Poppleton was involved in a claim filed against the UPRR by Brigham Young for non-payment of compensation and costs incurred by Young in building a portion of the UPRR track from Echo Canyon to the Great Salt Lake. The contract was signed by the parties in May 1868. Young submitted a claim in the amount of nearly $198,000 and the UPRR refused to pay. In August 1869, the parties agreed to meet in Omaha within thirty days, each side to bring their own referee to arbitrate the claim. Young's representatives arrived in Omaha on time, Sept 28, 1869, and stayed at the Cozzens Hotel. On October 5, 1869, Poppleton informed them that the UPRR referee, J.L. Wilson, had finally arrived in Omaha, but Young's representatives said they would not arbitrate the matter because the UPRR was in default of the 30-day agreement, and so they demanded payment in full. The UPRR officials in Boston said no to Young's demand. Nothing more happened between the parties until the following July when the UPRR made a final offer to settle the case for $70,000, accepted by Young's representative. (see *Stevens* for further discussion*).*

225 *The Deseret News*, Salt Lake City, Utah, May 19, 1869, 6.

226 Broadfield, 103.

227 A. Poppleton, *Reminiscences* 18.

228 A. Poppleton, *Reminiscences* 19.

229 In 1867, UPRR lobbyist George Frances Train believed Omaha needed a new first-class hotel where Eastern businessmen could stay when they came to Omaha on railroad and other commercial business ventures. After exchanging angry words with staff at the Herndon House Hotel, Train decided to build a rival hotel across the street on 9th & Harney Street. The **Cozzens House Hotel** was an ornate three-story building, with window awnings, balconies, and a ridge turret roof, but in a few years, issues of mismanagement forced its sale. Over time it was occupied by the Omaha Medical & Surgical Institute, later by the Omaha Presbyterian Theological Seminary. It was demolished in 1902.

230 A. Poppleton, *Reminiscences* 19-20.

231 A. Poppleton, *Reminiscences* 19.

232 A. Poppleton, *Reminiscences* 19.

233 A. Poppleton, *Reminiscences* 20.

234 A. Poppleton, *Reminiscences* 20.

235 A. Poppleton, *Reminiscences* 21.

[236] A. Poppleton, *Reminiscences* 21.

15 The Bridge Connecting the Nation

[237] *Omaha Bee News*, December 3, 1905.

[238] Klein, 1:268.

[239] A. Poppleton, *Reminiscences*, 9.

[240] Klein, 1:269.

[241] Klein, 1:269.

[242] A. Poppleton, *Reminiscences,* 21.

[243] Klein, 1:258.

[244] Site of **"Child's Mill"** varies depending on the starting point. Poppleton said it was "four miles south of Farnam Street." (A.Poppleton. *Reminiscences*, 21); while Klein said it was "eight miles south of Omaha." (Klein 1:259)

[245] A.Poppleton. *Reminiscences*, 22.

[246] A.Poppleton. *Reminiscences*, 22.

[247] T.E. Sickels and his brother Frederick E. Sickels worked together in building the bridge in Harlem, New York and were familiar with the importance of using iron piers which were vital to the safety of any bridge on the Missouri River. Frederick Sickels later served as a key investigator for Poppleton in the Snowplow patent case . (Klein 1:263).

[248] A.Poppleton. *Reminiscences*, 22.

[249] A.Poppleton. *Reminiscences*, 22.

[250] A.Poppleton. *Reminiscences*, 23.

[251] A.Poppleton. *Reminiscences*, 23-24.

[252] A.Poppleton. *Reminiscences*, 24.

[253] Woolworth, *Biography,* 103.

[254] Klein 1:277-78. Note: *The Omaha Daily Bee*, December 1, 1883, published a special edition to commemorate the 20th anniversary of the breaking of ground in Omaha.

255 *United States ex.rel. Hall et.al. v. Union Pacific Railroad Company,* 91 U.S. 343. (1875). The Petitioners moved for an Order of Mandamus to compel the UPRR to fulfill its duty to build and operate a connected and continuous line. U.S. Department of Justice: Civil Resource Manual 215 states that Mandamus is a motion filed in federal court used only in "exceptional circumstances of peculiar emergency or public importance" for which "there is a want of other remedies." The case was filed by the petitioners under the act of Congress of March 3, 1873 (17 Stat. 509, 4).

256 Section 14. of the **Pacific Railway Act of 1862**: "That the said Union Pacific Railroad Company is hereby authorized and required to construct a single line of railroad and telegraph from a point on the western boundary of the State of Iowa, to be fixed by the President of the United States, upon the most direct and practicable route." The Supreme Court in the Hall decision did not rule that the UPRR could never charge rates of toll for their passengers or freight cars, but rather if they decided to do so to help defray costs of doing business or reducing debts: "They were not allowed to charge rates of toll which they did not charge upon other portions of their line."

257 A. Poppleton to Sidney Dillon, December 10. 1875.

16 The Case of the Kidnapped Judge

258 A. Poppleton to Sidney Dillon, December 10, 1875.

259 After Colorado was admitted in the union as a state on August 1, 1876, the case which was originally filed in the Colorado Territorial Court was appealed to the Circuit Court for the District of Colorado as *Ames v. Colorado Central Railroad Company* 4 Dill 251 Case No. 324 (1876) and 4 Dill 260 Case No.325, (1877). See Lake, 19-26.

260 A. Poppleton, *Reminiscences*, 28.

261 Athearn, 221.

262 A. Poppleton, *Reminiscences*, 29.

263 A. Poppleton, *Reminiscences,* 30.

264 Testimony of A. Poppleton given in Omaha, July 1, 1887, in a *Report of the United States Pacific Railway Commission* complied by Robert E. Pattison, (Washington, U.S.G.P.O. 1887, 1466). In the report Poppleton was asked about vouchers submitted by F.E. Sickels for work done on this case. Poppleton replied: "The result of his work was that he gave me the materials out of which I was enabled to defeat that suit. And an equal amount of money was never better expended so far as Mr. Sickels was concerned." The chairman responded" "That is sufficient explanation of that." Frederick Sickels brother Theophilius, was known to A.J. as chief engineer for the recently built bridge across the Missouri River.

[265] F.E. Sickels to A. Poppleton, March 20, 1878..

[266] A. Poppleton, *Reminiscences*, 30.

[267] A. Poppleton, *Reminiscences,* 31.

[268] A. Poppleton, *Reminiscences*, 31.

17 Leader of the Bar

[269] Savage 263-64; and Andreas, *History of Nebraska-Douglas County*: 13,4. **Benjamin Eli Barnet Kennedy** (1827-1916) was born on April 20, 1827 in Bolton, Vermont. He read the law in a local law office and was admitted to the Vermont bar in 1853. He moved to Omaha in September 1858 and married Frances Nims (1832-1919) that same year. He was elected to the Omaha City Council in 1862 and served as Omaha's seventh Mayor in 1863. For nine years he was a member of the board governing Omaha schools and was instrumental in building public schools. After he left the mayor's office, he was elected to the territorial legislature from 1864 to 1866, served as Douglas County Surveyor in 1865, and Omaha City Attorney in 1867. He devoted his law practice to estate planning and probate. He was elected president of the Old Settlers Association in 1907 and helped preserve the stories and history of the original settlers. He and his wife Frances had three children. In 1888, their daughter Charlotte married Poppleton's son William. B. E. B. Kennedy died August 19, 1916, at age 89, and was buried in Forest Lawn Cemetery, Omaha.

Charles Frederick Manderson (1837-1911) was born in Philadelphia, Pennsylvania on February 9, 1837. He studied law in Canton and was admitted to the Ohio bar in 1859. He served in the Civil War and mustered out as Brevetted Brigadier General of Volunteers in 1865. He married Rebekah S. Brown (1840-1916) and resumed law practice in Canton, where he was elected county attorney before moving to Omaha in 1869. He was a member of the Nebraska Constitutional conventions in 1871 and 1875 and became City Attorney for three terms. He was elected president of the Nebraska Bar Association in 1880. Then, he was elected to the U.S. Senate from 1883 to 1895. He later served as solicitor for Burlington Railroad operations west of the Missouri River and was president of Omaha Savings Bank. In 1899, he was elected president of the American Bar Association, the second Nebraskan to hold that position (James M. Woolworth was the first from Nebraska in 1896). Manderson died on September 28, 1911, at age 74, while vacationing on a steamship in the harbor at Liverpool, England. He was buried in Forest Lawn Cemetery, Omaha. A street in Omaha is named in his honor.

[270] Catalogue of Books of The Omaha Law Library Association for 1877. 13-14.

[271] Catalogue of Books of The Omaha Law Library Association for 1877. 2-3.

[272] Catalogue of Books of The Omaha Law Library Association for 1877. 15-24. The State Reports included: California, Connecticut, Illinois, Indiana, Iowa, Kansas, Kentucky, Maine, Massachusetts, Michigan, Missouri, Nebraska, New Hampshire, New Jersey, New York, Ohio, Pennsylvania, Rhode Island, South Carolina, Wisconsin.

[273] Douglas County Bar Association Directory 1875, 1,7. **Clinton Briggs** (1828-1882) was born on September 9, 1828, in Washtenaw County, Michigan. He read the law in a law office in Detroit and was admitted to the Michigan bar in 1853. He moved to Auburn, New York, to practice law with William H. Seward, who later served as governor of New York and Secretary of State in the Lincoln Administration. In 1855, Briggs married Emily J. Manley (1838-1896), and they moved to Omaha that November. He served as a Douglas County Judge from 1857 to 1859, then practiced with John L. Redick from 1859 to 1869. Elected to the territorial legislature, he helped write the Code of Civil Procedure for the territory. Elected in 1860 as Omaha's fifth Mayor, he sent the first telegraphic message from Omaha to the officials of New York City and San Francisco. He often tried cases before the Nebraska Supreme Court and in many Federal courts. He was a member of the Nebraska Constitutional Convention (1875). Briggs died December 16, 1882, age 55, due to a train accident traveling to Chicago on business. He was buried in Prospect Hill Cemetery, Omaha. A street in Omaha is named in his honor.

[274] **Experience Estabrook** (1813-1894) was born April 30, 1813 in Lebanon, New Hampshire. He attended Dickinson College in Carlisle, Pennsylvania, and graduated from law school in Pennsylvania in 1839. For a few years he practiced in Buffalo, New York, then moved to Wisconsin where he became District Attorney, school commissioner, and a member of the constitutional convention in 1848. While a member of the Wisconsin territorial legislature, he led the debate in 1851 to grant citizenship and the vote to Black Americans. He married Caroline Augusta Maxwell in 1843 and they had two children. President Pierce appointed him to be the first U.S. Attorney General for the Nebraska Territory from 1854 to 1859. Historian Arthur C. Wakeley described him as a tall robust man who did everything with passion and vigor: "He arrived at Omaha on January 23, 1855, by walking across the Missouri River on the ice from Council Bluffs."(Wakeley, Arthur C. 322). In 1855, the Douglas County District Court appointed Estabrook, Solomon and Poppleton to a new committee to examine all applicants for admission to the bar. He was legal counsel for the Council Bluffs & Nebraska Ferry Co. and served in the Nebraska constitutional conventions of 1871 and 1875. Estabrook died on March 26, 1894, age 81. His funeral was held at Trinity Episcopal Cathedral and he was buried in Forest Lawn cemetery, Omaha.

[275] **Albert Swartzlander** (1843-1908) was born on May 3, 1843 in Bucks County, Pennsylvania. He served briefly in the Civil War but was honorably discharged because he suffered an eye injury, so he enrolled in Harvard law school and graduated in 1865. A year later he moved to Omaha and opened a law office specializing in real estate and estate planning. He practiced for a time with John I. Redick. Swartzlander was a founder and board member of the Omaha Public Library in 1871. He married Stella May in 1878. He died at age 65 in his home at 3612 N.24th Street on July 15, 1908, and was buried in Holy Sepulcher cemetery Omaha.

Herbert J. Davis shared offices over the years with a number of distinguished attorneys, including W. W. Keysor, a future judge, Henry D. Estabrook, and Judge James Savage. He was elected to the Omaha School Board in 1886 and was an organizer and general counsel from the Omaha Motor Railway Co. in 1887. He served as a Douglas County District Court Judge from 1892-1893. Judge Davis died in 1909.

[276] Douglas County Bar Association Directory 1875: Constitution Art. II, 7.

[277] Douglas County Bar Association Directory, 1875, 3.

[278] Douglas County Bar Association Directory, 1875: Constitution Art. III, Sec 3, 8.

[279] Douglas County Bar Association Directory, 1875, 5. **Original Members of the Omaha Bar Association**: George W. Ambrose, William O. Bartholomew, Clinton Briggs, Charles H. Brown, Leavitt Burnham, N.J. Burnham, E.H. Buckingham, Champion S. Chase, John C. Cowin, Edward T. Cowin, William J. Connell George W. Doane, Elmer S. Dundy, Experience Estabrook, Arthur N. Ferguson, George L. Gilbert, R.E. Gaylord, John D. Howe, B.E.B. Kennedy, George B. Lake, Charles F. Manderson, James Neville, Andrew J. Poppleton, George E. Pritchett, Thomas W.T. Richards, John L. Redick, James W. Savage, Charles H. Sedgwick, Silas A. Strickland, Albert Swartzlander, John M. Thurston, Eleazer Wakeley, John L. Webster, and James M. Woolworth.

[280] Douglas County Bar Association Directory, 1875: Constitution Art VIII, 9.

[281] Douglas County Bar Association Directory, 1875, 1. Words were attributed to Emory Washburn.

[282] Omaha City Directory 1878-79: 296-97.

[283] Omaha Bar Association Directory, 1889: Constitution Art. III, 4.

284 Omaha Bar Association Directory, 1889, 14. **Frank Irvine** (1858-1931) was born on September 15, 1858 in Sharon, Pennsylvania. He graduated from Cornell University in 1880 and the National University School of Law in Washington D.C. in 1883. He moved to Omaha the following year and practiced law. Poppleton's son William 'read the law' in Irvine's office. Governor James Boyd appointed Irvine judge of the Nebraska District Court in 1891, then he was appointed one of the three original Commissioners of the Nebraska Supreme Court from 1893 to 1899. For seven years, he was the New York State Public Service Commissioner and was legal counsel to several Utility companies. He returned to Ithaca, New York to teach at his alma mater, Cornell University. In 1907, he was appointed Dean of the Cornell Law School and served in that position until 1916. In his honor, the law school established 'The Frank Irvine Lecture'. He died in Ithaca on June 23, 1931, age 72. **Office of Supreme Court Commissioner**. In 1893, the Nebraska legislature granted the Nebraska Supreme Court authority to appoint three lawyers to serve as commissioners to help the court reduce its backlog of cases. The first three men appointed were Frank Irvine, Robert Ryan and John Ragan who served from 1893 to 1899. The court abandoned the use of commissioners in 1931.

James Woodruff Savage (1826-1890) was born on February 2, 1826 in Bedford, New Hampshire. After graduating from Harvard in 1847, he read the law in a New York City law office and was admitted to the New York bar in 1850. He served General John C. Fremont as his aide-de-camp during the Civil War and mustered out as Colonel of the 12th NY Cavalry in 1865. He moved to Omaha in 1867 and formed a partnership with Charles F. Manderson for six years and later with John C. Cowin. In 1875, he married Lucy Tucker Morris. He was appointed judge of the Third Judicial District of Nebraska from 1875 to 1883 but resigned because his health was failing and resumed private practice until his death. He also served as a director of the Union Pacific Railway Co. In 1888, he and John T. Bell began to research and write a history of Omaha published four years after Savage's death. At the time of his death, James Savage was president of the Omaha Public Library Association. He died, age 64, on November 22, 1890, and was buried in Forest Lawn Cemetery.

285 Omaha Bar Association Directory, 1889: By-laws Art II, Sec 1, 8.

286 Omaha Bar Association Directory, 1889: By-laws Art II, Sec 1, 8.

287 Omaha Bar Association Directory, 1889: Constitution Art. II, 4.

288 Constitution & By-Laws of Nebraska State Bar Association, 1876, 1.

289 Constitution & By-Laws of Nebraska State Bar Association, 1876, 1.

290 Constitution & By-Laws of Nebraska State Bar Association, 1876: Constitution Art VII, 5.

18 Business Community Leader

[291] First Annual Report of the Trade and Commerce of Omaha Nebraska for the Board of Trade for the year ending December 31, 1877, 3.

[292] First Annual Report of the Trade and Commerce of Omaha Nebraska for the Board of Trade for the year ending December 31, 1877, 4.

[293] First Annual Report of the Trade and Commerce of Omaha Nebraska for the Board of Trade for the year ending December 31, 1877, 5-8.

[294] First Annual Report of the Trade and Commerce of Omaha Nebraska for the Board of Trade for the year ending December 31, 1877. 17.

[295] First Annual Report of the Trade and Commerce of Omaha Nebraska for the Board of Trade for the year ending December 31, 1877, 18.

[296] First Annual Report of the Trade and Commerce of Omaha Nebraska for the Board of Trade for the year ending December 31, 1877, 21-22.

[297] First Annual Report of the Trade and Commerce of Omaha Nebraska for the Board of Trade for the year ending December 31, 1877, 22.

[298] First Annual Report of the Trade and Commerce of Omaha Nebraska for the Board of Trade for the year ending December 31, 1877, 22-23.

[299] First Annual Report of the Trade and Commerce of Omaha Nebraska for the Board of Trade for the year ending December 31, 1877, 49.

[300] U.S. Dept of the Interior, National Register of Historical Places Inventory – Nomination Form 1982. Its legal description was "Lot 1, Block 134, Original City of Omaha."

[301] U.S. Dept of the Interior, National Register of Historical Places Inventory – Nomination Form 1982.

19 Clients: The Barker Family

[302] Barker Letters. Introduction I:1-2.

[303] Barker Letters. I:2.

[304] Barker Letters. I: Introduction, 2.

[305] Barker Letters. II: 1235.

[306] Barker Letters. I:3 and see Map II:759. The site now includes Creighton Prep High School.

[307] Barker Letters. II: 1235.

[308] Barker Letters. II: 1235.

[309] Wakeley, Arthur C. 455-56.

[310] Barker Letters. I:82,90.

[311] Barker Letters. I:129.

[312] Barker Letters. I:424.

[313] Barker Letters. II:1185.

[314] Barker Letters. II:1268.

[315] Barker Letters. II:1235-40.

[316] Barker Letters. II:1235-40 and II:1266.

[317] Barker Letters. I:564. **The Barker Family** biographies are found in 1:640-643. **Reverend Barker** (1806-1875) was born on May 11, 1806 in Yorkshire, England and died on September 15, 1875 in the home of his daughter Mary Jane in Nebraska. **Mary Jane Barker Hamilton** (1833-1903) was born on June 21, 1833 in Bramley, England and died in Richfield, Nebraska on August 18, 1903. She married Thomas Hamilton, foreman for the Barker's family farm on 72nd Maple Street. **Frances Barker** (1802-1871) was born on November 16, 1802 in Staffordshire, England. She married the Rev. Barker in Halifax, England on October 12, 1830. In 1860, she returned with the family to Sheffield, England and died on October 25, 1871, buried in Nottingham. She never returned to Omaha. After his wife Frances died, Rev. Barker and Mary Jane returned to Omaha for the Rudowsky trial. **Joseph Barker Jr.** (1831-1896) was born on September 1, 1831 in Bramley, England. He was elected to the Omaha City Council in 1858. He married Lide Patrick in Omaha on September 23, 1875. In 1882, he was appointed to Omaha's first Board of Public Works. He died in Omaha on July 4, 1896. **George Barker** (1835-1927) was born on July 3, 1835 in Chester, England. He finished his education with his brother Joseph under a private tutor while the family lived in Ohio. When the family returned to England in 1860, George studied gas illumination, and later served as an officer and director for the Omaha Gas Manufacturing Co. He was involved with the creation of the Union Stock Yards Co., was president of the Bank of Commerce, and engaged in other banking activities in Omaha. He was also heavily involved in real estate development projects throughout the growing city. George was still playing golf at the Omaha Field Club until age 88. He died on November 27, 1927 in Omaha.

20 Commencement Speaker: Character and Education

[318] A. Poppleton Address, Character, 6.

[319] Savage, 571.

[320] A. Poppleton, Address Character, 6.

[321] A. Poppleton, Address Character, 6.

[322] A. Poppleton, Address Character, 6.

[323] A. Poppleton, Address Character, 6.

[324] Judge Samuel Maxwell to A.J. Poppleton, July 3, 1877.

21 Missing Caroline and Libby

[325] A.J. Poppleton to Caroline Poppleton, January 25, 1878.

[326] A.J. Poppleton to Caroline Poppleton, January 25, 1878..

[327] **Brownall Hall** was organized in 1863 by Trinity Episcopal Cathedral as a school for young ladies. It was located in Saratoga Springs on 24th and Grand Ave., 3 miles north of downtown Omaha. It was formally incorporated in 1868 by Bishop Clarkson, with James Woolworth, George Doane, Champion Chase, John Redick and Henry Yates as the incorporators. The school moved into a building on 16th and Jones Street the same year. Later, it moved into a larger building on 10th and Worthington Street. When Libby returned to live in Omaha, she supported the school financially and donated books and memorabilia for its library. **Elizabeth Butterfield**, the first female principal from 1869 to 1871, became a life-long leader in encouraging higher education for women, and later married James M. Woolworth.

[328] Circular of Brownell Hall, Omaha, Nebraska, September 17, 1867.

[329] Elizabeth "Libby" Poppleton to A.J. and Caroline Poppleton, November 12, 1877.

[330] Elizabeth Poppleton's work was titled *Thomas Carlyle: A Study of his Life and Work*. This 26-page study was published by F.C. Festner & Son of Omaha. In the flyleaf to her personal signed copy, she inscribed next to her name that she wrote it in Boston and "delivered first time in Poughkeepsie, N.Y. Dec 1878."

[331] Elizabeth "Libby" Poppleton to A.J. and Caroline Poppleton, November 12, 1877.

[332] Elizabeth "Libby" Poppleton to A.J. and Caroline Poppleton, November 12, 1877.

[333] A.J. Poppleton to Elizabeth Poppleton, February 9, 1878.

[334] Short Course on Shakespeare Invitation.

[335] In a scrapbook belonging to Caroline was a clipping from an un-named Omaha newspaper describing the first time Libby gave a lecture on Thomas Carlyle in Omaha. The event took place in December 1879 at the Academy of Music Hall. The room was "filled to overflowing, the list of reserved seats having been secured long before the hour of opening. None who were present can question the truth of the statement that a better audience or a more intellectual was never assembled in Omaha." Bishop Clarkson introduced Libby saying: "It seems unnecessary to introduce to you one whose name and fame are so well known, whose home is here, of whom we are so justly proud, and whom we shall be more and more proud as the years roll by – Miss Poppleton." The newspaper reported that Libby held "her hearers almost breathless for an hour and a half ... none were so wise but that they found the original and strong ideas expressed in clear and incisive language, and with an earnestness which could be best described in her own description of that characteristic of Carlyle himself – full of power to instruct and elevate the mind." She also wrote a manuscript (unpublished) on the *Life of Saint Paul* and gave lectures across the nation.

[336] Twenty-Fifth Annual Catalogue of Vassar College, 1889-1890. Poughkeepsie: A.V. Haight, Printer, 1890. Libby served on the Scholarship Standing Committee for the Board of Trustees.

[337] Together with two fellow alums, Libby wrote a Circular reviewing the growth and condition of Vassar for it 25th celebration on June 12, 1890. *Vassar at Twenty-Five. Review of it Growth and Condition.* Poughkeepsie Eagle-News June 1, 1890..

[338] C. Poppleton, *Diary,* January 2, 1879.

22 Standing's Bear Attorney

[339] Tibbles, *Ponca Chiefs*, 35.

[340] Tibbles, *Ponca Chiefs*, 34.

[341] Tibbles, *Ponca Chiefs*, 34-35.

[342] Tibbles, *Ponca Chiefs*, 34-35.

[343] A. Poppleton, *Reminiscences,* 32.

[344] Cherokee Nation, 1831.

[345] Blacks Law Dictionary 709; *Faye v. Noia*, 372 U.S. 391, 401-02 (1963).

[346] The Writ, Douglas County Historical Society, 6-7.

[347] Bourke, *Diaries*, 3:187; Omaha Daily Herald May 2, 1879.

[348] Omaha Daily Herald, May 4, 1879.

[349] Omaha Daily Herald, May 4, 1879.

[350] Omaha Daily Herald, May 4, 1879.

[351] Omaha Daily Herald, May 6, 1879.

[352] Omaha Daily Herald, May 6, 1879.

[353] Omaha Daily Herald, May 6, 1879.

[354] Omaha Daily Herald, May 7, 1879.

[355] Omaha Daily Herald, May 7, 1879.

[356] Tibbles, *Buckskin*, 201.

[357] Omaha Daily Herald, May 4, 1879.

[358] Case Determined, 5:468-69.

[359] Tibbles, *Ponca Chiefs*, 112-116; *Omaha Daily Herald*, May 20, 1879.

[360] Myron L. Learned to Clarence S. Paine, Secretary of the Nebraska State Historical Society, Lincoln, dated January 26, 1915: "Mrs. Caroline L. Poppleton, Mrs. Myron L. Learned, Mrs. Ellen E. Shannon, and William Sears Poppleton, to whom belongs the War Bonnet given the late Andrew J. Poppleton in 1879 by Standing Bear, desire to loan this War Bonnet to the Nebraska State Historical Society, and have asked me to deliver it to you, together with a statement in writing by Mrs. Caroline L. Poppleton concerning the presentation of the Bonnet by Standing Bear. You know the circumstances under which Mr. Poppleton became acquainted with Standing Bear, and the great service which he rendered Standing Bear and his tribe, and it seems most fitting that the priceless treasure of the great Chieftain should at least temporarily be in the possession of our historical society. Yours Very Truly, Myron L. Learned."

[361] C. Poppleton, *The War Bonnet,* 1-2.

[362] C. Poppleton, *The War Bonnet,* 1-2.

[363] C. Poppleton, *The War Bonnet,* 1-2.

[364] C. Poppleton, *The War Bonnet*, 1-2.

[365] A. Poppleton, *Reminiscences,* 32

[366] Poppleton and Webster are still role models for lawyers. In 2016, Garvin A. Isaacs, then serving as President of the Oklahoma Bar Association, wrote an article encouraging his state's attorneys to offer their services, pro-bono, to those residents who could not afford to hire a lawyer. Pointing to Poppleton and Webster as examples in history, Isaacs wrote: "Of great significance in the history of American jurisprudence are the two lawyers, John L. Webster and A. J. Poppleton, who gave back to the judicial system and became role models for all of us as lawyers." Issacs, Garvin A. "With Liberty and Justice for All."Oklahoma Bar Journal 87, No. 21 (2016): 1508, 1547.

23 Poppleton and Webster Fight for Native Americans

[367] U.S. Cong Senate. Report of the Secretary of the Interior. H.R. Ex. Doc. No.1, 47th Cong 1st Sess 1881.

[368] Ponca Tribe of Indians v. Makh-pi-ah-lu-tah, or Red Cloud, in his own behalf and in behalf of the *Sioux Tribe of Indians*, Fed. Dist. Ct. (D. Nebraska 1880)

[369] *Omaha Bee News,* December 4, 1888.

[370] U.S. Cong Senate. Report of the Secretary of the Interior. H.R. Ex. Doc. No.1, 47th Cong 1st Sess 1881.

[371] *Elk v. Wilkins*, 112 U.S. 94 (1884).

[372] *Elk v. Wilkins*, 112 U.S. 94 (1884). A **"Demurrer"** is an allegation of a defendant saying that even if all the factual allegations made in the plaintiff's petition are true, they are insufficient to establish a valid cause of action for the plaintiff to proceed with or force the defendant to have to answer. Today, the Federal Rules of Procedure do not provide for the use of the demurrer, but provide for the use of something similar- a Motion to Dismiss. *Black's Law Dictionary*, 432-33.

[373] *Elk v. Wilkins*, 112 U.S. 94 (1884).

[374] *Elk v. Wilkins*, 112 U.S. 94 (1884).

[375] *Elk v. Wilkins*, 112 U.S. 94 (1884). The previous year, Judge Harlan was the only justice who dissented when the Supreme Court struck down the 1875 Civil Rights Act (*Civil Rights Cases of 1883*, 109 U.S. 3.) During the next two decades, Judge Harlan earned the nickname "the Great Dissenter" in civil rights cases. In 1896, he dissented from the majority opinion in *Plessy v. Ferguson* which upheld segregation statutes and created the "separate but equal doctrine."

[376] Indian Freedom Citizenship Suffrage Act. of 1924 (Snyder Act). 8 U.S.C. ch.12, subch.111, 1041b. 68th Cong. 1st Sess. Hhtps://legislink.org/us/stat. See Lambertson, 183-85; Bodayla, 372-80; and Rollings, 126.

[377] *Who's Who In Omaha.* Baldwin Corporation Publishers: Omaha, 1928, 202. This author attended primary and secondary schools on Webster Street, one block from his home on Burt Street.

24 Promoter of Arts and Literature

[378] *Omaha Daily Heral*d, September 25, 1879.

[379] *Omaha Bee News*, September 11, 1879,

[380] *Omaha Bee News*, September 11, 1879. **Henry Whitefield Yates Sr.** (1837-1915) was President of the Nebraska National Bank of Omaha; an incorporator of the Omaha Library Association. He served in many roles at Trinity Episcopal Cathedral from 1866 to his death, including authoring its first history, and serving as treasurer of the Cathedral Chapter at the time of the art exhibition.

[381] *Omaha Bee News*, September 11, 1879

[382] Art Loan Catalogue 1879, 5.

[383] *Omahà Daily Herald*, September 25, 1879.

[384] Art Loan Catalogue 1879, 11-72.

[385] Art Loan Catalogue 1879, 34.

[386] Art Loan Catalogue 1879, 34.

[387] Art Loan Catalogue 1879, 48.

[388] Art Loan Catalogue 1879, 48.

[389] Art Loan Catalogue 1879, 45.

[390] Art Loan Catalogue 1879, 56.

[391] Art Loan Catalogue 1879, 56.

[392] Art Loan Catalogue 1879, 53.

[393] *Omaha Daily Herald*, October 10, 1879.

[394] *Omaha Bee News,* February 19, 1886.

[395] Kalish, 411-17.

[396] Omaha Library Association Catalog 1872.

[397] Omaha Library Association Catalog 1872, 45.

[398] Savage, History of the City of Omaha, Nebraska and South Omaha, 258.

[399] Savage, History of the City of Omaha, Nebraska and South Omaha, 258.

[400] Omaha Library Association Annual Report 1890.

[401] Omaha Library Association Annual Report 1890.

[402] John Grove to A. J. Poppleton, December 16, 1890.

[403] Savage, 261.

[404] *Omaha World Herald*, October 18, 1897.

[405] C. Poppleton, *Diary*.

25 Silver Wedding Anniversary

[406] **A.J. and Caroline Poppleton's Residences.** During their 41 years of marriage, they lived in a number of homes: **Dec 1855 - Feb 1856**: their first home was a one-room apartment in the Douglas House Hotel on 13th Harney Street. **Feb 1856 - May 1856:** three months later they moved into a one-room apartment in a brick building built by Jesse Lowe on 12th & Farnam Street. Later, the site was occupied by the U.S. National Bank. A.J. moved his law office to an adjoining room. **May 1856 - Dec 1866**: they built their first home on 15th & Capitol Ave. **Dec 1866 - April 1868:** they built a home across the street from Brownell Hall on 24th & Grand Avenue where Libby attended school. **April 1868 - May 1870:** Due to an outbreak of fever, they moved back into town and into a building they owned on 16th & Cass Street, which they remodeled into two homes – they lived on one side, and they rented the other side to their friend J.M. Ham, who worked for the Union Pacific. **May 1870 - January 1879:** They built a new home on 19th & Capitol Avenue, which they hoped would be their last residence after A.J. became full-time counsel for the UPRR. **January 2, 1879 - October 1880:** their home burnt to the ground with all their possessions, and they were forced to move into Roswell Smith's, a boarding house on the corner of 15th & Harney Street. **October 1880 – 1911:** they built their final home at 2232 Sherman Avenue, where A.J. died in 1896 and Caroline stayed until she moved in 1911 to live with Libby at 504 S. 26th Avenue, where she lived until her death in 1917. See C. Poppleton's *Diary* and C. Poppleton's interview with the *Omaha Bee News* on June 8, 1913.

[407] Thomas B. Lemon to A.J. and Caroline Poppleton, December 4, 1880. The friendship of the two wives continued after the death of their husbands. On December 30, 1908, Margaret Lemon wrote a holiday letter to Caroline: "My dear friend: Your token of remembrance came to me like good news from afar and it gave me great pleasure. To know I was not forgotten by the tried-and-true friends of the early days. I often go over that part of my life's history, and I assure you that you and your dear husband occupy a considerable space for Mr. L. was firmly devoted to Mr. Poppleton, not only admired but loved him as a brother." Rev. Lemon died in 1890 and Margaret Lemon died in Omaha in 1913. Rev. Lemon gave the opening prayer at the groundbreaking ceremony for the UPRR in Omaha on December 2, 1863.

[408] William Foote to Caroline Poppleton, November 27, 1889.

[409] Orrin Poppleton to A.J. Poppleton, November 30, 1880

[410] *Omaha Bee News*, December 3, 1880.

[411] *Omaha Bee News*, December 3, 1880

[412] *Omaha Daily Herald*, December 3, 1880.

[413] *Omaha Daily Herald*, December 3, 1880.

414 *Omaha Daily Herald*, December 3, 1880.

415 *Omaha Daily Herald*, December 3, 1880.

416 *Omaha Daily Herald*, December 3, 1880.

417 *Omaha Daily Herald*, December 3, 1880.

418 *Omaha Bee News*, December 2, 1919.

419 A. Poppleton, *Reminiscences,* 34.

26 Last Years of Practice

420 A. Poppleton to C. Poppleton April 3, 1882. **Samuel Blatchford** (1820-1893) was born in upstate New York, attended Columbia University and studied law under New York Governor William Seward. He was appointed to the U.S. District Court for the Southern District of New York (1867-1878) and then served on the U.S. Court of Appeals for the Second Circuit (1878-1882). He served on the U.S. Supreme Court for 11 years until his death July 7, 1893.

421 A. Poppleton, *Reminiscences,* 29. The Kansas Pacific Railway Company, owned by Jay Gould, together with the Denver Pacific Railway and Telegraph Company, filed a lawsuit in the Circuit Court for the District of Nebraska against the UPRR in 1868 that was later appealed to the U.S. Supreme Court in 1877 (at 95 U.S. 279) The two railway companies were represented by James M. Woolworth. What is of interest is that Poppleton submitted a 41-page document titled *"Suggestions submitted to the Hon. Charles Devens, Attorney General of the United States, on behalf of said Railroad Company,"* dated 1877 in which he attempted to set the record straight from the point of view of his employer, the UPRR, as to some complaints asserted by the Kansas and Denver companies. A few years later the two companies were acquired/merged into the UPRR.

422 UPRR Circular from Charles Francis Adams, November 21, 1885. Adams was the grandson of President John Quincy Adams.

423 UPRR Corporate Resolution, March 29, 1886.

424 A. Poppleton, *Reminiscence,* 29.

425 Charles Francis Adams to A. Poppleton, December 12, 1887.

426 A. Poppleton, *Reminiscence,* 33.

427 A. Poppleton, *Reminiscence,* 33

428 *Omaha Bee News*, January 14, 1888

429 *Omaha Bee News*, January 14, 1888

430 John Dillon to A. Poppleton, January 6, 1888.

431 Charles Adams to A. Poppleton, January 9, 1888.

432 W.H. Savidy to A. Poppleton, January 23, 1888.

433 Nebraska State Historical Society – Woolworth 1898, 104.

434 The *Omaha Excelsion,* October 17, 1888. William's marriage to **Charlotte Kennedy** lasted only 11 years as she died at age 32 from a brief intestinal episode on August 13, 1899. Their only child, Andrew Jackson Poppleton ("Jack") died three years earlier on January 10, 1896, at the young age of six. Both Charlotte and Jack were buried at Prospect Hill cemetery. On October 7, 1903, William married **Helen Clarke Smith**. They had one child, William Sears Poppleton Jr, born on June 18, 1905. A.J. and Caroline's son William S. Poppleton died on November 15, 1913, age 47. He had been ill for over a year. Funeral services were held at Trinity Episcopal Cathedral, interment in Prospect Hill cemetery. His second wife, Helen Clarke Smith Poppleton, died on November 23, 1936, and their son Will died on April 7, 1953 – both were buried in Prospect Hill cemetery.

435 Sorenson, 287-93. See also *Hotel Company v. Wade*, 97 U.S. 13 (1877), and *Omaha Hotel Co. and others v. Kountze and others*, 107 U.S. 378 (1883).

436 A. Poppleton, *Reminiscence,* 34.

437 Woolworth, *Biography,* 104-05.

438 A. Poppleton, *Reminiscence,* 34.

439 **Ed F. Morearty Sr.** in his memoirs tells the story about a matter Poppleton handled as city attorney. After the new city hall was built in 1891, the general contractor, John F. Coots, believed he lost money on the deal so he "entered into collusion with others with a view of furnishing the city hall with the necessary furniture on the pretense that the furniture would be made in Coot's mill in Omaha." Morearty wrote the furniture was going to be made in Michigan. The city let out bids. Coots bid $40,000. The low bid of $27,000 from Ketchum Furniture Company of Cleveland was accepted. Before Mayor James Boyd could sign the contract, he "was served with an injunction." A hearing was held before Douglas County District Judge George W. Donne who refused "to sustain the injunction." A.J. Poppleton, city attorney, represented Mayor Boyd won the argument. Morearty said "that was nearly twenty-five years ago, and the same furniture is doing service in the city hall at the present time; the taxpayers were saved $13,000." Morearty, 46.

440 Woolworth, *Biography*, 105. See the *Omaha World Herald* May 1890 edition which lists some of the details of Byron Reed's Last Will & Testament and his bequest to the city for a new public library building.

27 "My Life of Light Was Ended"

441 A. Poppleton, *Reminiscences,* 34.

442 Poppleton, Diary, March 1892.

443 Detroit Free Press, March 19, 1892, 3.

444 C. Poppleton, Diary, April 1892.

445 C. Poppleton, *Diary,* June 1892.

446 Green Court pamphlet 1892 of tribute in court record from Woolworth.

447 John Thurston to A. Poppleton, May 13, 1892.

448 Stephenson Burke to A. Poppleton, July 28, 1892.

449 William Rooker to A. Poppleton, October 14, 1892.

450 Olson, J. Sterling Morton, 30-31. Olson wrote that "Poppleton and Morton occasionally disagreed politically during the long years they spent in Nebraska but always they were friends."

451 Ballowe, 11. Carrie Lake Morton was born in Omaha in 1857 and died in 1915. She was buried with the Lake family plot in Prospect Hill cemetery. Her husband made a gift of $25,000 in her honor to Brownell Hall girl's school in Omaha from which Carrie had graduated in 1875. Joy Morton was born in 1855 and died in 1934.

452 J. Sterling Morton to A. Poppleton, June 9,1892.

453Andrew Raymond to A. Poppleton, May 9, 1895.

454 A. Poppleton to Raymond, May 15, 1895.

455 *Ann Arbor Courier,* June 29, 1895.

456 C. Poppleton, *Diary,* June 1891.

457 *Omaha Daily Bee,* April 23, 1893. **Myron L. Learned** (1866-1928) was born in Vermont on February 19, 1866. He was home-schooled until he enrolled in a public school in Massachusetts. He "read the law" in the office of Massachusetts attorney Daniel Bond, and later moved to Omaha and formed a partnership with John L. Kennedy. He was active in the state Republican party, chairman of its county central committee. He was a member of the Elks Club and the Omaha County Club of which he served for a time as its president. Myron was requested by N.H. Loomis, General Solicitor for the Union Pacific Railroad Company, to read excepts pertaining to the railroad from A.J. Poppleton's memoirs at a meeting held in the UPRR library on April 21, 1915, with the permission of Caroline. Mary and Myron were very active members of the Nebraska Audubon Society. After 33 years of marriage, Myron died suddenly of an appendicitis attack on February 9, 1928, age 61. They had no children. On January 15, 1960, Mary passed away at her home, 316 S. 50th Ave, age 86. She lived longer than her parents and siblings. Funeral services were held at Trinity Episcopal Cathedral and interment at Forest Lawn Cemetery, Omaha next to her husband.

458 *Omaha World Herald,* May 5, 1895 and May 9, 1895. **William Cummings Shannon** (1851-1905) was born in New Hampshire in 1851. After graduating from Bowdoin College, Maine in 1872, he attended medical school at Bellevue Hospital Medical College in New York and joined the Army as a surgeon. He spent two years providing medical care to the surveyors of the Intercontinental Railway Commission in Central America. He also did a residency in bacteriology at Johns Hopkins University. Libby and the Major lived on various Army posts until he retired in April 1898 from the military, due to Bright's disease. Major Shannon died April 21, 1905, age 53. They had been married only ten years and had no children. After her husband's death, Libby devoted the remaining thirty years of her life to supporting many charitable causes and helping take care of Caroline in her last six years. Elizabeth died on May 2, 1936, age 79. Funeral services were held at Trinity Episcopal Cathedral, with interment next to her husband at Forest Lawn cemetery.

459 A. J. Poppleton to C. Poppleton, September 11, 1895.

460 C. Poppleton, *Diary,* June 1892.

461 C. Poppleton, *Diary,* June 1892.

462 *Omaha Mercury*, October 9, 1986.

28 "He Has Been Blind – He Can See Now"

463 Washington D.C. *The Evening Times* September 30, 1896.

464 Death Certificate – Douglas County Dept of Vital Statistics. **Bright's Disease.** Named after Dr. Richard Bright, a British doctor who first described it in 1827 as a type of kidney disease. Notable people who were diagnosed as having this disease at time of death included baseball player Ty Cobb, Theodore Roosevelt's first wife Alice, poet Emily Dickinson, President Chester Arthur, English preacher Charles Spurgeon, scientist and educator Booker T. Washington, and Matthew Brady, photographer of Abraham Lincoln and civil war battlefields. *The Surgery Journal, NY,* December 19, 2017.

465 *Lincoln Journal* September 25, 1896.

466 *Omaha Mercury,* October 9, 1896. **Charles A. Baldwin**, a criminal defense attorney, was the first president of newly formed Prospect Hill Cemetery Association (1890). **Judge John Clay Cowin** (1846-1918) was the Douglas County Attorney from 1869 to 1873; Adjutant in The Grand Army of the Republic first formed in Omaha in 1867; Professor of Medical Law at the Omaha Medical College from 1880 to 1885; and attorney for the Omaha Motor Railway Company founded in 1887. He was buried in Forest Lawn Cemetery, Omaha. **William D. Beckett** was an attorney.

467 *Omaha Bee News* , September 26, 1896..

468 *Omaha Bee News* , September 26, 1896.

469 *Omaha Bee News*, September 26, 1896. **Rev. Alvin Foote Sherill** (1842-1928) was born in Quebec, Canada on December 24, 1842. He came to Omaha and assumed pastorship of the First Congregational Church in 1869. The church was organized by Rev. Reuben Gaylord in May 1856 and held it services in the old State House on 9th Douglas St., then moved into the dining room of the Douglas House Hotel. In August 1857, the congregation moved into a building on the corner of 16th & Farnam Street, considered to have been the first protestant church building in Omaha, (Savage, *History of Omaha*, 325). When Rev. Sherill assumed pastorship, he sold the Farnam Street building and built a brick church on the Northwest corner of 19th Street & Chicago Ave in 1870 – which the members occupied until they built a church on Davenport Street in 1888 (see Savage, *History of Omaha*, 326 for pencil drawing). Rev. Sherill was one of the clergymen who signed the telegram to U.S. Interior Secretary Carl Schurz on March 31, 1879 on behalf of Standing Bear and the Ponca prisoners. He became active in the Omaha Ponca Relief Committee and served as its treasurer. He was living in Galesburg, Illinois at the time of Poppleton's death. He died, age 86, on July 3, 1928, in Polk County, Florida.

470 *Omaha Bee News* , September 26, 1896.

471 *Detroit Free Press,* October 3, 1896

472 Historic Omaha Prospect Hill Cemetery Walking and Driving Guide.

[473] *Omaha Mercury,* October 9, 1896.

[474] *Omaha Mercury,* October 9, 1896.

[475] *Omaha Mercury,* October 9, 1896. .

[476] *Omaha Mercury,* October 9, 1896.

[477] *Omaha Mercury,* October 9, 1896.

[478] *Omaha Mercury,* October 9, 1896.

[479] C. Poppleton, *Diary,* September 1896.

[480] City of Omaha, Council Chamber, October 6, 1896.

[481] City of Omaha, Council Chamber, October 6, 1896.

29 Caroline – The Pioneer Woman

[482] A. Poppleton, *Reminiscences,* 12.

[483] *Omaha Bee News, June 8, 1913.*

[484] *Omaha Bee News*, June 8, 1913.

[485] *Omaha Bee News*, June 8, 1913.

[486] *Omaha Bee News*, June 8, 1913.

[487] *Omaha Bee News*, June 8, 1913.

[488] *Omaha Bee News*, June 8, 1913.

[489] *Omaha Bee News*, June 8, 1913.

490 Interview with Jill Jackson, Trinity Episcopal Cathedral Historian, July 17, 2024. Champion Spalding Chase and Algernon Sidney Paddock were active members of Trinity Episcopal Cathedral, civic and political leaders, and close friends of A.J. and Caroline Poppleton. **Champion Spalding Chase** (1820-1898) moved to Omaha from Wisconsin in 1866 and opened a law practice. 1867 he was appointed the State of Nebraska's first Attorney General and served until 1869. He was elected three times as mayor of Omaha (1874-77, 1879-81, and 1883-84). He also served on the University of Nebraska Board of Regents for six years from 1869 to 1875, and as President of the Nebraska State Humane Society in 1886. Chase was past Commander of the GAR and an Omaha Real Estate Owners' Association organizer. He was preceded in death by wife Mary Sophronia Butterfield, sister of James Woolworth's wife Elizabeth. His funeral was at Trinity Episcopal Cathedral, and his burial was in Prospect Hill cemetery. **Algernon Sidney Paddock** (1830-1897) moved to Omaha from New York in 1857. He was a graduate of Union College, as was A.J. Poppleton. He was elected to the House of Representative in the 1859 session of the Territorial Legislature. As editor of the Nebraska Republican newspaper from 1858 to 1859, he worked tirelessly for the election of Abraham Lincoln in 1860. He was rewarded by being appointed by President Lincoln, as Secretary of the Nebraska Territory from 1861 to 1867. He served as acting Governor for a portion of 1861. He was elected twice to the U.S. Senate (1875-81 and 1887-93). On December 22, 1869, he married Emma L. Mack -the first marriage ceremony held in the new Trinity church. She died in 1923. He died in 1897. They had two children. Both are buried in Prospect Hill cemetery.

491 Martin, *A History of Trinity Episcopal Cathedral*, 12. One of the first Catholic masses was said in Thomas and Marguerite Cuming's home in Spring 1856 by Father Scanlon of St. Joseph Missouri. Thomas Cuming was the son of an Episcopal minister and married Marguerite Murphy, a Roman Catholic. Both Thomas and Marguerite remained active members of their respective denominations, yet are buried side by side at Holy Sepulchre cemetery Omaha. Trinity Episcopal Church, the Cathedral for the Episcopal Diocese of Nebraska, and Saint Cecilia's Church, the Cathedral for the Catholic Archdiocese of Omaha, are located less than two miles apart in present day Omaha and have held several joint-ecumenical services over the years. The current Bishop of the Episcopal Diocese, Rev. Scott Barker, is a direct descendent of the Joseph Barker family spoken of in an earlier chapter - his installation ceremony, due to the large size of the audience, was held in St. Cecilia's Cathedral Church. This author attended the installation ceremony at the invitation of the Bishop's father, Joe Barker. This author and Joe Barker served on the board of directors of Douglas County Historical Society and were charter members of its Foundation.

492 Martin, *A History of Trinity Episcopal Cathedral*, 17, 31-32

493 Martin, *A History of Trinity Episcopal Cathedral*, 96.

494 Martin, *A History of Trinity Episcopal Cathedral*, 51.

[495] The Bishop Clarkson Memorial Hospital for Children, Twenty-Third Annual Report, Omaha, May 1, 1906. History of Bishop Clarkson Memorial Hospital,1935.

[496] The Bishop Clarkson Memorial Hospital for Children, Twenty-Third Annual Report, Omaha, May 1, 1906. History of Bishop Clarkson Memorial Hospital,1935.

[497] *Omaha Daily Bee News*, November 23, 1917.

[498] Omaha World Herald, November 26, 1917.

[499] *Omaha World Herald*, November 26, 1917.

[500] Bishop George Beecher to Elizabeth Shannon, April 1936. **Beecher** was Bishop of Trinity Episcopal Cathedral (1905-1910). He was elected Bishop of Western Nebraska in 1910. Charles Martin writes: " Dean Beecher was an exceptional man. He was very well-liked by the congregation ... He made a survey of Omaha and found opportunities for holding services in undeveloped neighborhoods. He started a mission among the employees of the South Omaha packing houses and another one in connection with the City Mission. Martin quoted the bishop saying: "During my Deanship in Omaha, I became vitally interested in the work of the Juvenile Court and attended the sessions as regularly on Monday mornings as I conducted services on Sunday." (Martin, 47-48) His activities for the poor and troubled children were a common interest with Caroline Poppleton, whose leadership of the church's aid society and willingness to open her house to social gatherings supported his work. Bishop Beecher and his wife Florence were close friends of Caroline and her children. **Elizabeth Poppleton Shannon** died on May 2, 1936, at age 79, just three months after receiving the Beecher's letter. She was buried in Forest Lawn Cemetery Omaha next to her husband Major Dr. William Shannon, who died in 1905. **Mary Poppleton Learned,** the last of the four Poppleton children, died January 15, 1960, age 86, at her home, 316 S. 50 Ave., and was buried in Forest Lawn Cemetery next to her husband Myron Learned, who died in 1928.

30 Reminiscences

[501] A. Poppleton, Reminiscences, 35.

[502] A. Poppleton, *Journal,* February 16, 1851, 53.

[503] A. Poppleton, *Journal*, February 16, 1851, 53.

[504] A. Poppleton, *Reminiscences*, 35.

[505] A. Poppleton, Address to Nebraska Bar Association, 1880, 9, 11, 18.

[506] A. Poppleton, Address to Nebraska Bar Association, 1880, 33-34.

[507] Charles F. Manderson Eulogy, September 28, 1896.

Epilogue

508 Sorenson, 251-52.

509 Constitution and By-Laws of The Sons of Omaha Catalogue, 1892-93.

510 *Omaha Bee News*, June 8, 1913.

511 Poppleton, Address on Character to 1877 University of Nebraska Commencement, 19.

512 Sheldon, 66-67; Larsen, 17. At the opening day ceremony of The Trans-Mississippi and International Expositions of 1898-1899, President of the Board of Directors Gurdon Wattles declared that "the Great American Desert is no more." Katz, 27-28. For a detailed study of Major Long's expedition see Nichols, *Stephen Long and American Frontier Exploration,* 51-63.

513 Poppleton, Address on Character to 1877 University of Nebraska Commencement, 19.

Made in the USA
Columbia, SC
28 March 2025

55793667R00159